Within the fields of education and psychology, the role that discourse plays in social processes of learning and teaching has emerged as a critical empirical and theoretical question. *Discourse, Learning, and Schooling* explores theoretical and methodological relationships between children's discourse – or socially used language – and their learning in educational settings.

The authors in this volume address from multidisciplinary perspectives a range of issues, including literacy, authorship, the construction of the self, and classroom interactional processes. Individual chapters range from research studies of classroom discourse to essayist reflections on discourse and literacies. Collectively, these chapters reflect both sociocognitive perspectives on the relations between discourse, learning, and schooling and sociocultural perspectives on discourse and literacies among diverse cultural groups.

Discourse, learning, and schooling

Discourse, learning, and schooling

Edited by

DEBORAH HICKS
University of Delaware

CAMBRIDGE
UNIVERSITY PRESS

Published by the Press Syndicate of the University of Cambridge
The Pitt Building, Trumpington Street, Cambridge CB2 1RP
40 West 20th Street, New York, NY 10011-4211, USA
10 Stamford Road, Oakleigh, Melbourne 3166, Australia

First published 1996

Printed in the United States of America

Library of Congress Cataloging-in-Publication Data

Discourse, learning, and schooliing / [edited by] Deborah Hicks.
     p.   cm.
   Includes bibliographical references and indexes.
   ISBN 0-521-45301-1
   1. Children – Language. 2. Oral communication. 3. Verbal
behavior. 4. Interaction analysis in education. 5. Literacy.
6. Learning, Psychology of. I. Hicks, Deborah.
LB1139.L3D54   1996
407–dc20   95-33579
                                             CIP

A catalog record for this book is available from the British Library.

ISBN 0-521-45301-1 Hardback

Contents

v

Part III   Discourse and literacies

Afterword

Contributors

Courtney B. Cazden
Harvard University
Graduate School of Education
Cambridge, Massachusetts

Catherine Dorsey-Gaines
Kean College
Office of Academic Affairs
Union, New Jersey

Joel E. Dworin
University of Arizona
College of Education
Tucson, Arizona

Frederick Erickson
University of Pennsylvania
Graduate School of Education
Philadelphia, Pennsylvania

Cynthia M. Garnett
Kean College
Early Childhood Development
Union, New Jersey

James Paul Gee
Clark University
Department of Education
Worcester, Massachusetts

Deborah Hicks
University of Delaware

College of Education
Newark, Delaware

Alex Kozulin
The International Center for the
    Enhancement of Learning
    Potential
Jerusalem, Israel

Brenda F. Kurland
Harvard University
Graduate School of Education
Cambridge, Massachusetts

Sarah Michaels
Clark University
Department of Education
Worcester, Massachusetts

Luis C. Moll
University of Arizona
College of Education
Tucson, Arizona

Mary Catherine O'Connor
Boston University
School of Education
Boston, Massachusetts

Catherine E. Snow
Harvard University
Graduate School of Education
Cambridge, Massachusetts

Acknowledgments

This volume grew out of a year-long colloquium series sponsored by the University of Delaware, College of Education. I am grateful for the financial support that enabled the development of intellectual ideas leading to the current volume. I am also grateful for the continual support of colleagues and graduate students throughout the year, and beyond, as this work emerged into textual form. This scholarly dialogue and support was by no means limited to my own institution. Other friends/ colleagues have been "contributors" to this volume through their engagement in critical dialogues about discourse and schooling. I owe a special debt to James Paul Gee in that respect. Hopefully, this volume will spark other dialogues, as colleagues (some known to me and others not) collectively explore and debate – grappling with questions related to discourse and its role in formal and informal processes of schooling.

I thank the relevant publishers for permission to reprint material from the following sources:

Chapter by Tony Burgess. In *Charting the Agenda,* H. Daniels (ed.), 1993. By permission of Routledge Press.

Cultural Politics of Everyday Life (p. 118), by John Shotter, 1993. By permission of University of Toronto Press.

Language and Learning: The Importance of Speech in Children's Development (pp. 303–4), by James Britton, 2nd ed. 1992. Copyright © by James Britton, 1970, 1992. By permission of Allen Lane The Penguin Press.

How Writing Shapes Thinking: A Study of Teaching and Learning (pp. 139–40), by Judith A. Langer and Arthur N. Applebee, 1987. NCTE Research Report No. 22. By permission of the National Council of Teachers of English.

Quote from article by James Baldwin, July 29, 1979, Op-ed. Copyright © by The New York Times Company. Reprinted by permission.

The Collected Works of L. S. Vygotsky (pp. 221–2. 223). R. W. Rieber and A. S. Carton (eds.), N. Minick (trans.), 1987. By permission of Plenum Press.

1 Introduction

Deborah Hicks

It is no secret to teachers and other educators who work with children that there is an intimate relationship between language, learning, and schooling. Indeed, one of the astounding achievements of children in the preschool years is their mastery of language. By the time children enter school, at the age of 5 or 6, they are masterful users of one, sometimes two, languages. Children in kindergarten or first grade control the use of a highly complex grammatical system, so complex that some linguists have maintained that some, if not all, aspects of this system must be part of the child's initial cognitive structures, present at birth and activated through exposure to language in use (Chomsky, 1982; Pinker, 1984). And yet, there is another aspect of children's language competency that has in past decades intrigued educators, psycholinguists, and anthropologists. From the earliest moments of language use, when children are using language to accomplish cognitive tasks such as labeling or requesting (see Bruner, 1983), they are participants in *discourse* contexts, which involve specific social usages of language. Thus, by the time they enter a system of formalized schooling, children are also adept at "doing things with words." Through recurrent participation in social activities at home and in certain "proximal" institutional settings (e.g., day-care centers, churches), children are cognitively apprenticed (Rogoff, 1990) into ways of using language that *makes sense* within particular social settings and particular cultures. Children's knowledge of a range of discourses, socially appropriate within the intimate contexts of their home and proximal communities, becomes an integral beginning point for their formalized schooling. The child's entrance into a larger society is largely mediated by discourse.

It seems intuitive that there should exist a relationship between language, noninstitutional learning in community settings, and formalized schooling. Any effort to imagine a classroom or other educational setting without language boggles the mind. Indeed, as philosophers, linguists, psychologists – and educators – have noted for centuries, lan-

1

guage is the uniquely human means of constructing knowledge. By contrast, understanding *how* discourse (or language used socially) mediates processes of learning and schooling is less intuitive. On the one hand, teachers and researchers can observe that children actively explore their world through language – questioning, hypothesizing, constantly interacting with more capable others in the process of constructing an understanding of a self and a social world. On the other hand, these same researchers, bolstered by the efforts of theorists working across disciplines, struggle to explain *how* discourse mediates children's informal learning and formal education.

This question of how discourse mediates learning in social context has become in recent years a topic of intense study and debate. Three theoretical and pedagogical strands of inquiry have been central to this study of discourse and learning, and these form the backdrop to the current volume. The first is what might be loosely termed *sociocognitive theories of learning,* studies of what one theorist has called the "social mind" (Gee, 1992). The second strand of scholarly inquiry is that of *sociocultural studies of language and literacy,* linking oral and written language to particular social contexts of use. The third domain of inquiry related to this question is *studies of classroom discourse,* what Cazden (1988) has termed the "language of teaching and learning." In each of these areas of inquiry, scholars have sought a deeper understanding of the role that discourse plays in *education,* broadly conceived.

The present volume was conceived as an effort to bring together these different strands of theoretical and pedagogical work in a way that would lend new perspectives to this question of how discourse is a cultural and cognitive mediator of learning and schooling. It addresses the need to explore the impact of sociocognitive theories of learning and sociocultural theories of language on educational theory and research (with *education,* again, being broadly conceptualized as learning and schooling in both informal and institutional settings). Although scholarly inquiry across disciplines has resulted in a wealth of knowledge about relationships between discourse, learning, and schooling, there is still work to be done. The emergence of sociocognitive perspectives on learning has resulted in a theoretical framework that is highly compatible with sociocultural perspectives on language and literacy. The translation of theoretical writings in psychology and philology from the former Soviet Union – namely, the work of Lev Vygotsky and his contemporary, Mikhail Bakhtin – has led to an explosion of scholarly inquiry into the social dimensions of knowledge construction. Because the work of these theorists was grounded in queries of how language used socially both mediates and constitutes the thinking self, discourse has become a fulcrum for much of this scholarly inquiry. Theorists working within a sociocognitive framework assume that learning is situational, both context and culture specific, and that it is mediated by language. Thus, sociocognitive studies of learning and sociocultural studies of language become natural parallels. In the arena of studies of educational processes, such melding of the two strands of scholarly inquiry provides a powerful means of investigating the *how* of relationships between discourse and learning. How do teachers and children construct situational understandings through their use of discourse? How do children become adept at the use of multiple discourses, some of which are tied to literacy? How does discourse mediate the child's evolving sense of self and her movement within an expanding social world?

The work of sociocognitive and sociocultural theorists can be mutually informative about such questions. Indeed, these two strands of scholarly inquiry are interwoven in educational theory and practice, as the chapters in this volume suggest. Like Vygotsky and other intellectual predecessors of sociocognitive and sociocultural inquiries, the contributors to this volume explore different dimensions, or "units," of social activity and educational processes. Some contributors address the face-to-face interaction that occurs in classrooms and other educational settings; others look at classrooms as cognitive and cultural communities constituted by language practices; still others explore more generally social experience and social discourses as mediators of human thinking. However, the differing dimensions of these focusing lenses on discourse, learning, and schooling should not be misleading with respect to a shared grounding in sociocognitive and sociocultural perspectives. The contributors to this volume are concerned with both the generalities and the particulars of how discourse mediates children's guided entrance into overlapping educational contexts – schools, churches, and other social and institutional settings. Hence, questions related more generally to relationships between discourse and learning, and questions related specifically to discourse and learning in *this* classroom or with *this* child, are overlapping areas of inquiry. The omnipresent distinction between theory and practice in education becomes more diffuse, as it was for Vygotsky, one of the central figures in this history of the melding of sociocognitive and sociocultural perspectives on learning. What emerges instead is a constant questioning about the complexities of how discourse mediates children's educational experience. The melding of sociocognitive and sociocultural perspectives reconfigures learning and education as inherently messy phenomena – complex, though not indescribable; something to be *understood* rather than explained causally through scientific inquiry (Bakhtin, 1986).

To reiterate, the current volume is an effort to explore the impact of these sociocognitive and sociocultural theories of discourse and learning on education as it is broadly conceived by the authors of individual chapters. To understand the individual contributions to this volume, it is therefore useful to first have an overview of the strands of inquiry that have contributed to the work represented here. In this initial chapter, I provide such an overview, a thumbnail sketch of scholarly inquiry within the overlapping fields of education, psychology, philology, and sociolinguistics, inquiry that foreshadows the work presented in this volume. This overview is by no means comprehensive; rather, it is a selective description of sociocognitive theories of learning, sociocultural theories of language and literacy, and studies of educational processes related to discourse. I begin with a discussion of the theoretical work in psychology, linguistics, and education that I (and others in the volume) have collectively termed *sociocognitive*.

Sociocognitive theories of learning

In his book *The Forbidden Experiment*, Roger Shattuck (1980) describes how a young French doctor, Jean-Marc Gaspard Itard, struggled to bring the "wild boy of Aveyron," captured in the woods in 1800, to a more socialized state of existence. Central to the motives of this physician were his efforts to teach the boy, whom he named Victor, language. Although the physician's efforts were only partially successful, his ambitious goal of educating a completely unsocialized, and therefore speechless, child attests to the importance placed on language as a symbolic tool of society. Throughout the history of psychology, language has been viewed as a crucial link in explaining how children become fully functional members of a social world.

Not all psychologists (or educators) would view language primarily as a means of socialization. In fact, the prevailing view in the field of psychology is that language functions as a catalyst for cognitive development, or alternatively, that cognitive development is reflected in language. In *The Language and Thought of the Child*, for instance, Piaget (1952) observed how 5- and 6-year-old children often spoke to themselves during their work and play in kindergarten settings, and he concluded that this *egocentric* speech reflected their cognitive inability to "decenter," that is, to take on the perspective of another. Other researchers working from a cognitivist perspective have explored how children's language and learning are dialectically interactive. Katherine Nelson and her colleagues, for instance (see Nelson, 1986, 1989), have examined in great depth how children's event knowledge is constituted in narrative form. In *Narratives from the Crib*, an intriguing collection of writing on the crib monologues of a 2-year-old, Nelson (1989) suggests that language and cognitive development are interwoven in complex ways. The young child's understanding of temporal relationships, for example, may be reflected in her use of temporal connectives like *when* (Nelson, chapter 8). On the other hand, the discourse organization of narrative, experienced first through the child's social interaction with caretakers, may provide the linguistic structure that facilitates her understanding of temporal relationships (Gerhardt, Chapter 5, this volume). Students of children's cognitive development throughout the history of psychology have been intrigued with the relationship between language and learning and have developed varying theoretical models to depict that relationship.

The story of Itard and his valiant efforts to educate Victor, the so-called "wild boy," brings up the particular aspect of this long-standing intrigue that provides grounds for the emergence of the present volume. Since language is a primary means of social communication, it must also be a central symbolic tool through which children become full members of society. Moreover, language is not a neutral means of expression in the way mathematical systems, for example, are considered to be detached from social and cultural values. Languages can be described as abstract grammatical systems, but language used socially, or *discourse*, is also laden with the values, beliefs, and intentions of its users. As Bakhtin (1981) has suggested, the language appropriated by its users is still "warm" with the meanings and intentions of others. The social foundations of language and thought are, for many current theorists, the key to developing an understanding of the role that discourse plays in children's learning.

A collection of work published in honor of Jerome Bruner, an early advocate of a social view of language and mind, attests to the intensification of interest in this topic during recent decades. In that volume, researchers and theorists across disciplines explored how, as suggested by editor David Olson (1977), "[social] foundations come to be represented in the structure of cognitive processes of particular individuals" (p. 3). Literacy was explored as a "cultural amplifier" (Cole and Griffin, chapter 15) and language as a means through which caretakers "scaffolded" children's learning (Wood, chapter 12). Interestingly, many contributors to this important collection cited the work of Soviet theorists, such as L. S. Vygotsky and A. R. Luria, as the theoretical (sometimes empirical) precedent to their own work. The writings of Vygotsky and his colleagues from formerly Communist lands was, for many contributors to that volume, an important influence on the ways language and learning were viewed.

Indeed, since the publication of English translations of Vygotsky's collected works (see Vygotsky, 1962, 1978, 1986, 1987), there has been a virtual explosion of research and writing in what might be considered a "post-Vygtoskian" vein. Scholars working across disciplines have appropriated Vygotsky's sociocultural psychology as a beginning point for studies of language and learning processes. In part, this explosion may be due to the extraordinary way in which Vygotsky's writings seem to capture some of the basic institutions about discourse and learning held by theoreticians and educators alike. There is no need here to provide an in-depth review of the tenets of Vygotskian theory, since a variety of writers have done just that (e.g., Kozulin, 1990; Minick, 1989; Moll, 1990; Wertsch, 1985; Yaroshevsky, 1989). Briefly, however, Vygotsky's sociocultural and sociohistorical theories of learning were grounded in his intense interest in how language and other culturally significant symbolic systems mediated human thinking. Unlike animals, who were limited to lower biologically determined forms of thinking, human thinking was transformed, or *interrupted* (Emerson, 1993), by the introduction of language. By language, or *speech*, Vygotsky referred not to an abstract grammatical system, what Saussure would term *langue*, but to social means of communication imbued with cultural and historical meaning. Thus, the study of word meanings and their effect on learners' cognitive processes became the central topic of inquiry (Vygotsky, 1986, 1987). Over the course of his extraordinarily short professional career, Vygotsky studied children's development of "higher mental processes" (as opposed to "lower," more elementary ones) through their social interaction with more mature others in language-filled social environments, including formal educational settings. In Vygotsky's developmental theory, the movement inward of social forms of communication was the child's means of reorganizing her thinking. It is perhaps this extremely powerful *idea* that has so influenced educators and psychologists, rather than the specifics of Vygotsky's theory. This idea is compatible with the observations of educators about how children learn through participation in social contexts.

It is interesting to note here that Vygotsky considered himself an educator as well as a psychologist. The hybrid term *pedologist* was used to describe the field that Vygotsky considered his domain of study. Indeed, Vygotsky was centrally concerned with the education of handicapped children, as well as with the impact more generally of formal education on children's thinking. Thus, it is perhaps fitting that many scholars in more recent times who have taken up the study of the social mind (Gee, 1992) have engaged in such hybrid forms of scholarly inquiry. The work of researchers and theoreticians such as Bruner (1990), Gee (1990, 1992), Forman, Minnick, and Stone (1993), Moll (1990), Rogoff (1990), and Wertsch (1985, 1991), to name only some of the prominent scholars working in this interdisciplinary field of sociocognitive learning, has spanned the fields of psychology and education, often venturing into the neighboring fields of literary theory and anthropology. The child's social construction of knowledge through participation in activity mediated by language has become, for these and other researchers, a critical focusing issue.

Moreover, this issue has often been considered in the context of pressing societal and educational issues, as it was by Vygotsky and his colleagues. Scholars like James Paul Gee, for instance, have explored how the social discourses of particular communities function simultaneously as cognitive resources and as social "goods." Children from socially and politically marginalized communities may find that their rich store of cognitive resources, embodied in these primary discourses, are not valued by the larger educational community. Other scholars, like James Wertsch, have explored the social and cognitive processes through which discourses are internalized by children. In *Voices of the Mind*, Wertsch (1991) explores as one example of his "sociocultural approach to mediated action" an episode of classroom discussion. In that episode, the classroom teacher skillfully socializes a young kindergarten child into a certain *way* of talking about a natural object (a piece of volcanic rock). Discourse and learning are explored by Gee, Wertsch, and other sociocognitive theorists as processes integrally related to education and fundamentally linked to societal and political issues.

As I suggested earlier, studies of discourse have played an extremely important role in this evolving history of sociocognitive theories of learning. Some of the interest in studies of the role of discourse in children's informal and formal institutional learning undoubtedly is related to the now extremely rich accumulation of sociocultural studies of discourse and literacy (see the following discussion). As Luis Moll and Joel Dworin point out in their contribution to this volume, literacy has become one of the truly interdisciplinary domains of scholarly inquiry. Scholars working in the fields of education, psychology, and anthropology have inquired into the cultural and historical contexts in which literacy has arisen and the cognitive and pedagogical consequences of literacy-based discourses (Cole & Griffin, 1980; Gee, 1989, 1990; Graff, 1987; Heath, 1982, 1983; Moll, 1990; Olson, 1977; Scollon & Scollon, 1981; Scribner & Cole, 1981). From these interdisciplinary studies of literacy, there has emerged an interest in literacy not only as a modality (e.g., written versus oral language) but also as a repertoire of discursive "positionings," or what Heath (1983) has termed "ways with words" (see also Tannen, 1982b). According to many theorists engaged in the cross-disciplinary study of the cognitive, social, and educational consequences of literacy, it is the way one situates oneself socially through discourse that is of central import (Gee, 1990; Scollon & Scollon, 1981). Thus, along with a specific interest in the cognitive consequences of literacy has emerged an interest more generally in the role that particular *forms* of discourse play in children's learning and socialization. For instance, in a book on the unique place that narrative holds in human cognition, Bruner (1986) has moved from the more general theoretical position embraced by Vygotsky (that social forms of speech are internalized by the child) to a more specific study of the role that this particular discourse form has on learning, thinking, and self-formation (see also Miller, 1994).

This question of how particular forms of discourse mediate the construction of knowledge is central to the work of many of the contributors to this volume. Having adopted the theoretical position that discourse mediates children's informal and formal learning (a sociocognitive perspective), many theorists are now delving into the specifics of this mediational process. In the current volume, psychologists and educators like Catherine Snow and Brenda Kurland ask questions about how "science talk" between mothers and their 5-year-old children is a social and cognitive facilitator of children's learning about science; and sociolinguistic researchers like Mary Catherine O'Connor and Sarah Michaels ask about the role that specific kinds of classroom discussion play in children's learning about mathematics and science. The work in this volume on the discourses of learning and schooling parallels an emergent interest among educators in the forms of talk (and writing) that provide the means for learning math and learning science (see Lampert, 1990; Bill, Leer, Reams, & Resnick 1992; Lemke, 1990; Rosebery, Warren, & Conant, 1992) – indeed, learning in any academic discipline. As Mikhail Bakhtin stated, abstract systems like mathematics do exist, but it is impossible to engage in "doing math" outside of a socially and historically situated discourse (see Bakhtin, 1981). Strikingly, researchers who might formerly have concentrated on children's cognitive representations of knowledge have begun to look closely at how children and teachers coconstruct knowledge in language-filled social environments.

In research focused on the role of discourse in learning and schooling, the work of Mikhail Bakhtin (1981, 1986) and his colleagues (see, in particular, Vološinov, 1973, 1987) has emerged as an important theoretical resource. I noted earlier that Bakhtin was a contemporary of Vygotsky, also working in the former Soviet Union in the 1930s (and well beyond for Bakhtin). There is no clear evidence that the two scholars had any direct communication or that their work was mutually influential (Morson & Emerson, 1989, 1990). Nonetheless, perhaps because of the shared cultural and intellectual climate in which their work arose, the theories developed by Vygotsky and Bakhtin are often considered highly compatible ones (e.g., Emerson, 1983; Wertsch, 1991). Both theorists are thought to be centrally concerned with the role that speech, inbued with the meanings (or "senses") particular to social and historical moments of utterance, plays in the emergence of a thinking, agentive *self*. Unique to Bakhtin's work, however, is an emphasis on this process of self-formation as an inherently dialogic one. For Bakhtin in particular, the conscious self is constituted by discourses imbued with the intentions and meanings of others but then subjected to active questioning and response. Dialogue and understanding (creative listening and response) become metaphors for individual cognitive thought. As Morson and Emerson (1990) suggest, Bakhtin's theory of the conscious self is a prosaic one: centrally concerned with discourse (dialogue) and with the origination of the conscious self in everyday, quotidian experience – what historians like Fernand Braudel (1980) refer to as *la longue durée*, as opposed to the more cataclysmic stages of which developmental theorists often write.

Since the appearance of translations of two volumes of Bakhtin's writing (see Bakhtin, 1981, 1986), an increasing number of educators, typically those interested in issues related to discourse and literacy, have begun to explore the ramifications for their work of his dialogical theories of discourse. To date, most researchers who draw on Bakhtin's work do so mostly in the spirit of understanding more completely the role that social and historical discourses play in learning and thinking. Thus, for many sociocognitive theorists and researchers, the work of Bakhtin and his colleagues has been utilized as a means of extending Vygotsky's emphasis on the internalization of social speech. The rich depiction in *The Dialogical Imagination*, for instance, of the appropriation of social and historical discourses has been used to extend the theory of how language becomes the means for achieving a thinking, conscious self (see Wertsch, 1991). Whereas Vygotsky wrote more generally about the role of social speech as a mediator of cognitive development, Bakhtin addressed the specificity of these social speech genres and their dialogic interaction in an individual consciousness. In fact, Bakhtin deliberately critiqued the distinction between "individual" and "social" that often provides the grounds for the central question in sociocognitive inquiry today: How is the individual child's learning mediated by social speech genres? Without a doubt, the writings of Bakhtin have had a significant impact on theory and research in education and psychology. However, the cognitive and pedagogical consequences of Bakhtin's theories of a dialogic self have yet to be fully articulated in the field of education, in part because Bakhtin's own work has been consistently aligned with the more Marxist theories of his close colleagues (see the discussion in Morson and Emerson, 1990) and in part because Bakhtin's writing has been viewed as primarily literary in nature, removed for many scholars from their interests in learning and schooling. And yet, as the work of Alex Kozulin in this volume suggests, literary texts are a valid metaphor for human consciousness, equal in importance to psychological metaphors grounded in the physical sciences (e.g., the mind as a computer). The theoretical writings of Mikhail Bakhtin and the work of Kozulin in this volume both point to the convergence of humanistic studies with the study of discourse and psychology. Such a convergence holds exciting possibilities for theory and practice in education.

The theoretical writings of Bakhtin, even given the limits of how these writings have thus far been utilized, suggest new venues for the exploration of discourse, learning, and schooling. If the work of scholars of literacy and discourse is to be taken seriously, the role of social discourses in the constitution of a thinking self is a crucial developmental and pedagogical question. *Texts*, literary and otherwise, might therefore come to be viewed as a central metaphor for scholars documenting the development of a conscious self in social contexts. Such discursively oriented depictions of human thinking and learning have begun to appear in the field of psychology, though at this point in the history of the discipline they are afforded a more marginal status. However, such discursive or "literary" models for psychology (see Edwards & Potter, 1992; Harre & Gillett, 1994; in addition to Kozulin, this volume) could potentially be extremely informative for the field of education. Questions about the *how* of the relationship between discourse and learning permeate the current volume, just as they are beginning to permeate the field of education more generally. How is the process of education mediated by discourse in general and by social discourses more specifically? What is the relationship between the child's thinking and her discursive interaction with a social world? How do the discourses of classroom instruction in part constitute environments for learning, and how are these discourses appropriated by children? How does the appropriation of multiple languages and multiple discourses transform children's participation in an expanding social world? Due to the profound impact of socioculturally oriented theories of psychology and language, questions such as these have become central to contemporary sociocognitive inquiry into learning. The humanistically oriented theories of Bakhtin provide an interesting research lens from which to extend the exploration of these kinds of questions. Viewing children as agentive selves engaged in dialogic response to the social discourse of classrooms and communities may be a necessary move away from the determinism of both sociological and psychological theory (see Rosaldo, 1989, for a discussion of similar movements in the field of anthropology; see Bruner, 1990, for a discussion of related issues in the field of psychology).

Sociocultural research on language and literacy

Earlier, drawing on similar comments by Luis Moll and Joel Dworin in this volume, I suggested that studies of the social and cognitive consequences of literacy have come to constitute an interdisciplinary field of research. Psychologists, sociolinguists, and educators – with individual researchers often representing more than one discipline area – have in recent decades begun to explore literacy as a complex but extremely important tool of society. As I mentioned earlier, some of this cross-disciplinary work on literacy is directly related to the impact of the sociocultural psychological theories developed by Vygotsky and his colleagues. For instance, the now famous studies by A. R. Luria, a former student of Vygotsky, of the impact of literacy on Uzbekistan and Kirghizia peasants are often cited in current studies of the cognitive consequences of literacy (see Luria, 1976). Perhaps the best-known descendant of this work from the former Soviet lands is the large-scale research study conducted by Sylvia Scribner and Michael Cole among the Vai in West Africa. In *The Psychology of Literacy,* Scribner and Cole (1981) explored, through a wide array of research methodologies, the impact of literacy, or *literacies* (since there were multiple forms of literacy among the Vai), on cognitive functioning. Their conclusion that particular forms of literacy have local, culture-specific cognitive consequences as opposed to sweeping transformations of cognitive functioning has often been cited in context-specific studies of literacy.

Not all scholars of the social and cognitive consequences of literacy would by any means agree with the central thesis of this groundbreaking work. Scholars like David Olson, for instance (see Olson, 1977), would argue that writing systems more generally have altered the relationships between language and thought. Because written language is available for reflection and analysis in a way that oral language is often not, it lends itself to a certain discursive and intellectual stance. As Kozulin points out in this volume, Olson suggests that written discourse tends to be more decontextualized, removed from the immediate contexts of everyday dialogue. However, regardless of the theoretical position that one assumes, studies of the social and cognitive consequences of literacy constitute a fascinating domain of inquiry within the more general area of studies of discourse, learning, and schooling. Indeed, a number of the contributors to this volume draw directly from this domain of scholarly inquiry. Luis Moll and Joel Dworin, for example, explore the social and cognitive consequences of *biliteracy*, or literacy in two languages – Spanish and English. Courtney Cazden examines through historical analysis the impact of Vygotskian theory on educators' positions with respect to the teaching of writing in schools. Finally, as I mentioned earlier, Alex Kozulin explores theories of the impact of literacy (notably the theoretical position articulated by David Olson) as he articulates his own "literary model for psychology." Thus, inquiries into the cognitive and social consequences of literacy are an important theoretical and empirical thread in the current volume.

At the same time, a related strand of scholarly inquiry on literacy, and on discourse more generally, is of equal import to this volume. Concomitant with the emergence of sociocognitive theories of learning, a field of research that one might broadly term *sociocultural studies of language and literacy* has arisen in recent decades. This field of research and inquiry has been, sometimes explicitly, other times more indirectly, rather intimately related to research and writing in sociocognitive learning theory. Unlike the first group of studies in psychology, however, these studies of language and literacy in social contexts draw their intellectual ancestry from the fields of anthropology and sociolinguistics more than from psychology.

Anthropological studies of the languages and social practices of various cultures have a long history in the larger field of social science research. However, beginning in the 1960s, a parallel hybrid domain of study emerged within the field of linguistics. Linguistics during this period, partly in response to the heavy emphasis on abstract, generative grammars in theoretical linguistics, began to explore the variability of languages within cultures, and even among social groups within a single culture. The field of sociolinguistics emerged as an alternative to the heavy emphasis among many theoretical linguists on *langue*, or language as an abstract system. Sociolinguists still focused largely on culture-specific variability in *grammatical* systems. Thus, topics such as the variable use of inflections (-*ing*) or auxiliary verbs (*be*) were explored as culture- and context-specific linguistic phenomena (see Fasold, 1969; Labov, 1972; Wolfram & Fasold, 1974). "Variable rules" were incorporated into grammars of languages, such that linguistic competence was presented in part as a process of selection among various options available to a native speaker. However, because of the emphasis on context specificity within the field of sociolinguistics, *discourse* (as opposed to syntax, morphology, or phonology) was from the beginning of this hybrid domain of inquiry an important unit of analysis. Rather than simply intuiting linguistic rules from one's knowledge as a native speaker (the primary method of analysis in generative linguistic theory), sociolinguists, like their intellectual counterparts in anthropology, conducted field-based research. Sociolinguists recorded speakers in varied settings – in conversation, doing shopping, telling stories, participating in a formal interview. Thus, concomitant with the emergence of this hybrid field of inquiry was an emerging interest in the analysis of discourse. Books such as *Discourse Strategies* (Gumperz, 1982) attest to the importance placed on studies of discourse by linguists working within this hybrid disciplinary area (see also Tannen, 1982a).

Along with an interest in the analysis of discourse, however, there was a strong interest in the social, political, and even pedagogical implications of linguistic variability. Sociolinguists like Labov (1972) and Fasold (1969), for instance, attempted to dispel the myth that what they termed *Vernacular Black English* was grammatically incorrect (for instance, the use of the auxiliary *be* in *she be going to church every Sunday*). Rather, these linguists explored grammatical systems much as anthropologists explored cultures: as systems of communication specific to social groups and inherently correct for native speakers within groups. It is not surprising, then, that the field of sociolinguistics developed as one of its principal means of inquiry *ethnographies of communication*. Combining research methodologies and theories from the fields of sociolinguistics and anthropology, scholars conducted holistic studies of communities' ways of using language socially. Rather than being limited to studies of particular events (such as a dinner table conversation) or even particular interlocutors (such as women versus men), these ethnographic studies of language use sought to establish a broader research lens. Entire speech communities were studied, with the goal of documenting the "interaction of language and social life" (Hymes, 1974).

Out of these traditions of sociolinguistic studies of linguistic variability, discourse, and language and social life within speech communities has emerged an interest among educational researchers in the acquisition of language and literacy in social context. As I have suggested, sociolinguistic research was never divorced from pedagogical issues. Schools and classrooms were viewed as speech communities in themselves, and language use in classroom settings was studied as one dimension of sociolinguistic research (see, for instance, Cazden, John, & Hymes, 1972). Such sociolinguistic research on classroom communication is, in fact, an important predecessor of the research on *classroom discourse*, which I will discuss later. Along with studies of classrooms as unique speech communities, educators conducted ethnographic studies of language use within communities. Such studies were often directly related to issues of classroom learning and teaching. For example, Shirley Brice Heath's (1983) ethnographic study of language and literacy learning in the Piedmont was both a sociolinguistic study and a social and pedagogical statement. Conducted just after the implementation of desegregation in the late 1960s, Heath's study explored, through ethnographic inquiry and sociolinguistic analysis, the forms of discourse used by members of three neighboring communities and acquired by children within those communities. Central to this work was its pedagogical implications. Children from two of the communities studied, a working-class white community and a working-class black community, did not typically fare as well in school as their middle-class classmates. Heath's study both explored the reasons for these differences and suggested an alternative pedagogy for addressing children's varied language backgrounds.

What has occurred in the field of education since the inception of sociolinguistic work parallels the explosion of research and writing conducted within a sociocognitive framework. The study of language use and literacy learning in social context, particularly in classroom settings, has become a major area of focus among educators. The sheer magnitude of research and writing on this topic speaks to its importance for educators (e.g., Bloome, 1987; Cook-Gumperz, 1986; de Castell, Luke, & Egan, 1986; Dyson, 1993; Schieffelin & Gillmore, 1986). One reason for the importance placed on this topic is undoubtedly its power to be informative about pressing social issues in education. From these sociolinguistic studies of culture-specific ways of using language has emerged a deeper understanding of questions such as why some children are successful in school and others are not. Sociolinguistic and educational researchers like Au (1979), Dyson (1993), Gee (1989, 1990), Heath (1982, 1983), Michaels (1981), and Scollon and Scollon (1981), for instance, have addressed the relationship between community-based language practices and children's classroom learning. Much of this research has been centered on the crucial role that literacy learning plays in children's classroom participation. Educational theorists have developed descriptive and theoretical models in their attempts to understand how and why the community-based discourses acquired by children in differing communities have different degrees of consonance with school, often literacy-based, discourses.

From the beginning of the history of this grouping of research, what I have here termed sociocultural studies of language and literacy, the field of anthropology has been an important source of theory and particularly of research methodology. Many educators who have pursued research questions related to classroom discourse, language socialization, and literacy learning have utilized methods of inquiry drawn from anthropology. Indeed, the ethnographic study of language and educational processes has emerged as a field of inquiry in its own right (see Erickson, 1988; Green & Wallat, 1981). And yet, the field of anthropology has itself undergone major changes in recent decades (see Ortner, 1984) as traditional views of ethnography have been questioned. Research in anthropology since the 1960s has begun to adopt a somewhat alternative and critical stance toward the observer and the observed. The traditional analytical role of the more distal participant-observer has been called into question, as has the resultant interpretive text developed by this presumed outside observer (see Clifford & Marcus, 1986). Perhaps more important for the purposes of the current volume, recent work in anthropology has begun to critique the illusion that cultures are static, contained entities. In contrast, the fluidity and overlap of cultures has been emphasized, as well as their constant historical change (Geertz, 1994; Rosaldo, 1989). One can simultaneously be female, working class, straight, and Latina. Each of these cultural identities carries with it an associated discourse, or set of discourses, that in part constitutes that identity.

This more recent work in anthropology is integrally related to some new questions that are currently being developed in the field of language and literacy studies. Educational theorists and researchers are exploring the multiple discourses that children acquire in home and institutional settings. Drawing on both a sociolinguistic framework and one consonant with this "new wave" of anthropological and ideological studies, theorists such as Gee (1989, 1990) have suggested that literacy is the masterful control of certain secondary discourses (i.e., the discourses of socially sanctioned institutions, like schools) rather than mastery of the conventions of written language. These scholars have pursued questions related to the multiple *literacies* that define full, successful participation in classrooms and workplaces. Rather than focusing exclusively on classroom discourse that involves the use of written texts, they have explored the discursive contingencies of multiple classroom activities and institutional settings. The contributions of O'Connor and Michaels and of Dorsey-Gaines and Garnett to this volume are examples of this theoretical framework. O'Connor and Michaels examine the discourse of instruction in mathematics, in particular the linguistic and social structure of a unique kind of classroom discussion. Dorsey-Gaines and Garnett explore the discourses of the Black Church that are an integral part of growing up in African-American communities. Though not all sociolinguistic and educational researchers have drawn on critical anthropological theory in their pursuit of questions related to discourse, many have begun to question in serious ways what it means to be literate or what is required to be a successful participant in classroom instructional activities. Among classroom researchers in particular, the more familiar questions related to children's literacy learning (i.e., *How do children gain mastery of written symbol systems?*) and classroom discourse have given way to questions about multiple discourses and varied task and participation structures. Things have begun to get unruly in educational research, as they have in ethnography.

And yet, the inherent messiness of current sociocultural research on language and literacy learning strikes me as consonant with the day-to-day lives of children and teachers in classrooms. In her book *Classroom Discourse*, Cazden (1988) points out that there is no parallel in the adult world to the linguistic and interactional structures of classrooms. Up to 30 children, some of them as young as 5 or 6 years of age, are social participants in an environment that is directed (with differing degrees of direction, dependent on individual pedagogical beliefs and practices) by one teacher (though sometimes with the help of a teaching assistant). Classrooms are crowded, often boisterous environments, with teachers attempting both to facilitate children's learning and socialization and to maintain order. Again dependent on individual instructional beliefs and practices, much classroom discourse is facilitated by classroom teachers. Through the establishment of regular activity and discussion frameworks, teachers attempt to create social environments conducive to learning. These activity and discussion frameworks, though orderly and systematic, are also "improvisations" on the part of children and teachers (Erickson, 1982). Some children compete to get the floor, and teachers struggle to make certain that other children are not lost in the fray.

Frederick Erickson, in his contribution to this volume, describes the complexities of classroom discourse in the context of one combined kindergarten–first-grade classroom. Erickson's work, and current work in general among sociolinguistic and educational researchers, addresses the complexity and unruliness of discourse in educational settings as much as it addresses its order and systematicity. Classroom discourses do not adhere to the idealized speaker–hearer interchange that is often depicted in transcriptions of speech: You speak, I respond, and then you develop a counterresponse. Language use in classrooms is overlapping, sometimes confusing, often indeterminate. It is directly linked to the demands of varied settings, where teachers and students often have different situational understandings and differing goals. The multiple discourses of teaching and learning are indeed as complex and fluid as the cultures once studied by anthropologists as static, structurally definable wholes.

My discussion of current theoretical questions and methodological approaches within the grouping of research on language that I have termed sociocultural has led me to the topic of classroom discourse, and it is here that I will also conclude. I suggested earlier that sociolinguistic research on speech communities' ways of using language led to efforts to understand the structure and functions of classroom discourse. Out of the overlapping fields of educational research on language and literacy and ethnographic research on language use in social context developed a body of research and writing devoted to classroom discourse processes. This body of work is summarized by Cazden (1986, 1988), and there is no need to review that literature here. Moreover, much of the literature on classroom discourse overlaps significantly with what I have already described here in terms of sociocultural research on language and literacy (e.g., Au, 1979; Michaels, 1981). However, some notable aspects of that body of work are worthy of brief discussion, if only to highlight the work that is currently being done, and also remains to be done, in studies of language use in classroom settings. One of the most familiar and significant findings that resulted from earlier studies of classroom discourse was the unique structural and functional properties of the forms of talk typically found in classrooms. Since many classroom discussions were and continue to be teacher-directed, a prominent social interactional construct that emerged from this research was the *IRE* (Initiation–Response–Evaluation) sequence (Mehan, 1979; see also the discussion in Cazden, 1988). This interactional sequence is an extremely familiar one to scholars studying language in educational settings, either from a research perspective or from the perspective of personal experience. The classroom teacher initiates a question or issue (to which he or she often already has an answer or a set of possible answers), a student replies to this query, and the teacher responds to the student's remark, often with an evaluative comment (*good, that's right*). Such interactional sequences exist, in a sense, as what linguists would refer to as the *unmarked* case. They constitute somewhat of a norm.

What has happened since the publication of this important research on language in classroom settings is that both classroom teachers in their practice and educational researchers in their descriptive analyses have begun to deviate from this norm. I have already discussed the new frameworks for analyzing discourse and learning that have emerged in consort with developments in social theory. Alongside these new research developments, there have emerged among classroom teachers new kinds of activity structures, some of which do not adhere to the teacher-directed IRE framework. Teachers like those described in this volume by O'Connor and Michaels have constructed participant frameworks that defy the more traditional social roles of teachers and students. In these discussion formats, teachers' *revoicings* of students' comments are nonevaluative and nonfinal. Students have the last word. Social participant frameworks such as these suggest that researchers' studies of classroom discourse must be extremely adaptive. The multifarious activity structures found in classrooms – small cooperative learning groups, student-led whole-class discussions, teacher-facilitated group discussions – and the inherent unruliness of any classroom discursive activity should be reflected in researchers' inquiries. And this seems to be exactly what is happening among many educators and psychologists studying classroom discourse processes. The chapters by Erickson, Hicks, Moll and Dworin, and O'Connor and Michaels in this volume are representative of the many possibilities that exist for examining the diversity and even unruliness of language use in classrooms.

All of these remarks about sociocognitive and sociocultural perspectives on language, learning, and schooling suggest that there is still a great deal of work to be done as educators and developmental theorists attempt to understand *how* discourse mediates children's learning. Over the past two decades, an impressive body of work has been amassed in the overlapping fields of education, psychology, and sociolinguistics. And yet, the convergence of work in these fields, through the recognition of scholars that such convergence is ultimately necessary if their questions are to be adequately addressed, continues to suggest new and powerful opportunities for innovative forms of inquiry. The chapters in this volume demonstrate this possibility inherent in the merging of sociocognitive and sociocultural studies of discourse. Collectively, this work suggests that, if not explicable in a causal, scientific sense, the complexities of relationships between discourse, learning, and schooling are worthy of at least deeper understanding.

Organization of the volume

Rather than organizing the volume around issues of theory and practice (as is often the case with education volumes), I have grouped the chapters according to three broad topics and modes of inquiry. Part I deals with classroom discourse, but the chapters in this part reposition classroom discourses as improvisational social constructions in which rhythmic timing, shifting relationships among actors, and the dialogic response to one's milieu are central. Part II presents studies in an essayist mode, explorations by two interdisciplinary scholars of the relationship of literacy to both theories of psychology and theories of pedagogy. Part III deals with the multiplicity of discourses that play an important role in literacy learning, with *literacy* broadly viewed as engagement with written texts and as participation in the social practices that collectively are constitutive of formal educational processes.

The chapters in Part I explore issues related to the discourses of learning and formal instruction, the kinds of discourse that one typically finds in classrooms and other formal institutional settings. Like all of the authors in this volume, the authors of the chapters in Part I dialectically explore issues related to developmental and educational theory and issues related to pedagogical practice. Frederick Erickson (Chapter 2) and Mary Catherine O'Connor and Sarah Michaels (Chapter 3) revisit the topic of classroom discourse that is a mainstay of research on language and education. However, as I intimated earlier, the authors of both chapters portray something other than the normative IRE sequences typically associated with classroom teaching and learning. Erickson depicts classroom discussion as a rhythmically timed interactional achievement, with students and their teacher coconstructing a "zone" through both successful and unsuccessful attempts to contribute. His analysis of one young student's attempts to enter successfully into the discourse amid the attempts of more experienced "turn sharks" attests to the complexity of group discussions that might previously have been characterized as IRE sequences. O'Connor and Michaels present a compelling analysis of group discussion that is not based on an IRE model. In their chapter, the sociocognitive work of learning about science and math (in this case, torque) is described as being mediated by particular discursive moves in which classroom teachers linguistically position students' contributions as competing *theories*. My contribution to this volume (Chapter 4) explores the relationship between oral and written discourse and classroom learning both empirically – through case studies of two first graders – and theoretically. Grounding my work in a sociocognitive theoretical framework, I focus on issues of methodology: How can one, methodologically speaking, explore children's construction of knowledge through discourse? This chapter provides exemplars of *contextual inquiries*, multifaceted interpretive analyses, that are consonant with the theoretical tenets of a sociocognitive psychology and with a humanistic approach to the study of learning.

The chapters in Part II focus on interdisciplinary studies of literacy, psychology, and pedagogy, explored in an essayist mode of inquiry. In Chapter 5, Alex Kozulin examines a topic that has been widely explored by psychologists working within a sociocultural or sociohistorical framework: the cognitive consequences of literacy. However, Kozulin extends his depiction of the intellectual consequences of literate discourse to a broader model for psychology. Drawing largely on the work of Bakhtin, he proposes that the development of a conscious, socially responsive self be viewed as a process of authorship ("life as authoring"). In developing this model, Kozulin explores the impact of forms of literature on cognitive thought, and he addresses the pedagogical consequences of such a "literary model for psychology." Like Kozulin's chapter, Courtney Cazden's (Chapter 6) is primarily essayist in nature. She reviews differing interpretive "readings" of Vygotskian theory among prominent writing researchers (mostly educators), relating these alternative readings to the theoretical positions they imply. Her chapter is interesting for educators working within sociocognitive or sociocultural perspectives in that it reveals the multifarious ways in which Vygotsky's work can be applied to educational problems. In this case, contradictory pedagogies have been constructed from writing researchers' alternative readings of the "same" texts.

Part III also focuses primarily on the topic of literacy but shifts from the essayist orientation of the previous two chapters to one grounded in educational research. The chapter by Catherine Snow and Brenda Kurland explores scientific talk, of the sort that is sanctioned in classroom settings, from an empirical basis. Rather than examining science talk in the classroom, as did O'Connor and Michaels, Snow and Kurland (Chapter 7) look at science-related discourse among younger children and their mothers in a task setting. They constructed a task that was constrained only by the presence of a large magnet and varied objects – like coins, sponges, and paper clips – some of which readily adhered to the magnet. The resulting talk between mothers and their 5-year-old children provides a fascinating glimpse into the more everyday ways of talking about scientific phenomena that might be predecessors of the highly valued "process talk" that characterizes science as an academic discipline. The empirical relationships between extended science talk about processes of magnetic attraction and school-based literacy that are explored in this chapter are important ones. They suggest, more generally, a complex view of relationships between children's discursive experiences in the preschool years and their participation in school-based literacy practices, such as reading.

Luis Moll and Joel Dworin (Chapter 8) also discuss literacy, but their research focus is on the sociocultural practices that define literacy in classroom settings. In their chapter, they explore *biliteracy*, or literacy in two languages. Through classroom-based studies of the development of biliteracy among children in the primary and middle school grades, they critique the position held by many educators of minority children that literacy education should focus on developing mastery of literacy of one language only – the dominant language of mainstream society. Their studies of biliteracy among Latino children in bilingual school settings suggest an alternative view: that the simultaneous development of literacy in two languages amplifies the cultural and intellectual resources available to children. Their case studies of the biliteracy of two Latino children provide valuable insight into a central question explored in this volume: how discourse, in this case multiple literacies, mediates children's learning in educational settings. In Chapter 9, Catherine Dorsey-Gaines and Cynthia Garnett continue with the theme of *literacies* and their educational consequences. Their work explores literacy not only as a modality but also as a set of discourses, or socially defined ways of using language. They provide an historical overview of the development of literacies in the Black Church, a prominent educational institution in the African-American community. They also delve into the unique attributes of the discourses of the Black Church, and into how these have impacted the literacy-related experiences of its members. Finally, their narrative studies of the discourses unique to the Black Church are linked to an exploration of literacy education among African-American children. Dorsey-Gaines and Garnett propose a research model that allows for the existence of multiple ways of defining literacy education as a set of pedagogical practices.

In his closing remarks, James Paul Gee (Chapter 10) moves from a discussion of literacies (as in Part III of this volume) to a discussion of what could be called *critical literacies*. Drawing on the work of Vygotsky and Bakhtin, whose work is integral to many, if not all, of the chapters in this volume, Gee moves to questions of the value of educational practices. Educators have begun to realize that instruction (whether of the more traditional/overt or the more progressive/implicit variety) entails the "learning" of certain discourse practices. The mastery of school-based literacies is for most educators the goal of formal schooling. Vygotsky and more recent sociocognitive theorists and researchers have, as Gee suggests, maintained that the internalization of school-based literacies (e.g., "talking" and "thinking" science) enables the student to engage in new forms of thinking, ones that may be enabling for their participation in formal institutional settings. However, Gee raises questions about the costs of this apprenticeship (or overt instruction) into school-based literacies. Is it the case, for instance, that students' "internalization" of scientific literacies enables them to critique those literacies? Do non-spontaneous forms of thinking (as described by Vygotsky) necessarily entail critical dialogue *about* those new forms of thinking? Gee's remarks remind us that discourses are always embedded in ideologies. His afterthoughts suggest that inquiries about discourse and schooling necessarily entail difficult questions about the social and political values embedded in instructional practices and theories.

References

Au, K. (1979). Participation structures in a reading lesson with Hawaiian children: Analysis of a culturally appropriate instructional event. *Anthropology and Education Quarterly, 11*, 91–114.

Bakhtin, M. M. (1981). *The dialogic imagination: Four essays by M. M. Bakhtin* (M. Holquist, Ed.; C. Emerson & M. Holquist, Trans.). Austin: University of Texas Press.

Bakhtin, M. M. (1986). *Speech genres and other late essays* (C. Emerson & M. Holquist, Eds.; V. McGee, Trans.). Austin: University of Texas Press.

Bill, V., Leer, M., Reams, L., & Resnick, L. (1992). From cupcakes to equations: The structure of discourse in a primary mathematics classroom. *Verbum, 1–2*, 63–85. Pittsburgh: Learning Research and Development Center.

Bloome, D. (Ed.). (1987). *Literacy and schooling*. Norwood, NJ: Ablex.

Braudel, F. (1980). *On history* (S. Mathews, Trans.). Chicago: Chicago University Press.

Bruner, J. (1983). *Child's talk: Learning to use language*. New York: W. W. Norton.

Bruner, J. (1986). *Actual minds, possible worlds*. Cambridge, MA: Harvard University Press.

Bruner, J. (1990). *Acts of meaning*. Cambridge, MA: Harvard University Press.

Cazden, C. (1986). Classroom discourse. In M. E. Wittrock (Ed.), *Handbook of research on teaching* (3rd ed.). New York: Macmillan.

Cazden, C. (1988). *Classroom discourse: The language of teaching and learning.* Portsmouth, NH: Heinemann.

Cazden, C., John, V. P., & Hymes, D. (Eds.). (1972). *Functions of language in the classroom.* New York: Teachers College Press. (Reprinted by Waveland Press, 1985.)

Chomsky, N. (1982). *Lectures on government and binding.* Dordrecht, The Netherlands: Foris.

Clifford, J., & Marcus, G. (Eds.). (1986). *Writing culture: The poetics and politics of ethnography.* Berkeley: University of California Press.

Cole, M., & Griffin, P. (1980). Cultural amplifiers reconsidered. In D. Olson (Ed.), *The social foundations of language and thought: Essays in honor of Jerome S. Bruner.* New York: W. W. Norton.

Cook-Gumperz, J. (Ed.). (1986). *The social construction of literacy.* New York: Cambridge University Press.

de Castell, S., Luke, A., & Egan, K. (Eds.). (1986). *Literacy, society, and schooling: A reader.* New York: Cambridge University Press.

Dyson, A. H. (1993). *Social worlds of children learning to write in an urban school.* New York: Teachers College Press.

Edwards, D., & Potter, J. (1992). *Discursive psychology.* Newbury Park, CA: Sage.

Emerson, C. (1983). The outer word and inner speech: Bakhtin, Vygotsky, and the internalization of language. *Critical Inquiry, 10,* 245–264.

Emerson, C. (1993). *Bakhtin and Vygotsky in the context of post-communist education.* Paper presented at the College of Education Colloquium Series, University of Delaware.

Erickson, F. (1982). Classroom discourse as improvisation: Relationships between academic task structure and social participation structure in lessons. In L. C. Wilkinson (Ed.), *Communicating in the classroom.* New York: Academic Press.

Erickson, F. (1988). Ethnographic description. In H. von Ulrich Ammon, N. Dittmar, & K. Mattheier (Eds.), *Sociolinguistics.* Berlin: Walter de Gruyter.

Fasold, R. (1969). Tense and the form *be* in Black English. *Language, 45,* 763–776.

Forman, E., Minick, N., & Stone, A. (1993). *Contexts for learning: Sociocultural dynamics in children's development.* New York: Oxford University Press.

Gee, J. P. (1989). What is literacy? *Journal of Education, 171(1),* 18–25.

Gee, J. P. (1990). *Social linguistics and literacies: Ideology in discourses.* New York: Falmer Press.

Gee, J. P. (1992). *The social mind: Language, ideology, and social practice.* New York: Bergin & Garvey.

Geertz, C. (1994). Life on the edge. [Review of *In the realm of the diamond queen: Marginality in an out-of-the-way place* (A. L. Tsing).] *The New York Review of Books.* April 7.

Graff, H. (1987). *The legacies of literacy: Continuities and contradictions in Western culture and society.* Bloomington: Indiana University Press.

Green, J., & Wallat, C. (Eds.). (1981). *Ethnography and language in educational settings.* Norwood, NJ: Ablex.

Gumperz, J. (1982). *Discourse strategies.* New York: Cambridge University Press.

Harre, R., & Gillett, G. (1994). *The discursive mind.* Thousand Oaks, CA: Sage.

Heath, S. B. (1982). What no bedtime story means: Narrative skills at home and at school. *Language in Society, 11(2),* 49–76.

Heath, S. B. (1983). *Ways with words: Language, life, and work in communities and classrooms.* New York: Cambridge University Press.

Hymes, D. (1974). *Foundations in sociolinguistics: An ethnographic introduction.* Philadelphia: University of Pennsylvania Press.

Kozulin, A. (1990). *Vygotsky's psychology: A biography of ideas*. Cambridge, MA: Harvard University Press.

Labov, W. (1972). *Language in the inner city: Studies in the Black English vernacular.* Philadelphia: University of Pennsylvania Press.

Lampert, M. (1990). When the problem is not the question and the solution is not the answer: Mathematical knowing and teaching. *American Educational Research Journal, 27(1)*, 29–63.

Lemke, J. L. (1990). *Talking science: Language, learning, and values*. Norwood, NJ: Ablex.

Luria, A. R. (1976). *Cognitive development: Its cultural and social foundations*. Cambridge, MA: Harvard University Press.

Mehan, H. (1979). *Learning lessons: Social organization in the classroom*. Cambridge, MA: Harvard University Press.

Michaels, S. (1981). "Sharing time": Children's narrative styles and differential access to literacy. *Language in Society, 10*, 423–442.

Miller, P. (1994). Narrative practices: Their role in socialization and self construction. In U. Neisser & R. Fivush (Eds.), *The remembering self: Construction and accuracy in the self-narrative*. New York: Cambridge University Press.

Minick, N. (1989). *L.S. Vygotsky and Soviet activity theory: Perspectives on the relationship between mind and society*. Technical Reports, Special Monograph No. 1. Newton, MA: Literacies Institute.

Moll, L. (Ed.). (1990). *Vygotsky and education: Instructional implications and applications of sociohistorical psychology*. New York: Cambridge University Press.

Morson, G. S., & Emerson, C. (Eds.). (1989). *Rethinking Bakhtin: Extensions and challenges*. Evanston, IL: Northwestern University Press.

Morson, G. S., & Emerson, C. (1990). *Mikhail Bakhtin: Creation of a prosaics*. Stanford, CA: Stanford University Press.

Nelson, K. (1986). *Event knowledge: Structure and function in development*. Hillsdale, NJ: Erlbaum.

Nelson, K. (Ed.). (1989). *Narratives from the crib*. Cambridge, MA: Harvard University Press.

Olson, D. (1977). From utterance to text: The bias of language in speech and writing. *Harvard Educational Review, 47*, 257–281.

Olson, D. (Ed.). (1980). *The social foundations of language and thought: Essays in honor of Jerome S. Bruner*. New York: W. W. Norton.

Ortner, S. (1984). Theory in anthropology since the sixties. *Comparative Studies in Society and History, 26(1)*, 126–166.

Piaget, J. (1952). *The language and thought of the child*. New York: Humanities Press. (Original work published 1926)

Pinker, S. (1984). *Language learnability and language development*. Cambridge, MA: Harvard University Press.

Rogoff, B. (1990). *Apprenticeship in thinking: Cognitive development in social context*. New York: Oxford University Press.

Rosaldo, R. (1989). *Culture and truth: The remaking of social analysis*. Boston: Beacon Press.

Rosebery, A., Warren, B., & Conant, F. (1992). Appropriating scientific discourse: Findings from minority classrooms. *Journal of the Learning Sciences, 2(1)*, 61–94.

Schieffelin, B., & Gilmore, P. (Eds.). (1986). *The acquisition of literacy: Ethnographic perspectives*. Norwood, NJ: Ablex.

Scollon, R., & Scollon, S. B. (1981). *Narrative, literacy, and face in interethnic communication*. Norwood, NJ: Ablex.

Scribner, S., & Cole, M. (1981). *The psychology of literacy.* Cambridge, MA: Harvard University Press.

Shattuck, R. (1980). *The forbidden experiment: The story of the wild boy of Aveyron.* New York: Farrar Strauss Giroux.

Tannen, D. (Ed.). (1982a). *Analyzing discourse: Text and talk.* Washington, DC: Georgetown University Press.

Tannen, D. (1982b). The oral/literate continuum in discourse. In D. Tannen (Ed.), *Spoken and written language: Exploring orality and literacy.* Norwood, NJ: Ablex.

Voloshinov, V. N. (1973). *Marxism and the philosophy of language.* (L. Matejka & I. R. Titunik, Trans.). New York: Seminar.

Vološinov, V. N. (1987). *Freudianism: A critical sketch.* (I. R. Titunik & N. R. Bruss, Eds.; I. R. Titunik, Trans.). Bloomington: Indiana University Press.

Vygotsky, L. S. (1962). *Thought and language* (E. Hanfmann & G. Vakar, Ed. and Trans.). Cambridge, MA: MIT Press.

Vygotsky, L. S. (1978). *Mind in society: The development of higher mental processes* (M. Cole, V. John-Steiner, & E. Souberman, Eds.). Cambridge, MA: Harvard University Press.

Vygotsky, L. S. (1986). *Thought and language* (rev. ed.) (A. Kozulin, Ed. and Trans.). Cambridge, MA: MIT Press.

Vygotsky, L. S. (1987). *Thinking and speech* (N. Minick, Trans.). New York: Plenum Press.

Wertsch, J. (1985). *Vygotsky and the social formation of mind.* Cambridge, MA: Harvard University Press.

Wertsch, J. (1991). *Voices of the mind: A sociocultural approach to mediated action.* Cambridge, MA: Harvard University Press.

Willis, P. (1977). *Learning to labor: How working class kids get working class jobs.* New York: Columbia University Press.

Wolfram, W., & Fasold, R. (1974). *The study of social dialects in American English.* Englewood Cliffs, NJ: Prentice-Hall.

Yaroshevsky, M. (1989). *Lev Vygotsky* (S. Syrovatkin, Trans.). Moscow: Progress Publishers.

Part I

Classroom discourses

2 Going for the zone: the social and cognitive ecology of teacher–student interaction in classroom conversations

Frederick Erickson

Introduction

Social interaction as a learning environment

Research and theory construction along neo-Vygotskian lines[1] has presented cognition in a new light: as socially situated (a kind of production that makes purposive use of tools, including those others have made) and as transpersonal (a distributed phenomenon, not simply something residing within a single head). This makes for a profound change in how we think about thinking, about learning, and about teaching – participation by teachers and pupils in nonverbal interaction and in oral and written conversation – the interaction among people that fosters learning.

Learning becomes not simply the internalization of knowledge and skill by an isolated mind interacting with a physical surround or even with a surround containing humanly produced artifacts. Rather, the organism–environment relation is one of interpenetration and of reflexively constitutive activity. The learning environment is not one designed at a distance by a curriculum developer or by a teacher as a First Cause and Unmoved Mover, as if the educator were analogous to the eighteenth-century Deist's conception of a watchmaker God who builds the universe, winds it up, and then stands at the margins of Creation, letting it run its course.

This view of relations between teacher and learner, expert and novice, is a radically proximal one in which there is conjoint participation and influence, one in which no mover is unmoved. In such a view of teaching and learning the Word is indeed made Flesh, that is, immanence replaces distal transcendence in our understanding of the relations between teacher and learner. Moreover, the learner is seen as having the same agentive footing in the interaction as the teacher. In the former view of teaching, the teacher was seen as the subject and agent and the pupil as the object and patient. In the new view, the student is seen as active, influencing the teacher while being influenced by the teacher.[2]

How does the mutual influence we call teaching and learning actually take place in and through immediate social interaction? Neo-Vygotskian work has emphasized the importance of social interaction in learning. It points to the engagement of expert and novice in the *zone of proximal development* (ZPD), through which the more expert party in the interchange helps to complete and extend the actions and insights of the less expert one.

Yet, if social interaction is seen as crucial for learning, we must not leave unexamined the notion of social interaction itself. My sense is that in much of the neo-Vygotskian work, what has occupied the foreground of attention is the cognitive or linguistic changes that occur in the learner rather than the processes of interaction through which such changes are seen as being stimulated. Analyses of transcripts of expert–novice dialogue focus on the content of speech rather than on the process of interaction in tandem with its manifest content. In other words, interaction as a social and behavioral process seems to be treated as a residual category in discussions of engagement in the ZPD. Thus it is possible that unexamined assumptions about the nature of social interaction (and of conversation) as a medium for learning and teaching may be constraining the ways in which pedagogical transactions are being viewed.

It seems to me that conceptions from recent work in the study of the organization of immediate social interaction can make more rich the notions of activity and of engagement in the ZPD that are being used by those I have been calling *neo-Vygotskians* and who might even more appropriately and inclusively be called *neo-interactionist* researchers on learning. In the remainder of this chapter, I will review certain issues in the conception of human interaction in face-to-face conversation. Then I will illustrate those issues with an example of conversation from a kindergarten–first-grade classroom.

Conceptions of social interaction

Neo-Vygotskian discussions of engagement in the ZPD place special emphasis on two aspects of social interaction – the dyadic and the reciprocal. Perhaps because of the origins of the notion of ZPD in the interactive experiments of Vygotsky, the learning situation is seen as one involving a single expert and a single novice (see, e.g., Vygotsky 1978; Wertsch 1985; Wood, Bruner, & Ross 1976).

Dialogue is a powerful and evocative metaphor for the transformative engagement that happens in conversation. Yet the organization of talk in classrooms is not literally dialogic, that is, classrooms are not just settings for verbal exchanges between pairs of individuals in isolation from others around them. That view comes in part from idealized images of pedagogical conversations such as that of Mark Hopkins and a student sitting on either end of a log, or of the teacher–student dialogues from classical, medieval, and renaissance educational texts (which themselves probably derive from Plato's idealized presentation of Socrates in dialogue with one primary interlocutor at a time). Prescriptive models of "good teaching" often treat classroom conversation as if it were a series of one-on-one engagements between the teacher and a succession of students. Classroom etiquette for recitation (nowadays considered an aspect of classroom management) and the ubiquity in whole-class discussion of what many researchers call the *IRE* discourse sequence (known information question initiated by the teacher, followed by a response by a student, followed in turn by evaluation of the response by the teacher) may imply a cultural model of "one speaker at a time and pairs of speakers in dialogue" for the social participation framework of ordinary classroom conversation.[3]

Admittedly, some empirical research on classroom discourse does show sustained interaction between a teacher and a single child that has the overall appearance of dialogue. A wonderful example comes from the work of Wertsch (1990, 113–114) who shows a scene of classroom interaction in which a student is appropriating the voice of the teacher more and more completely across successive turns at talk in dialogue with the teacher.

Danny, a kindergartner, has brought a rock from home for "Show and Tell." He first presents the rock in terms of its relation to himself: "My mom went to the volcano and got it . . . I've had it ever since I was . . . I've always been taking care of it. It's never fallen down and broken." Then the teacher shifts referential perspective to an objective, taxonomic one. Danny adopts this perspective in his next utterances (17, 19, 41), appropriating the teacher's voice:

(14) T: Uh hum. Okay. Is it rough or smooth?
(15) C1: (Danny): Real rough and it's . . . and it's . . . and it's sharp.
(16) T: Okay. Why don't you go around and let the children touch it.
          Okay? (*C1 takes it around the group, which is sitting on the floor.*)
          Is it heavy or light?
(17) C1: It's heavy.
(18) T: It's heavy.
(19) C1: A little bit heavy
          (*As discussion continues, the teacher opens a child's dictionary and reads from it under the heading "lava."*)

(40) T: Okay. Wow. Wait till you hear what this says. . . . It says, "Lava is
            melted rock that comes out of a volcano when it erupts. It is rock
            formed by lava that has cooled and hardened." . . . Once it cooled
            off it got hard and, and now it's rock.
(41) C1:   And it's . . . know what? And it's still . . . it's still . . . Look . . .
            Shows from where it got . . . from where it was burned.

In presenting a short form of Wertsch's transcript, I have eliminated
some of the side comments of the teacher to children other than Danny,
as well as the comments of those other children. But in spite of the
presence of other students in the transcript, Wertsch's analysis of the
interaction puts the dialogue between the teacher and Danny at the
center of analytic attention. Wertsch's commentary foregrounds the
voices of Danny and the teacher and, in a sense, abstracts them from
their situation in the midst of the voices of other students in the classroom. This portrays the dialogue between Danny and the teacher as in
effect uninterrupted by the other students. That may be warranted in
this instance, for the scene portrayed came from what appears to be a
classroom characterized by easy politeness among the participants. But
as our attention was drawn centrally to how the teacher and a single
student engaged one another in the ZPD, the information presented and
organized in Wertsch's transcript and discussion (which, in showing the
appropriation of the teacher's voice, is a luminous tour de force analytically) did not enable us to consider how others in the scene may have
been leaning on and even interpenetrating the interaction occurring
between the focal characters.

In my experience, much classroom interaction is far messier than this,
even when children are being nice. Children stumble over each other in
conversation. They may complete each other's clauses and turns at talk.
They may take turns away from each other. The pullings and coun-
terpullings, the ebbs and flows of mutual influence in the conversation,
are not just between one student and the teacher at a given time but
rather among many students – sometimes among teams of students –
and the teacher. How, then, does a single student get to a ZPD with a
teacher? And need the single student get there alone or can multiple
students enter a ZPD together? Do we mean only dyadic engagement
when we conceive of interaction in the ZPD?

The other notion about interaction implicit in the neo-Vygotskian
work is that it is reciprocal in a sequential sense; that is, one party's
action is seen as being followed by another's in response across successive moments in real time. From this point of view (the usual one),

human social interaction is conceived as a ping-pong match. Successful participation by speakers, and the influence of one speaker on another, are seen as involving syntagmatically appropriate matchings of one person's initiation with another person's response across successive moments in real time, (e.g., if person X asks a question, then person Y is accountable for answering it at the next appropriate moment).

Yet this emphasis on sequential reciprocity (which centers our attention on turntaking in oral discourse) overlooks the complementarity of simultaneous participation in interaction by interlocutors. More than turntaking is going on. At the same moments in which the speaker is speaking, the listener is listening. Because the speaker can see as well as hear, whatever the listener is doing nonverbally (and verbally) is available as evidence that what the speaker is saying is being received by the auditor.

Thus mutual influence between interlocutors happens simultaneously as well as successively as they converse. The issue for the practical speaker in articulating his or her actions with those of other participants is not just to take account of what someone has done the moment before, what I need to do now, and what they will do next. Articulation of action also involves taking into consideration what others are doing while I am doing something in the present moment (see Condon & Ogston, 1967; Erickson, 1986; Erickson & Shultz, 1982, 70–77).

In sum, as teachers and students interact in classrooms, they construct an ecology of social and cognitive relations in which influence between any and all parties is mutual, simultaneous, and continuous. One aspect of this social and cognitive ecology is the multiparty character of the scene – many participants, all of them continually "on task," albeit working on different kinds of tasks, some of which may be at cross purposes with others. Although teachers in group discussion may attempt to enforce a participation framework of successive dyadic teacher–student exchanges, often the conversation is more complicated than that. The conversations that take place are multiparty ones, and they may be ones in which various sets of speakers and auditors are engaged simultaneously in multiple conversational floors (see, e.g., Shultz, Florio, & Erickson, 1982, for a discussion of conversation in the classroom that will be considered in detail in this chapter, and see Au & Mason, 1981, for a discussion of reading group conversation in classrooms of native Hawaiian pupils).

Another aspect of the social and cognitive ecology of interaction in the classroom – a system of relations of mutual influence among participants – involves the combination of what I have called here the *reciprocal* and *complementary* aspects of the organization of immediate social interaction in real time. Interaction, it would seem, always involves the articulation of both successive and simultaneous actions, verbal and nonverbal, by those engaged in it.

Given the complexity of reciprocal and complementary organization that is necessary to accomplish a multiparty conversation successfully, we must ask, "How does the sociocognitive ecology work in classroom conversations? How is the collective action done so that interactional (and cognitive) traffic jams do not occur and so that there is an opportunity for understanding and learning?" In attempting to answer such questions, we may come to see how insights gained from analysis of the workings of interactional traffic management in classroom conversations can inform a theory of cognition and learning as situated, collective, and purposive human activity.

Traffic management in interaction: timing and contextualization cues

Timing appears to be what holds the whole ecology of interaction together in its performance. The relative temporal location of the various actions of interlocutors is an important aspect of the ordering of the collective activity of conversation in both its reciprocal and its complementary aspects. We can speak of timing as one aspect of a dialectical process in interaction that has been called *contextualization* by Gumperz (1982; see also Erickson, 1992), entailing a system of signals he calls *contextualization cues*. The notion of contextualization follows that of Bateson (1956), who observed that because of an inherent ambiguity in systems of communicative signs, those engaged in interaction need to regulate it by signals that point to the relevant context of interpretation in which other signs are intended to be "read." Thus sets of communicative displays contain, within the surface structure of their performance, certain behavioral features that function as cues that point to their proper interpretation. In other words, the enactment of communication reflexively creates its contextual framing at the same time as it is being framed by its context.

In the timing of immediate social interaction, such as in face-to-face conversation, an especially important contextualizing function appears to be performed by the temporal placement of points of emphasis in speech prosody (volume and pitch shifts) and in body motion (postural shifts, gaze, changes in direction of motion in gesture). The points of emphasis appear to function as contextualization cues that signal expectations at various levels. Not only do individual cues of verbal or nonverbal emphasis enable one to anticipate immediate next moments, but because they tend to cluster together in regular intervals of occurrence, the clusters of points of emphasis in speech and body motion often can be perceived as a cadence. This cadence is a rhythmic underpinning that enables the various participants in a conversational interchange to anticipate the projected courses of action of individual interlocutors and of the conversational group as a whole (see the discussion in Erickson, 1991).

The presence within communicative behavior of contextualization cues for the regulation of interactional timing enables interlocutors to "read" the ongoing course of the conversational roller coaster as they are riding along in it. This makes it possible for interlocutors to act on their anticipations by "going for" crucial functional places that are turning points in the reciprocal (syntagmatic) order that will occur as oncoming moments ahead in the interaction's ongoing course. (This is akin to the way in which a pianist "goes for" the next chord in a harmonic sequence, temporally in terms of the flow of the music as well as kinesically and spatially by reaching for the keys on the piano keyboard. See Sudnow, 1978 and 1980, for discussion.)

In terms of the organization of discourse in conversation, the cadence stress pulses usually occur at points of midcourse correction, points of turn completion and turn exchange, and points of crucial information and "keying" (e.g., irony, seriousness). In terms of nonverbal activity, cadence emphasis often occurs at points of exchange of objects (such as one person handing another a hammer) or of one person opening to a page in a book as another person is calling out the page number. Somewhat as traffic lights signal the timing of the flow of cars across intersections (the regular timing of the light change enabling drivers to take strategic account of what the next light on the road ahead is doing), the contextual cues of what can be called *verbal* and *nonverbal prosody* seem to signal the timing of crucial functional moments in syntagmatic sequences of individual actions in a conversation so that they can be done in a jointly articulated fashion rather than haphazardly. Such concerted action is *social* in that the various social actors take intended (read "meaningful") actions in account of the intended actions of others.

Thus, as we are engaged in the moment-by-moment unfolding of an actual conversation, it is not only necessary to have an abstract capacity to understand a speech sound or comprehend a grammatical string. It is also important to be able to hear *just this* strip of speech and/or see *just this* strip of gesture *at the right time.* Given the limits on human information processing and the huge number of verbally and nonverbally communicated information bits in the air at any one moment in a conversation, for an interlocutor to receive intelligible information or to produce it requires the capacity to "go for" crucial moments in the discourse, attentionally and in uttering, and to disattend and not utter in other moments that are noncrucial. Otherwise, we would be continually overwhelmed by data we could not even handle perceptually, let alone process cognitively.

This sense of "rightness" of time is pointed to by a distinction in Greek between time in a technical or physical sense and in a social and phenomenological sense. The former conception of time is meant by the term *chronos,* from which we derive terms for clock time and for the quantitatively uniform measurement of units of time. The latter understanding is meant by the term *kairos,* which refers to the developing or unfolding quality of time: change of seasons, of weather, of crucial turning points in history. This is time as humanly experienced: "in the fullness of time"; the emergent "not quite yet"; the "now" that, once arrived, feels right.

In human social interaction, *kairos* timing results from the mutual activity of the interactional partners. It is not absolutely regular chronometrically; there is an ebb and flow of speeding up and slowing down that in music is called *rubato.* Yet conversational partners share a mutually enacted timing that is remarkably predictable. At some moments, it is almost chronometric, but not quite. At other times, rhythmic stress in speech and in body motion (i.e., posture, gesture, and gaze) is virtually metronomic in its chronometric regularity. At this point, the significance of *kairos* timing for the organization of interaction is only beginning to be realized (see the discussion in Auer, 1992; Cooper-Kuhlen, 1992; Erickson, 1982, 1992; Erickson & Shultz, 1982, 72–74; Scollon, 1982).

In sum, we can say that timing enables nothing less than the social organization of attention and action in conversation. Moreover, we can say that the timing of interactional performance is accomplished by contextualization cueing. Hence when we say that cognition and action are situated in sociocognitive learning environments, we mean, among other things, that they are situated in real time – not an ideal "time-out" condition for reflection and deliberation but an actual, ongoing development of sequences of interaction, moment by moment, in which one is never completely sure of where the interaction is going next and during which the time clock never stops.

A classroom example

"I can make a 'P' "

This example comes from a kindergarten–first-grade classroom in a working-class Italian-American neighborhood in a suburb of Boston. Other aspects of interaction in this classroom and in the homes of focal children in the class have been reported separately.[4]

This particular classroom is an especially appropriate setting for illustrating the multiparty organization of interaction at the ZPD. This is for two reasons. First, the classroom was one in which what the teacher called "interrupting" happened frequently, that is, students often spoke overlappingly, blurring the boundaries between sequential turns at talk. The teacher noted this with some exasperation. One reason for the ubiquity of overlapping talk may have been, in part, the ethnic cultural communication style. Evidence from observation of two of the Italian-American students while they were interacting at home with family members suggests that speaking when someone else was speaking was usually seen in the family as an indication of interest and agreement (cf. Shultz et al., 1982). Another intention in overlapping talk may have been less benign in the classroom, however. Overlapping another speaker, as well as other conversational moves that were even more overtly aggressive, may have been a strategy for taking a turn at talk away from the student who was the teacher-designated speaker of the moment. (In the ensuing discussion, I will characterize as *"turn sharks"* those who tried to steal turns from other children who were teacher-designated speakers. The use of *"shark"* rather than *"bandit"* as a metaphor here emphasizes the more violent action quality of attack rather than the less violent action quality of theft of another's turn.)

The second reason this classroom provides an apt example for our discussion here is that it contained students with two different levels of expertise in student conversational roles. Among the students were those who were experts and those who were novices in the social management (and manipulation) of classroom talk. In any given year the kindergartners were newcomers to the classroom, unfamiliar with the customary conversational arrangements that obtained there. The first graders, however, were second-year veterans in classroom conversations. During the previous year, they had become familiar with the routine participation structures or frameworks – the allocation of communicative roles among conversational partners – by which classroom conversations usually proceeded (see O'Connor & Michaels, this volume, for further discussion).

The first graders' conversational expertise gave them a distinct tactical advantage over the kindergartners. Some of the first graders had become adept at getting a turn from other students during a whole-group conversation with the teacher. Often those other students were kindergartners, especially at the beginning of a new school year. In other words, in the conversational ecology of large-group discussion in this classroom, any student speaker of the moment had to be on the lookout for other students who were conversational "turn sharks." They would swim around looking for damaged turns. When they saw one, they would attack the speaker who was uttering it and attempt to take the turn away. The turn sharks were on the lookout for blood in the water. To be effective as an interlocutor with the teacher, a student had to know how to deal with the turn sharks of the classroom, and so did the teacher.

As the example begins, the teacher, Miss Wright, was asking questions of a kindergartner named Angie. Not only was Angie new to this classroom, she was relatively new to classrooms of any sort. Unlike some of the other kindergartners, she had not gone to preschool, although she had come in the previous summer for a few weeks of preschool in a class taught by Miss Wright. But then, of course, there were no first graders in the room. Thus Angie was new to the scene of kindergarten–first grade and to this particular classroom's turn sharks.

The discussion with Angie occurred at the beginning of the first named classroom event of the day. The teacher sat on a small chair, with students gathered on the rug around her. In many classrooms, such an event is called *Sharing Time.* In this classroom it was called *First Circle.* In the example that follows, perhaps because it was the first time that Angie was wearing a wireless microphone, the teacher engaged her in a series of questions to get her to talk a little. The teacher began by asking Angie what she had done outside school. That was a standard topic for discussion in First Circle.

Before presenting the transcript, a brief summary of transcription conventions is appropriate:

> Transcription is done in breath group units rather than in whole lines horizontally across the page. Usually there are two lines per breath group, with the *tonal nucleus,* the syllable receiving primary volume and pitch stress, appearing at the left margin. Even more special stress on a syllable or word is indicated by an underline. (Such transcription by breath group, with the tonal nucleus made visually prominent, enables the reader to read the text aloud and get a sense of the cadence organization that obtains within and between turns at speaking.)
> Occasionally, when a second speaker begins to talk in response to a prior

speaker, the second speaker's first word begins just to the right of the
last word uttered by the prior speaker, as at (29–31) and (64–66)
Overlapping speech is indicated by this symbol: [
Alternation between speakers with no gap and no overlap ("latching")
is indicated by this symbol: ⌐

The teacher was seated on a low chair and the students sat around her
on the floor.

(1) T: What did
              you do yesterday Angie? . .
(2) A: um . . (*shrugs shoulders, then speaks softly, with breathy voice*)
                                            I went over to
              Grammy's . .
(3) T: (*Whisper voice*) Talk a little bit
              louder. . . . I can't
              hear you. . . .
(4) A: (*a bit louder, still breathy*) I went over 'a
              Gramma's
(5) T: Does your Gramma live
              near you? . . .
(6) A: (*shakes head, "No"*)
(7) T: Do you have to go in the
              car to her house? . . .
(8) A: (*nods head, "Yes"*)
(9) T: What did you
              do . .
                            did you tell her all about
              school? . . .
(10) A: (*nods head, "Yes"*)
(11) T: What did you tell her that you like
              best about school?
(12) A: . . um that I
              colored
(13) T: That you
              colored and what else
(14) A: Read a
              story . .
(15) T: Right . . remember the
              story we read? . . What was the
              name of it? . . .
(16) A: (*shrugs shoulders*)
(17) T: The one about the
              bus. . . .
(18) A: (*nods head twice, "yes"*)
(19) T: The one about the three
              billy goats
(20) other S: I told my
              mo/
      other S: /———that
(21) T: (*turns to her right, points right finger,
                                       makes "sh" with lips but no speech*)

(22) other S: I told my
mother that too
(23) T: (*looks back to L*)
                              What
else do you like about school? . . .
(24) A: Play. . . .
(25) T: What do you like to do
best in school?
(26) A: Play
blocks . .
(27) T: Play with the
blocks . . is that your favorite thing? . .
(28) T: (*turns to her left, then points left hand to chalkboard behind her*)
          You remember what the name of that
letter is . .   that looks like a
snake? . .   (*Angie does not speak*)
What . .   (*Angie does not speak*)
(29) S-1:   S . .
(30) S-2:   S . .
(31) S-3:   S . .
(32) T: (*looks around to her right at speakers,*
shakes head, "No," . .and smiles)
Sh . .You're
right but let's let
Angie tell it . .
S . .   we're going to learn a-
nother letter today . .
(33) A: What's inside this
microphone?
(34) T: (*looking at Angie*)
Batteries . .like in your flashlight
(35) Li: um Miss
Wright
(36) T: (*looking at Liza*)
What?
(37) Li: That's still_____
(38) T: (*looking at Liza*)
                               I
know I . .I can't find the e-
raser Liza . .
that's what the trouble is . . I'll have to get
rid of it
(38) S: _____
(39) T: (*T looks around to her right at speaker*) What?
(40) S: _____(*same as child (38)*)
(41) T: Do you know how to
ride the two-wheeler?
Does it still have
training wheels on it?/
(42) S: /Miss Wri/ght
(43) S: /Miss Wright

(44) S: _____*(same child as (38))*
(45) T: You're a big
                   boy . .
(46) S: Miss Walsh *(this speaker is not Bobby)*
(47) T: Bobby's been waiting . . let's . let's let
                   Bobby talk . what *(as Bobby speaks Angie looks at chalkboard*
                   and continues to do so as Bobby continues)
(48) B: My_____
(49) T: <u>Bro-ther</u> *(heavy emphasis)*
(50) B: _____turtle
(51) T: *(looks intently, curiously at Bobby)*
                             Brought a
                   <u>turt</u>le to school? . .is it a-
                   <u>live</u>?
(52) B: *(shakes head, "no")*
(53) T: a
                   <u>dead</u> turtle?
(54) B: he's a-
                   <u>live</u>
(55) T: *(smiles)* Well he is alive then . . yes he's/
(56) B: ⌐/he's a
                   jumping turtle
(57) T: *(slight frown)* a jump/ . I never
                   <u>heard</u> of a <u>jump</u>ing turtle
                   _____

(58) S: Miss Wright
(59) T: _____
(60)   *(Angie looks at the teacher. Before she speaks, she has been*
                   looking at the chalkboard, not at Bobby or at the other students)
     A: I can make a "P"
(61) T: *(louder, smiling, still looking at Bobby)*
                             Oh . but I don't be
                   <u>lieve</u> you . . I never heard of a/ . .
                   <u>Turt</u>les don't fly . . they don't have
                   <u>wings</u> . . I think you're making up a
                   <u>non</u>sense story
(62): T: *(looks to her left, away from Bobby to another student who is*
                   sitting to Angie's left. Thus the teacher looks around toward An-
                   gie, but not as far around as the place where Angie is sitting)
(63) S: I have a fish down cellar . .
(64) T: You have a
                   <u>fish</u> in the cellar? . .
(65) A: I can⌐make a "P"
(66) T: ⌊I'll have to come and see this spe-
                                            cial house
(67) T: *(turns to another child who wants to speak, not to Angie)*

Notice that at the very beginning of this sequence (at 1–2) Angie did
two things that made her turns especially vulnerable to interruption by
the turn sharks. First, she hesitated at the beginning of her answer to the

teacher's question (at 1), "What did you do yesterday Angie?", by say-ing "um" (at 2) and then shrugging her shoulders in silence. Only after that silence did she say, "I went over to Grammy's." Silence at the beginning of a turn designated by the teacher provided an opportunity for interruption by another student. At this moment in the conversation no students availed themselves of the opportunity for interruption, but Angie had made that opportunity available at the very outset of her colloquy with the teacher. This could have been seen by the turn sharks as the first evidence of blood in the water.

The other thing that might have invited interruption was the volume and voice quality of Angie's speech. She spoke low enough that the teacher asked her to speak louder (at 3). In addition, Angie's speech had a breathy quality that could be heard as hesitant. While she complied (at 4) with the teacher's request to speak louder, she continued to speak in a breathy, "little girl" voice.

(3) T: (*Whisper voice*) Talk a little bit
         <u>louder</u>. . . . I can't
         <u>hear</u> you. . . .
(4) A: (*a bit louder, still breathy*) I went over 'a
         <u>Gramma's</u>

After the opening interchanges in this sequence, Angie continued to do some of the things she had done at the beginning. At (6), (8), (10), (16), and (18) she answered the teacher's questions nonverbally, nod-ding or shaking her head and (at 16) shrugging her shoulders a second time. We cannot know Angie's communicative intentions for certain, but it seems as if her shrugs followed by silence may have been taken by other pupils as an invitation for someone else to answer the question.

Shrugging and waiting for something to happen next was a strategy that Angie employed frequently in the first few months of school. It may be significant that her second shrug (at 16) followed the first question by the teacher in this sequence that was truly teacherlike: "Remember the story we read? What was the name of it?". That is a special type of request for information. As noted in note 3, it is one characterized in research on classroom discourse as a "known information question."[5]

Miss Wright waited as Angie shrugged. Then, still looking at Angie, the teacher prompted, "The one about the bus?". Angie nodded her head twice, as if to say, "Yes" (at 18), while Miss Wright paused for her answer. Then (at 19) Miss Wright gave another prompt: "The one about the three billy goats?". Immediately, (at 20) with no gap or overlap, two other students began to speak: "I told my mo/". They were sitting to

Miss Wright's left. As they spoke Miss Wright turned to look at them, pointing her right finger in a "hold it" gesture and pursing her lips to make the "sh" shape, although she did not utter the "sh" sound.

(15) T: Right . . remember the
story we read? . . What was the
name of it? . . .

(16) A: (*shrugs shoulders*)

(17) T: The one about the
bus. . . .

(18) A: (*nods head twice, "yes"*)

(19) T: The one about the three
billy goats

(20) other S: I told my
mo/

other S: _____that

(21) T: (*turns to her right, points right finger,
makes "sh" with lips but no speech*)

This seems to have stopped the other two students from continuing to speak. Yet notice that (at 20) Angie had not answered the teacher's question, either verbally or nonverbally. The other two students then began to fill in Angie's silence with their own talk.

Turning around to her left to look again at Angie, at (23) Miss Wright asked another question, "What else do you like about school?". This was not a known information question. Angie had information the teacher did not know and she immediately said, "Play." Then at (25) Miss Wright asked another question to which Angie alone possessed the answer, "What do you like to do best in school?". Again Angie answered immediately, "Play blocks." "Play with the blocks," the teacher said, expanding Angie's utterance slightly and thus modeling a more elaborated form of speech.

At (28) Miss Wright turned further to her left to look at the chalkboard behind her. Now she asked another question, and it was a known-information one: "You remember what the name of that letter is?". She paused and Angie did not answer." [The letter] that looks like a snake?" she prompted, tracing the sinuous letter with her hand. Angie still did not answer. "What . . ," Miss Walsh began with another prompt.

In the silence of the turn allocated to Angie, three other students answered at (29–31): "S! . .S . . . S . . ." Miss Wright looked away from Angie and around to her right at the speakers, shaking her head, "No," and saying "Sh . .You're right but let's let Angie tell it." The turn sharks had struck again.

(23) T: (*looks back to L*)
                                          What
            else do you like about school? . . .
(24) A: Play. . . .
(25) T: What do you like to do
            best in school?
(26) A: Play
            blocks . .
(27) T: Play with the
            blocks . . is that your favorite thing? . .
(28) T: (*turns to her left, then points left hand to chalkboard behind her*)
                         You remember what the name of that
            letter is . .   (*Angie does not speak*)   that looks like a
            snake? . .   (*Angie does not speak*)
            What . .   (*Angie does not speak*)
(29) S-1:   S . .
(30) S-2:   S . .
(31) S-3:   S . .
(32) T: (*looks around to her right at speakers,
            shakes head, "No," . . and smiles*)
                         Sh   . .   You're
            right but let's let
            Angie tell it . .

Notice (at 28–31), the time at which Angie did not speak and the
other students did. At (28) the teacher asked Angie, "You remember
what the name of that letter is?". The pause after that question was the
kairos time in which an answer was appropriate. But Angie did not
answer then, nor did she do so after a prompt by the teacher that was
followed by another prompt, " . . that looks like a snake? . . What/".
Finally, three other students said the answer, "S."

Someone needed to answer, and do so in the right time. But not just
anyone. As indicated by the prior verbal exchanges with the teacher and
by the teacher's nonverbal signals of posture and gaze orientation, it was
Angie who had been designated by the teacher as the appropriate utterer of the answer that was summoned by the question. The teacher had
been looking at Angie. When she looked away to her left (at 28), she did
not look at another student, which might have been taken as an implicit
cue nominating someone other than Angie as the next designated
speaker. (Often the teacher signaled that one child's air time was over
and another's was beginning by looking away from the prior speaker to
another student whose air time would be next.) But in this case, in
looking away from Angie, the teacher looked at the chalkboard. Thus,
even though gaze and full frontal postural orientation with Angie were
broken by the teacher, her glance to the board can be taken as maintain-
ing rather than changing Angie's right to the floor. Angie was still being

framed by the teacher's cues as the designated next speaker – the person who should answer the question just asked, and who should do so in the next moment of the discourse.

How do we know it is a *next* moment? How did the teacher, Angie, and the other students know when that "next" moment had arrived? We can infer that their inferences about the *when* of the answer slot have to do with the *kairos* timing cues discussed earlier. A succession of stressed syllables of speech mark a cadence together with markers of kinesic prominence, such as change in the direction of motion in a gesture, with shifts in postural position, and with shifts in gaze direction. Prior time intervals in that cadence could be taken as if they marked a metronome beat. Thus a succession of rhythmic, regularly spaced beats on prior moments enabled one, in the current moment of a "now" beat, to estimate how long it would be until the "next" beat would occur. Interactants could thus hold an expectation of the actual occurrence of a "next" and "go for" it, reaching for it by speech or gesture that projects a trajectory that will be completed on the cadence point of the next beat.

The following transcription (Figure 2.1), using musical notation, shows how the next moment for the answer "S" was being projected in Angie's and the teacher's interactional behavior. The transcription begins with the question by the teacher at (23), "What else do you like about school?".

Notice that in measure (2) there were two stressed syllables in the teacher's speech, "else" and "school." In measure (3), after a pause of exactly the same duration as the interval between "else" and "two" in the previous measure, Angie said "Play," thus answering the teacher's question. Notice a similar pattern in measure (5), where in the pause after the stressed word "best" in the teacher's question "What do you like to do *best* in school?", Angie said, "Play *blocks*." In this case the word "play" was unstressed – said as a "pickup note" to the stressed word that followed, "*blocks*." That stressed word came at the same time interval as that between the previous stressed word, "*best*," and the pause in the teacher's speech that followed. From this it would seem that the appropriate time for an answer to be uttered to a question by the teacher is either the next "beat" after the end of the teacher's question or the next "beat" after that. If the cadence established across stressed syllables or words is approximately 1 second, then the student has 1 second, or at most 2 seconds, to respond to the teacher's question. After 1 or 2 seconds, either the teacher will prompt the designated answerer (often beginning the prompt on the next beat after the silence by the student) or another student will attempt to answer.

In these cases, the questions asked for information that Angie alone

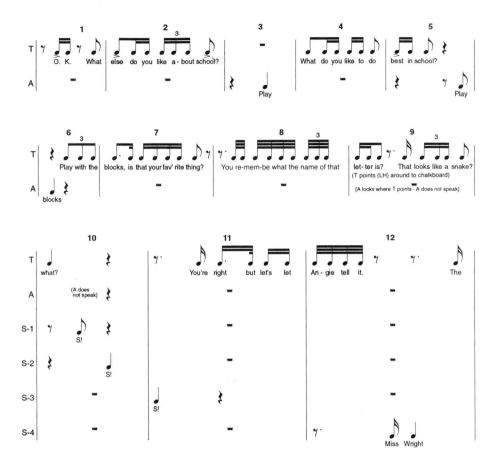

Figure 2.1 Rhythmic organization of questions and answers about school and letter name.

knew, and she answered them with a stressed word uttered on the "beat" immediately after the end of the teacher's question. This left no room either for a prompt by the teacher or for an attempt by another student to take away the answer turn by filling the rhythmically cued answer slot with an answer of his or her own.

Then the teacher revoiced Angie's utterance, "Play *blocks*," with a slight syntactic expansion, "Play with the *blocks*." (Notice that in making this slight paraphrase, a shift to a more formally elaborated style by including the conjunction and definite article, the teacher echoed the rhythmic placement of Angie's utterance; in the teacher's utterance, primary stress still fell on "blocks," with the previous syllables uttered as a triplet of "upbeats" preparing for the stressed word, "blocks.") At measure (8) the teacher began to ask another question: "You remember what the name of that letter is?" Unlike the previous questions, this was a teacherlike known-information question. As the teacher uttered the question, she turned and pointed to the board.

Angie's eyes followed the sweep of the teacher's arm as Angie directed her gaze to the chalkboard where the teacher was pointing. But notice the first beat of measure (9) – the beat immediately after the end of the teacher's question. Unlike the two previous occasions when Angie had answered on the next beat after the last stressed syllable in the question (measures 2–3 and 5–6), this time on the next beat after the teacher's question Angie did not answer. In measure (9) the teacher responded to Angie's silence with a prompt, " . . that looks like a *snake*?". Still no answer. On the next beat the teacher started another prompt: "what." As she said this, one other child answered "S" just after the beat. On the next beat, the second beat of measure (10), another child answered. Finally, on the next beat (measure 11), the teacher, who had by then looked away from Angie to the other speakers, addressed them by saying, "You're *right*," and went on to say, "but let's let *Angie* tell it." As the teacher said "you're *right*," she placed the stressed word on the immediately next beat, just as had Angie and the other children when they were filling answer slots after the teacher's questions. Thus the teacher's utterance, "you're *right*," on the second beat of measure (11) can be heard as an "answer" to the students' saying "S" in answering the question that had originally been directed at Angie.

The turn sharks had been partially successful; they got the answer turn away from Angie with only a slight rebuke from the teacher. Thus we see that in a classical sequence of classroom discourse, an IRE sequence (teacher initiation, student response, teacher evaluation; see Mehan, 1979), informationally crucial syllables in the discourse sequence occur on the beat, that is, the *let* in "letter" in the initiation slot, the "S" in the answer slot, and the "right" in the evaluation slot, "you're *right* but let's let *Angie* tell it." (Notice in the evaluation utterance that not only is the informationally crucial word "right" uttered on the beat, but so is the other informationally crucial word, "Angie," as the teacher indicates who the designated answerer was. Thus volume stress in that utterance underscores an item not only of academically relevant information, showing that the answer "S" was correct, but of social organizationally relevant information as well, showing who the designated answerer was.)

To provide further evidence of the importance of the cadence of stressed syllables in setting up the appropriate *kairos* moment for an answer slot in an IRE sequence, let us look at an earlier instance in the conversation in which Angie's answers were interrupted by turn sharks. In the complete transcript this appears at (10–22). It is the strip of conversation just prior to the question about the letter "S."

At (10) teacher asked a question of Angie that was not teacherlike: "What did you tell her you liked *best* about school?". Only Angie knew the answer and she answered promptly, on the next cadence "beat," "Um, that I colored."

In measure (3) of figure 2.2 we can see that Angie produced a stressed syllable on the second cadence beat, the syllable "um" and the syllable "co-" in the word "colored." (Perhaps the "um" was uttered as a rhythmic placeholder in order to occupy the answer slot and gain time to formulate an answer.) In measures (3–4) the teacher repeated "That you colored and what else?" On the next beat after "else" Angie answered, "read a story," and on the next beat after that (the second beat of measure 5), the teacher confirmed the correctness of Angie's answer by saying, "Right." Then the teacher asked a different kind of question – a teacherlike known-information question: "Remember the story we read? . . What was the name of it?" In the next beat after the end of that question (beat 2 of measure 7), Angie did not speak. Then on the next beat she shrugged her shoulders. The teacher responded with a prompt: "The one about the bus." Angie immediately nodded twice (measure 9) on the first beat of the measure.

That answer was half right: by nodding "yes," Angie showed that she remembered the story, but by not speaking Angie did not demonstrate that she knew the name of the story, which was the point of the question. (Angie may have been interpreting the teacher's question literally, rather than as an indirect request that she give the name of the story aloud.) "The one about the three billy goats?" On the next beat after that (second beat of measure 10) Angie did not answer, and on the next

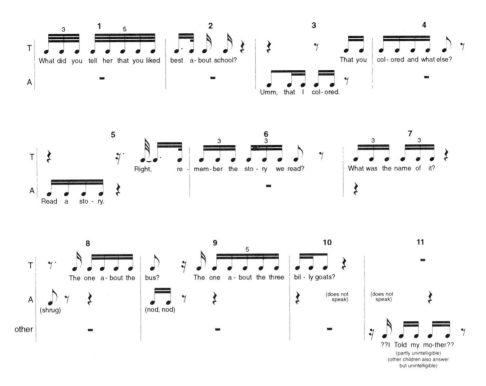

Figure 2.2   Rhythmic organization of questions and answers about school.

beat (the first beat of measure 11), one other child and then other children began to say something. They were in the process of taking Angie's turn away. The teacher looked at them and smiled but brought her finger to her lips in a "Sh" gesture. Angie was still the designated answerer, even though she had not spoken in the cadentially signaled answer slots given her by the teacher. When the other children began to speak on the beat that indicated an answer slot, they had become turn sharks who used their cultural knowledge of the customary timing of IRE utterances to attack Angie's turn at answering.

On the marriage of true minds in classroom discourse: Are turn sharks impediments to learning or not?

From the perspective on the ecology of social interaction presented here, and as illustrated in the previous examples of classroom discourse, the interactional difficulty – or at least the fragility – of engagement between teacher and student in the ZPD should be apparent. Both Angie and the teacher were "going for" engagement in the zone. On two occasions the teacher turned to Angie and asked a series of questions to which Angie alone knew the answer. That simplified Angie's interactional task of holding the floor while other students were vying for the teacher's attention and conversational engagement. Angie answered those questions promptly, with words or nods that occurred on the next beat after the last stressed syllable in the teacher's question. After a few questions that Angie alone could answer, the teacher asked a "teacherlike" known-information question. In both instances (the question about the names of stories read aloud yesterday by the teacher and the question about the name of the letter on the chalkboard), Angie hesitated. Immediately, other children – the turn sharks – filled in the answers. To be successful in going for the zone, Angie not only had to know the right answers to the questions, she also had to utter the answers in the right time so that the teacher could hear her utterance as an answer to the question asked and so that other students would not take away her turn.

We can speculate on the cognitive consequences of someone uttering the answer other than the answerer that was officially ratified by the teacher. If out of the group comes the information or idea needed to complete the discourse of the moment, it may not matter, for purposes of other students' learning, which student's voice actually utters the answer. Indeed, for the designated answerer who appears not to know the answer, like Angie, to have someone else answer could not only take her off the hook of being stuck without an answer, but also, by modeling the right answer, could give Angie an opportunity to learn. In such cases it would be fellow students who, by uttering a correct answer or by extending a fellow student's answer (e.g., by elaboration), would be functioning as the teacher's expert voice in the expert–novice dialogue ideally conceived as dyadic interaction in the original Vygotskian conception of interaction in the ZPD. In other words, the work of voicing and revoicing as scaffolding provided by the expert to the novice (whether the expert be a teacher, as in the chapter in this volume by O'Connor and Michaels and in the classroom example of Wertsch, or by a mother, as in the chapter by Snow and Kurland) can be done by various parties in the classroom, not just by the teacher. (This was especially the case in Angie's classroom, where there were first graders as well as kindergartners.) This may explain why heterogeneous grouping can create a stimulating learning environment for students who are less adept than others.

In the heterogeneous group, there will be more adept students who will voice and revoice the ideas and information to be learned.

Conversely, the teacher (nominally considered the expert) can do the work of a novice relative to the student, thus validating the student's expertise. Angie's teacher could be seen as taking on the role of novice in her initial questions about what Angie did after school and what she told her grandmother. In asking a student for information the teacher does not already know, the teacher becomes the learner. This recalls a strategy Cazden employed repeatedly in the inner-city class she taught in San Diego in 1974 (as reported in Mehan, 1979), the same year in which Angie's classroom was being videotaped in Boston. After a child gave a correct answer to a question by the teacher, Cazden would often say, "That's right. How did you figure that out?" Then the child would explain the reasoning or computation process that led to the correct answer. This was a strategy to get the child to articulate reasoning the child might otherwise have taken for granted and to have that child model and explain that successful line of reasoning for other children in the class. But in terms of the Vygotskian model of expert–novice dialogue, such a question by the teacher in effect switches the two roles, with the student becoming the expert and the teacher becoming the novice who doesn't yet know the new information – how the student "got" it (see also O'Connor and Michaels, this volume).

Thus we can see that in a conversational participation framework in which teachers and students are able to alternate the roles of expert and novice, members of the learning group can learn even if the one who utters the correct answer is not the designated answerer and even if the revoicing of a partially correct or cryptic answer is done by another student rather than by the teacher. In such a participation framework, scaffolding, appropriating voicing, and revoicing can be done alternately by varying members. In a sense these functions in interaction, which appear to be cognitively stimulating, are being done collectively rather than dyadically. This may be the way in which group learning takes place, with the group as a whole, as well as individual members, learning.

In the light of all this, we might want to rethink the metaphor of "turn shark," since what the students did in taking away Angie's answering turns may not have entirely inhibited her learning. Possibly the turn sharks, rather than being seen as attackers, might be better seen as rescuers – conversational dolphins. Their interventions did get Angie off the hook of being exposed as not knowing the right answer. In uttering the correct answer, the other children were modeling content knowledge for Angie, if not proper deportment as the teacher defined it.

Should we then give the turn sharks friendly faces in our analysis and reconsider them as dolphins?

Perhaps not. A final observation from the transcript may suggest that, at least from Angie's point of view, having her answer turn taken away was not a positive experience. After the "remember the story we read" sequence (15–22) and the "letter S" sequence (28–32), in both of which the turn sharks answered in Angie's turns, Angie tried on three occasions to reengage the teacher's attention. The first of these instances occurred at (33), just after the other children had answered the "letter S" question:

(31) S-3:   S . .
(32) T: (*looks around to her right at speakers,*
             shakes head, "No," . . and smiles)
                         Sh   . .   You're
             right but let's let
             Angie tell it . .
             S . .   we're going to learn a-
             nother letter today . .
(33) A: What's inside this
             microphone?
(34) T: (*looking at Angie*)
             Batteries . . like in your flashlight
(35) Li: um Miss
             Wright
(36) T: (*looking at Liza*)
             What?

As the teacher (at 32) began to move on to another topic ("We're going to learn another letter today"), Angie asked, "What's inside this microphone?" It could be that she did this because she had just been the recipient of a long series of questions from the teacher and figured it was now her turn to ask the question. It could be that she asked about the microphone to refocus the teacher's attention on her after the turn sharks had answered correctly the question she was unable to answer. We cannot know Angie's intention for certain. It does appear at (33) that after the intervention by the turn sharks, Angie was trying for more interaction with the teacher.

The other two instances in which Angie tried to get the teacher's attention are shown at the end of the full transcript. The conversation had turned to topics concerning what various children had at home: a bicycle and a pet turtle. From (47) to (61) Bobby was telling about his brother's pet turtle. He and his account got into trouble as he revealed that the turtle could jump. At (57) Miss Wright said, "I never *heard* of a *jump*ing turtle." (This was because she operated on the principle that in these conversations at the beginning of the school day, fantasy topics should not be allowed. That prohibition prevented talk about television cartoons the children had seen at home. Non-television-derived fantasy talk was encouraged at other points in the school day.

Immediately after Miss Wright questioned the legitimacy of Bobby's turtle story, a number of other children began to vie for the floor, raising their hands and swaying forward and calling, "Miss Wright!" As the other children did this, so did Angie. She said (at 60) "I can make a P."

(57) T: (*slight frown*) a jump/. I never
<u>heard</u> of a <u>jump</u>ing turtle

(58) S: Miss Wright
(59) T: <u>   </u>
(60)   (*Angie looks at the teacher. Before she speaks, she has been looking at the chalkboard, not at Bobby or at the other children*)

     A: I can make a "P"
(61) T: (*louder, smiling, still looking at Bobby*)
                           Oh . but I don't be
<u>lieve</u> you . . I never heard of a/ . .
<u>Tur</u>tles don't fly . . they don't have
<u>wings</u> . . I think you're making up a
<u>non</u>sense story
(62) T: (*looks to her left, away from Bobby to another student who is sitting to Angie's left. Thus the teacher looks around toward Angie, but not as far around as the place where Angie is sitting*)
(63) S: I have a fish down cellar . .
(64) T: You have a
<u>fish</u> in the cellar? . .
(65) A: I can⌈make a "P"
(66) T: ⌊I'll have to come and see this special house
(66) T: (*turns to another child who wants to speak, not to Angie*)

When Angie said "I can make a P" at (60), the teacher was still facing Bobby. She did not react to Angie's utterance. Then at (62) the teacher looked away from Bobby to another student, who began to tell about a pet fish. At (65) Angie again said, "I can make a P." But the teacher continued to look at the child talking about his pet fish and then turned further away from Angie to look at another child who would become the next speaker.

In these instances, the timing of Angie's utterances seemed not incorrect (notice that at 65 Angie started to speak just after the pause after the teacher's question at 64). But another dimension of appropriateness besides conversational rhythm needed to be taken into account. This was the teacher's gaze and postural position relative to a designated speaker. Gaze and postural orientation were a signal of the direction of the teacher's attention. Both times that Angie spoke, the teacher was not looking directly at Angie. At (60) the teacher was looking at Bobby, who was seated in the circle at one o'clock in relation to the teacher, while Angie was sitting at eight o'clock relative to the teacher. At (62) the teacher looked back around the circle in Angie's direction, but only back around to about nine-thirty, not all the way around to eight o'clock, where Angie was sitting. Moreover, Angie's comment was not at all topically relevant at either of the two times she uttered it. It is no wonder, therefore, that the teacher did not "hear" the topic and give Angie attention and a turn at speaking.

What might Angie have been trying to accomplish when she said "I can make a P" at these inappropriate moments? We can see her talk as an attempt to get the teacher's attention after the previous debacles in which her turns at answering were taken away. We can also see her as answering another content question about letter recognition (even though it was a question unasked by the teacher). In effect, Angie may have been trying to say, "I didn't recognize the letter 'S' but I do know the letter 'P'." In her persistent attempts to show that she knew and to try to get the teacher's attention again, Angie may have been indicating that she did not regard the intervention of the other children during her answer turns as rescuing but rather as interference. The classroom ecology in this example of conversation thus appears to contain turn sharks rather than turn dolphins, from Angie's point of view.

Conclusion

This has been an attempt to make visible the social interactional medium in which cognition and learning might be taking place in classroom conversation. That medium has been considered here as an ecosystem of relations of mutual influence between speakers who are also hearers and viewers. Classroom conversation is more than a dialogue or a series of successive dialogues, although there are dialogic aspects to the organization of classroom discourse. That organization involves more than just a reciprocal or sequential dimension of conversation, as well as a reciprocal one.

What appears to hold both aspects of organization together in performance is *time*, especially the cadential patterns produced by points of emphasis in the verbal and nonverbal behavior stream. These, I have argued, function as contextualization cues. They seem to allow participants in conversation to make *kairos* judgments so as to anticipate when the "next" appropriate moments for communicative action are likely to arrive. As participants orient their attention and action to a common temporal framework, their contributions in listening and speaking behavior occur together, and interaction proceeds smoothly and coherently.

In terms of the organization of discourse, we saw that the "next" organization of question–answer routines (IR and IRE sequences) appears to be strongly patterned by the cadence organization of verbal and nonverbal behavior in interaction. Crucial information items within question slots tended to occur in syllables uttered "on the beat." Answer slots tended to be initiated (or the key word in the answer slot tended to occur) on the immediately next beat after the end of the question or on the next beat after that. Participants held each other accountable for that expectation about the timing of question and answer slots, as evidenced by the successful attempts by the turn sharks to give answers at points in time that, according to the teacher's official designation of speaking rights to students, belonged to Angie. My purpose in the analysis of the stolen turns, as illustrated both by the transcript and by the musical notation, was to argue that if there was no regular relationship of timing between question slots and answer slots, the turn sharks would not have been able to seize the *kairos* moments so adeptly in taking away Angie's turns at answering.

Angie's lack of success in reengaging the teacher's attention as she said "I can make a P" also shows something fundamental about the organization of interaction in classroom conversation. This involves the postural orientation and gaze of a listener in relation to the current speaker, an aspect of organization on what I have called the complementary dimension of interaction. When the teacher was facing Angie and looking directly at her, Angie was able to get the teacher to respond even if Angie's utterance was not topically relevant (e.g., when she asked, "What's inside this microphone?"). When the teacher's postural focus and gaze were directed to other students, however (e.g., when Angie said, "I can make a P"), Angie's utterances received no response from the teacher. (When the teacher looked away from Angie to the chalkboard while asking the question about the letter S, that was a different matter, for although the teacher was no longer facing or gazing at Angie, she was not facing any other student and returned her gaze to Angie almost immediately.) From such instances, we can infer that students who are successful in classroom conversation attend not only to what the teacher is saying but also to the direction of the teacher's posture and gaze as the teacher is speaking.

In the transcripts and in the discussion of them, much was made of the organization of interaction as an environment for cognition and learning. However, other than in the discussion in the immediately preceding section (concerning the possible cognitive consequences of alternation of novice and expert roles by kindergartners, first graders, and the teacher), little has been said here about learning or cognition itself. This is due in part to the limitations of the empirical evidence. We cannot look inside the participants' heads to see what they are thinking at any given moment, nor can we see directly how sets of interacting individuals might be thinking collectively. In addition, the heavier emphasis on interaction than on cognition in this chapter is due to the focal interests of its author. I know more about the real-time organization of interaction as an environment for thinking than I do about the real-time organization of thinking itself. As this chapter concludes, however, I can speculate on how thinking and learning may be working within the kind of interaction that occurs in classroom scenes such as the one presented here. This involves considering directly the cognitive ecology of classroom discussion in relation to its social interactional ecology.

A way to approach this is to consider the social organization of attention in face-to-face interaction. Recall that, as perceivers and thinkers, we have severely limited information processing capacity at any given moment. Participation in face-to-face interaction provides us with far more potential information than we can handle perceptually and cognitively. Accordingly, our attention must be limited strategically – focused on some sets of information in our environment and not on others.

One way of focusing attention is by distributing it differentially across successive moments of time. It may be that the cadence organization of points of emphasis in oral discourse and in nonverbal actions reflects a temporal ebb and flow of selective attention among interlocutors. The analysis of classroom conversation presented earlier showed how syllables containing crucial information in a clause, or the onsets or endings of turns, often occurred on a cadence point in the verbal and nonverbal behavior stream. It may be that listeners (and watchers) focus their attention especially at those points. Consider the following examples, which are taken from utterances that occurred in the classroom conversation I have discussed here:

1. What   is the name   of that   letter
                                          story
                                          monkey
                                          tool
2. What   did you tell   your   mother
                                          father
                                          sister

Notice that at key turning points in the grammatical structure of these utterances, at differing hierarchical levels (noun phrase/verb phrase and, within the noun phrase, the noun that is the object of the verb), syntactic boundaries are marked by the prosodic cadence structure of the utterance. (This is indicated by the musical notes and by the accent marks in Figures 2.1 and 2.2.) Chomsky's insight that grammar is the foundation of the intelligibility of sentences can be amended here by saying that, in speech performance, the grammar of an utterance appears to be underscored (i.e., reinforced) by prosodic emphasis. By the co-occurring structures of syntax and prosody, the hearer's ear (and eye and mind) can be led to listen for and attend to a crucial next moment. In processing the first example, the hearer needs to know whether the question is about a letter or a monkey. What the object of the verb will be cannot be known by the interlocutor until the moment of uttering of the crucial noun (letter/monkey). That is a moment the hearer must "go for" attentionally in order to comprehend the utterance that is being heard.

Sight as well as hearing needs to be directed in focusing attention during engagement in the ZPD. If the "that" in the question "What is the name of that letter?" is a grapheme written on the chalkboard, then if a student is to understand the question, the student's gaze must be directed to the place on the chalkboard where the letter is written. (This seems so obvious as to go without saying. What is not obvious is that the gaze of the student will be directed to a particular place on the chalkboard at a particular moment in time, as was Angie's as her eyes followed the sweep of the teacher's left arm in its pointing gesture.)

In groups of interlocutors it is reasonable to assume that, if conversation is to be understood by the various participants, a temporally regulated process of "going for" certain moments attentionally must be participated in by the various auditors. Their attention needs to be focused collectively at certain moments if they are to understand what is going on. Thus the collective organization of attention would seem to be necessary for the group to learn; that is, if more than one pupil is to get the information available at a given moment, the attention of more than one pupil must get to the same moment.

Teachers who lead large-group discussions seem to sense that the collective organization of attention is important for students' understanding, as indicated by such commonly occurring directives as "I want all eyes up here." Yet our folk pedagogical understanding of attention may presume that attention is a unitary and continuous phenomenon – either attention is there for a span of time or it is not. It may be that attention in conversation is much more labile, ebbing and flowing within a given time span.

Some research suggests that the timing, and perhaps even the cadential rhythmicity, of conversational action is important for comprehension of meaning. In prior research on gatekeeping interaction in academic advising sessions, Shultz and I studied the comments of the adviser and the student in a simulated recall session during which they viewed and commented on a videotape of the advising session. We found that when the smooth flow of cadence broke down in the conversation between adviser and student, one party or the other reported not having understood what the other party had just said or characterized what was happening in very different terms from those used by the other party. In those moments, the adviser and student appeared to have been making different kinds of sense of the same potential information in the communicative behavior that was occurring as the cadence of conversation fell apart (see Erickson & Shultz, 1982, 136–143, 191–192).

In research on classroom interaction, Kounin identified a capacity in skilled teachers that he called *withitness* (Kounin, 1970). This referred in part to the behavioral smoothness with which the teacher conducted classroom events. Kounin thought that the teacher's sense of timing was an important component of withitness. Teacher educators sometimes speak of this as *orchestration*. The use of that musical analogy may point indirectly to the rhythmicity of teacher–student interaction, since as I have argued here, it is that rhythmicity that allows the interdigitation of the actions of the various participants into a coherent collective performance.[6]

In research on Head Start classes, Ruiz (1971) compared fifty 1-hour videotapes from classrooms in which the teacher was experienced with fifty tapes from classrooms in which the teacher was inexperienced. What struck her as the most salient contrast across the two sets of tapes was the periodicity with which the experienced teachers moved around the classroom. These teachers moved from place to place in the classroom in rhythmically regular cycles, whereas the movement of the inexperienced teachers was much more erratic, both spatially and temporally. The phenomenon Ruiz observed may have been an index of the overall cadential regularity of the verbal and nonverbal activity of the experienced teachers.

In the literature about research on teaching, there is also a suggestive observation about interactional timing that involves classroom discourse directly. This is Rowe's observation concerning *wait time*, the time a teacher gives a student to answer a question (Rowe, 1974). Rowe claimed that by allowing more wait time in mathematics lessons, the intellectual quality of students' answers was improved. Yet increased wait time may seem artificial precisely because of the cadence cues for the "immediate next moment as answer slot" that we have been considering in the classroom example shown in this chapter. It is possible that more wait time might have helped Angie to formulate answers to the teacher's known-information questions, but perhaps not. It does seem likely that increased wait time would have decreased or eliminated entirely the turn sharks' opportunities for turn seizing afforded by the "immediate next" organization we saw in the rhythmic organization of question–answer sequencing.

In our example, it seemed that even getting to the ZPD, much less doing anything cognitively stimulating in it, was a major interactional achievement. The teacher and the student had to "go for" the zone in real time, as others (notably the turn sharks) were also "going for" it. Indeed, there is no zone at all unless people construct it interactionally, "going for" crucial *kairos* moments both as listeners and as speakers. Unless experts and novices "go for the zone" in real time, the "zone" never happens.

One is left wondering what the temporal organization of classroom conversations might look like when what is being taught and learned is more cognitively complex than in the example given here. In fifth-grade mathematics lessons such as those reported by Lampert (1990), for example, what happens to the conversational rhythm as ideas in the discourse become more complex, or as students and the teacher shift from being more authoritative or more tentative in their presentation of new ideas? I wonder not only about what that talk is like, as various scholars are now reporting from the point of view of classroom discourse and pedagogical strategy. I also wonder about the timing of that talk.

If the timing of classroom conversation falls apart, it may be that the ZPD bursts like a bubble. How the temporal organization of classroom conversation works as a learning environment – as the locus of engagement in the ZPD – remains an issue for exploration. How the teacher and multiple learners are more or less able interactionally to engage in intellectually stimulating conversation, and how cadence and conversational rhythm may be working in the social and cognitive ecology of group learning as it takes place in classroom conversation, are issues that may well be related. Taken together they present intriguing possibilities for further research.

Notes

1 To illustrate this stream of work, a list that is representative but not exhaustive includes Brown et al. (1989), Moll (1990), Newman et al. (1989), Rogoff (1990), Tharp and Gallimore (1988), Vygotsky (1978), Wertsch (1991), and Wood et al. (1976).

2 This view is new in that it differs dramatically from the "process-product" orientation in recent research on teaching. One can argue, however, that this seemingly new view is a classic one, in the spirit of Dewey's interactionist conception of learning, teaching, and the nature of learning environments (see, e.g., his discussion of the "total social set-up of the classroom" in Dewey, 1965, pp. 43, 45).

3 Questions to which the asker knows the answer are ubiquitous in classroom discourse, as observed by Bellack et al. (1966), Sinclair and Coulthard (1975), and Mehan (1979), among many others. The known-information question frames a power–knowledge relationship that is constitutive of the conventional classroom; that is, it presumes and manifests the belief that "There is a body of knowledge to be mastered and the teacher has mastery of it. It is that mastery which justifies the teacher's authority in the classroom." How difficult it is to break this frame – to teach without invoking the existence of right answers – is attested to in current studies of attempts to "teach for understanding" (Lampert, 1990; see also Lemke, 1990).

4 Interaction in this classroom is reported in the doctoral theses of Florio (1978) and Dorr-Bremme (1982), as well as in Bremme and Erickson (1977), Shultz and Florio (1979), and Shultz, Florio, and Erickson (1982). Primary support for this work came from a junior faculty research award to Erickson from the Spencer Foundation and from an NIMH postdoctoral fellowship to Shultz. Additional support came to Florio and to Erickson from the Institute for Research on Teaching, Michigan State University, which was funded by the National Institute of Education.

5 As stated in note 3, the known-information question occurs commonly in classrooms. It may or may not occur commonly in family interactions at home. Heath has claimed that such questions were not usually asked of children in working-class African-American families that she studied (Heath, 1983). Cazden has speculated that this may be characteristic of working-class families more generally (Cazden, 1988, p. 197). This seems to have been the case in Laurie's family, which was Italian-American and working class. In two home visits we made in which interaction was videotaped from the time after school until Laurie's bedtime, no known-answer questions were addressed to Laurie by any of the adults present – her father, mother, and her mother's sister. It is reasonable to infer, then, that at the beginning of the school year Laurie was rather unfamiliar with known-answer question sequences as a speech genre and that her shrug was a tactical response in a situation in which she was not sure what to do. By November she had begun to answer known-answer questions, and by February she was active in doing so. But the transcribed example presented here comes from the second day of school in September.

6 Unfortunately, this analogy is partly misleading, since orchestration – the assignment of differing notes to different instruments in the orchestra by a composer or arranger – is a decision process that occurs before the performance of the music. It may be that what is meant by "orchestration" as a characterization of the teacher's leadership of collective classroom activity is more like what a conductor does in leading the orchestra in performance. But that analogy doesn't hold fully either, since in an orchestral performance the notes to be played by the various performers have been determined in advance. That is unlike ordinary conversation, which is a more improvisational kind of performance.

References

Au, H., & Mason, J. (1981). Social organizational factors in learning to read: The balance of rights hypothesis. *Reading Research Quarterly, 17,* 115–152.

Auer, P. (1992). Introduction: John Gumperz' approach to contextualization. In P. Auer and A. DiLuzio (Eds.), *The Contextualization of Language.* Amsterdam/Philadelphia: John Benjamin Publishing Company.

Bateson, G. (1956). The message "this is a play." In B. Schaffner (Ed.), *Group processes.* New York: Josiah Macy, Jr., Foundation. (Republished in G. Bateson, *Steps to an ecology of mind.* New York: Ballantine Books, 1972)

Bellack, A., Kliebard, H., Hyman, R., & Smith, F. (1966). *The language of the classroom.* New York: Teachers College Press.

Bremme, D., & Erickson, F. (1977). Behaving and making sense: Some relationships among verbal and nonverbal ways of acting in a classroom. *Theory into Practice, 16,* 153–161.

Brown, S. B., Collins, A., & Duguid, P. (1989). Situated cognition and the culture of learning. *Educational Researcher, 18,* 32–42.

Cazden, C. B. (1988). *Classroom discourse: The language of teaching and learning.* Portsmouth, NH: Heinemann.

Condon, W. S., & Ogston, W. D. (1967). A segmentation of behavior. *Journal of Psychiatric Research, 5,* 221–235.

Cooper-Kuhlen, E. (1992). Contextualizing discourse: The prosody of interactive repair. In P. Auer and A. DiLuzio (Eds.), *The contextualization of language.* Amsterdam/Philadelphia: John Benjamin's Publishing Company.

Dewey, J. (1965). The relation of theory to practice in education. In M. L. Borrowman, (Ed.), *Teacher education in America: A documentary history.* New York: Teachers College Press. (Original work published 1904)

Dorr-Bremme, D. (1982). *Behaving and making sense: Creating social organization in the classroom.* Unpublished doctoral dissertation, Harvard University.

Erickson, F. (1982). Money tree, lasagna bush, salt and pepper. Social construction of topical cohesion in a conversation among Italian-Americans. In D. Tannen (Ed.), *Analyzing discourse: Text and talk.* Washington, DC: Georgetown University Press.

Erickson, F. (1986). Listening and speaking. In D. Tannen & J. Alatis (Eds.), *Georgetown University Round Table in Languages and Linguistics 1985.* Washington, DC: Georgetown University Press.

Erickson, F. (1992). They know all the lines: Rhythmic organization and contextualization in a conversational listing routine. In P. Auer and Aldo di Luzio (Eds.) *The contextualization of language.* Amsterdam/Philadelphia: John Benjamin Publishing Company.

Erickson, F. and J. Shultz (1982). *The counselor as gatekeeper: Social interaction in interviews.* New York: Academic Press.

Florio, S. (1978). *Learning to go to school: An ethnography of interaction in a kindergarten/ first grade classroom.* Unpublished doctoral dissertation, Harvard University.

Gumperz, J. J. (1982). *Discourse strategies.* Cambridge: Cambridge University Press.

Heath, S. B. (1983). *Ways with words: Language, life and work in communities and classrooms.* Cambridge: Cambridge University Press.

Kounin, J. S. (1970). *Discipline and group management in classrooms.* New York: Holt, Rinehart and Winston.

Lampert, M. (1990). When the problem is not the question and the solution is not the answer: Mathematical knowing and teaching. *American Educational Research Journal, 27,* 29–63.

Lemke, J. I. (1990). *Talking science: Language, learning and values.* Norwood, NJ: Ablex.

Mehan, H. (1979). *Learning lessons: Social organization in the classroom.* Cambridge, MA: Harvard University Press.

Moll, L. (1990). *Vygotsky and education: Instructional implications and applications of socio-historical psychology.* New York: Cambridge University Press.

Newman, D., Griffin, P., & Cole, M. (1989). *The construction zone: Working for cognitive change in school.* New York: Cambridge University Press.

Rogoff, B. (1990). *Apprenticeship in thinking: cognitive development in social context.* New York: Oxford University Press.

Rowe, M. B. (1974). Wait-time and rewards as instructional variables. *Journal of Research in Science Teaching, 11,* 81–94.

Ruiz, S. (1971). Use of space in the classroom. *Research report 11.* Lansing: Center for Urban Affairs, Michigan State University.

Scollon, R. (1982). The rhythmic integration of ordinary talk. In D. Tannen (Ed.), *Georgetown University Roundtable on Languages and Linguistics.* Washington, DC: Georgetown University Press.

Shultz, J., & Florio, S. (1979). Stop and freeze: The negotiation of social and physical space in a kindergarten/first grade classroom. *Anthropology and Education Quarterly, 10,* 166–181.

Shultz, J., Florio, S., & Erickson, F. (1982). Where's the floor?: Aspects of the cultural organization of social relationships in communication at home and at school. In A. Glatthorn & P. Gilmore (Eds.), *Ethnography and education: Children in and out of school.* Philadelphia: University of Pennsylvania Press.

Sinclair, J. M., & Coulthard, R. M. (1975). *Toward an analysis of discourse: The English used by teachers and pupils.* Oxford: Oxford University Press.

Sudnow, D. (1978). *Ways of the hand: The organization of improvised conduct.* Cambridge, MA: Harvard University Press.

Sudnow, D. (1980). *Talk's body: A mediation between two keyboards.* Harmondsworth, Middlesex, U.K.: Penguin Books.

Tharp, R., & Gallimore, R. (1988). *Rousing minds to life: Teaching, learning, and schooling in social context.* New York: Cambridge University Press.

Vygotsky, L. S. (1978). *Mind in society: The development of higher psychological processes* (M. Cole, V. John-Steiner, S. Scribner, & E. Souberman, Eds.). Cambridge, MA: Harvard University Press.

Wertsch, J. V. (1985). *Culture, communication, and cognition: Vygotskian perspectives.* Cambridge: Cambridge University Press.

Wertsch, J. V. (1991). *Voices of the mind: A sociocultural approach to mediated action.* Cambridge, MA: Harvard University Press.

Wood, D., Bruner, J. S., & Ross, G. (1976). The role of tutoring in problem solving. *Journal of Child Psychology and Psychiatry, 17,* 89–100.

3   Shifting participant frameworks: orchestrating thinking practices in group discussion

Mary Catherine O'Connor and Sarah Michaels

Steven: I think that I don't agree with Janette's idea that we don't need to use Paulina's concentrate value, because I think it would be unfair to just *not* use Paulina's concentrate . . . if you make a concentrate over with different amounts of lemon juice and sugar, then it'll just be a totally different concentrate, like Ted said. . . .

Introduction

Ethnographic studies of social interaction and everyday cognition amply demonstrate that children are capable of complex and abstract reasoning in their everyday, out-of-school activities (Bloome & Horowitz, 1991; Cook-Gumperz, 1986; Goodwin, 1990; Heath, 1983; Rogoff & Lave, 1984; Saxe, 1988). But how do children come to take on the particular roles and discourse forms that are valued in problem posing and problem solving in school? Although children do bring their out-of-school reason-

Our thinking and writing for this chapter have been influenced by many people. First and foremost, we are grateful for the cooperation, collaboration, and insights of the two teachers, Lynne Godfrey and Judith Richards, who generously opened up their classrooms to us and made their thinking about their own teaching practices part of our socialization as researchers. We attribute our interest in participant frameworks largely to the fact that this notion makes possible a level of analysis that meshes well with their own way of thinking about group discussion and the need to create a conversation that makes room for all of their students. In turn, we are indebted to their students, who have let us watch their participation in that conversation. We have also benefited from the comments and suggestions of many colleagues, among them Carolyn Baker, Courtney Cazden, Allan Collins, Jenny Cook-Gumperz, Valerie Crawford, Jim Gee, Marion Guerra, Lowry Hemphill, Deborah Hicks, Jay Lemke, Susan McEwen, Joan Merrill, Kevin O'Connor, Pamela Paternoster, Maureen Reddy, Leslie Rupert, Marty Rutherford, Chikako Toma, Jim Wertsch, and the students in LS 726 at Boston University, spring 1994. During the years in which we studied in the classrooms of Lynne Godfrey and Judith Richards, O'Connor received support from a Spencer postdoctoral fellowship, and both O'Connor and Michaels were supported by a grant from the Mellon Foundation to the Literacies Institute. We gratefully acknowledge the support of these organizations. None of these individuals or institutions necessarily agree with the positions we hold here, and none are responsible for our errors or infelicities.

ing abilities into the classroom, this thinking is often not taken up and developed as part of the classroom work unless children can display it in ways that teachers recognize (Michaels, O'Connor, & Richards, 1993).

How do students come to appropriate and publicly communicate with the forms of talk or text that are part of being a competent hypothesizer, evidence provider, maker of distinctions, checker of facts? For some children these discursive practices never become natural, yet for others they seem to fit from the first day of school. Research suggests that language socialization patterns in the home provide a basis for some of these roles and actions (Heath, 1983; Ochs, Taylor, Rudolph, & Smith, 1991). But whatever the intellectual socialization provided in the family context, exemplary teachers see it as their responsibility to provide all children with access to these roles in the context of school learning, and to the rights and responsibilities that go with them.

For students to gain facility in these intellectual practices, they must receive social support in the form of scaffolded opportunities to perform and practice the relevant ways of talking and thinking. Classroom researchers are increasingly coming to realize the importance of conditions of entry provided by teachers into speech activities associated with complex thinking and problem solving (Brown, 1993; Erickson, 1982; Goldenberg & Gallimore, 1991; Lampert, 1990; Lemke, 1990; Martin, 1989; O'Connor, 1993; Wells, 1993). Following a long tradition in sociocultural and sociocognitive studies, originating with Vygotsky's work (1978) (summarized well in Resnick, Levine, & Teasley, 1991; Wertsch, 1985, 1991), we assume that facility in particular types of complex thinking follows from repeated experience in taking on various roles and stances within recurring social contexts that support those types of intellectual give-and-take and its proto-forms. This kind of learning requires that students take positions or stances with respect to the claims and observations made by others; it requires that students engage in purposive action within a social setting (Brown et al., 1992; Collins, Brown, & Newman, 1989; Lave & Wenger, 1991; Wells, 1993).

Following assumptions made more generally within research on language socialization (Ochs et al., 1991; Schieffelin, 1984; Schieffelin & Ochs, 1986), we assume that students who are frequently and successfully inducted into such activities are learning interactional routines and practices that will continue to work for them in other settings. In other words, we assume here that each instance of student participation, fostered and scaffolded by the teacher, represents an opportunity for an increment of learning, however small. (Whether or not this opportunity results in learning in any particular individual case, and whether we can know when it does, are two ever-present and crucial questions in this kind of research. We will revisit this issue in the discussion section of this chapter.)

On this view, teachers are thus continually engaged in a form of language socialization: socialization that is directed to bringing children into school-based intellectual practices manifested in ways of talking. We are interested in understanding the kinds of activities that foster the practices of externalizing one's own reasoning, inquiring into the reasoning of others, and comparing positions and perspectives on an issue or problem. We are particularly concerned with settings in which a teacher is actively present, and is purposefully organizing tasks and participation to foster these thinking practices. Central among these is the orchestration of group discussion: It provides a site for aligning students with each other and with the content of the academic work while simultaneously socializing them into particular ways of speaking and thinking (O'Connor & Michaels, 1993).

Involving students in these sorts of activities in elementary settings is quite complex and has not been fully characterized in the research literature.[1] Consider a first-order description of the task. Imagine a teacher who is using the activity of large-group discussion to foster students' participation in thinking through a particular problem. Imagine further that the teacher is committed to giving each child equal access to the intellectual enterprise, and that the students present a wide range of linguistic backgrounds, attitudes, and academic resources. The teacher must give each child an opportunity to work through the problem under discussion (whether publicly or privately) while simultaneously encouraging each of them to listen to and attend to the solution paths of the others, building on each other's thinking. Yet she must also actively take a role in making certain that the class gets to the necessary goal: perhaps a particular solution or a certain formulation that will lead to the next step. She may need to make judgments about what to avoid, or to lead them away from topics or methods for which too many of them are not prepared, while not squelching those who made the problematic contribution. Finally, she must find a way to tie together the different approaches to a solution, taking everyone with her. At another level – just as important – she must get them to see themselves and each other as legitimate contributors to the problem at hand.

Success in this complex realm involves more than simply creating a friendly or non-threatening setting for discussion and problem solving. One attempt to lead a group discussion is usually enough to convince the skeptic that the teacher's positive disposition toward discussion does not ensure student participation. Moreover, even students who do participate do not necessarily engage deeply or productively with the academic content. Thus we see the successful teacher as doing more than simply making discussion available for students. The complexity of this task probably explains the relative rarity of productive classroom discussion as a site for intellectual socialization in elementary school; it is rare even in many secondary and college settings.

As discussed by O'Connor and Michaels (1993), there are at least two independent components to this complex orchestration, components that must be integrated with each other. First, the teacher must skillfully align students with each other and with her, as proponents of a particular hypothesis or position relative to the problem at hand. She thus orchestrates students in taking on the target intellectual roles. But participation in such discourse activities cannot be fully specified independent of propositional content and, thus, academic content. One can only be a hypothesizer in virtue of one's support of a particular hypothesis. One cannot externalize one's reasoning without being in possession of some contents of reasoning. The teacher engaged in this language socialization process thus has to orchestrate and integrate both the academic content and the participation of students simultaneously. And both of these must be accomplished against a background in which students vary widely in the discursive and academic resources they bring to the classroom context.

We are interested in describing and understanding the ways that teachers purposefully and strategically use language to create contexts for intellectual socialization. We have developed this research topic during multiple-year observations and collaborations with two elementary school teachers, Judith Richards and Lynne Godfrey, who themselves have thought extensively about the importance of pedagogical practices that will develop in students the ability to participate fully in the thinking practices of the school.[2] Both teachers have developed sophisticated ways of orchestrating large- and small-group discussions as a means of bringing students into shared intellectual work.

In this chapter, we attempt to explicate and give a theorized account of some of the purposeful strategies used by these teachers. To do this, we use the notion of a *participant framework* (Goffman, 1974, 1981; Goodwin, 1990), contrasting it with other constructs commonly used in analyzing classroom discourse. We use the construct of a participant framework to analyze one particular, recurring move in both teachers' classrooms, a move we call *revoicing*. This analysis was first developed by O'Connor and Michaels (1993). Here we summarize and extend that analysis in two ways: We look more closely at the way revoicing moves create a complex participant framework in the two classrooms we have observed, and then we consider similar participant frameworks and conversational moves in two other classrooms. We contrast these particular uses of language and the participant frameworks they create with the much discussed initiation–reply–evaluation (IRE) sequence that commonly occurs in teacher-led group discussions. We suggest that a focus on participation frameworks allows an analysis of classroom discourse that more effectively links language (both form and function) with participation roles and socialization into thinking practices.

Participant frameworks and the analysis of classroom discourse

Numerous aspects of classroom discourse may be important to the induction of students into complex thinking practices. The notion of a participant framework (Goffman, 1974, 1981; Goodwin, 1990) is fairly new to the study of classroom discourse. Here we briefly introduce the idea of participant framework and then place that aspect of conversational process and structure in the context of other important analytic descriptors of classroom discourse, including *participant structure, speech activity,* and *speech event.*

We will begin with Goffman's formulation: "When a word is spoken, all those who happen to be in perceptual range of the event will have some sort of participation status relative to it. The codification of these various positions and the normative specification of appropriate conduct within each provide an essential background for interaction analysis" (Goffman, 1981, p. 3). For him, the participation framework for a particular moment within an encompassing social gathering is the amalgam of all members' participation statuses relative to the current utterance (ibid., p. 137).

In Goodwin (1990), we find a further development of Goffman's observation that linguistic description is the tool necessary to find some structural basis for the fluid and subtle shifts in footing that speakers are capable of (Goffman, 1981, p. 147). Goodwin systematically shows how linguistic structure at various levels of detail is used to create social organization among a group of peers through the moment-to-moment creation of participant frameworks. Her work painstakingly demonstrates how linguistic expressions open up roles and stances with respect to the content expressed in the utterance.

The term *participant framework,* as used by Goodwin (1990, p. 10), subsumes two constructs found elsewhere in the classroom discourse literature: (1) *participant structures,* the conventional configurations of interactional rights and responsibilities that arise within particular classroom activities as these are set up purposefully by the teacher; and (2) speakers' depictions of others through what Goffman (1981) called *animation*. In Goffman's puppeteering metaphor, a speaker animates self or other as a *figure* or character by simple linguistic means. Through talk *about* each other, speakers give each other participant roles and social identities relevant to the moment. The following examples from Goodwin demonstrate both aspects of a participant framework: the creation of roles and relationships in talk directed from one speaker *to* another and in talk by one speaker *about* another.

In example (1) a participant framework arises during the speech activity Goodwin calls "he-said–she-said," a gossip-reporting activity engaged in by the children Goodwin studied. The activity involved them as parties to reports of past events of a particularly charged kind. In this example, Annette, a young girl, is engaging in the activity of "he-said–she-said" by giving such an account. In her actual utterance she animates herself, her addressee, and a third-party bystander as *reported* speaker, addressee, and third-party bystander. But these are not simply speakers and addressees of an ordinary sort. The activity of "he-said–she-said" itself brings with it roles such as *accuser* and *defendant*. So the current participants, animated by Annette as speakers and addressees, are cast in the roles of accuser and defendant by virtue of their historical connection with the participants animated in the actual utterance.

(1)   *In the midst of play, Annette*
                 confronts Benita.

        Annette: And Arthur said that you said
                   that I was showin' off just because
                   I had that bl:ouse on.
                 (Example 4, Goodwin, 1990, p. 195)

This single utterance thus accomplishes a complex positioning of the participants. In (2) we provide Goodwin's display of Annette's move. Annette has animated Benita as a defendant in this activity by casting Arthur as a witness to a past speech act of Benita's – Benita's original animation of Annette as a show-off.

(2)   Annette → Benita   Annette is speaking in the present to Benita
           |
      Arthur → Annette   about what Arthur told Annette
           |
       Benita → Arthur   that Benita told Arthur
           |
         Annette   about Annette.

                                           (Goodwin, 1990, p. 196)

Simply put, the participant framework encompasses (a) the ways that speech event participants are aligned with or against each other and (b) the ways they are positioned relative to topics and even specific utterances. One of Goffman's points was that the categories of "speaker" and "addressee" grossly underdetermine the range of ways that humans use talk to create alliances and oppositions and to connect utterance acts with various participants.[3] In the previous example, those alliances are created both through the roles and rights embedded in the activity itself and by the speaker's explicit depictions and characterizations of other participants, utterance by utterance. Thus this notion provides a useful tool for explicating what goes on *inside* more extended speech activities. It also provides a tool for explicating how those activities are actually instantiated within the particulars of utterance sequences. This will prove to be an advantage for the analysis of teachers' orchestration of group discussion.

Why add the construct of participant framework to an already well-populated array of analytic approaches to classroom discourse? It may at first appear to be quite similar to the notion of participant structure (Au, 1980; Erickson, 1982; Gumperz, 1981; Philips, 1983). Both involve the rights and responsibilities of the interactants in a speech situation. Yet in work on participant structures in classrooms, the emphasis is on the ways that particular roles and alliances tend to arise out of fairly stable arrangements in classroom organization. For example, small-group work provides a different set of opportunities for learning and interaction than teacher-centered lecturing. Classroom arrangements that emphasize a student's individual work tend to produce different kinds of roles and relations than classrooms that institutionalize collaborative emphases. These are undoubtedly very important aspects of the creation of a learning environment. Yet it's clear that the choice of configuration (small groups, large-group discussion, lecture, or other) drastically underdetermines the character of interactions – and learning – that we see in classrooms. A more microanalytic level of description is needed to study the creation and maintenance of learning opportunities for children within classroom interaction. Goodwin's work stresses both speech activities and smaller units, such as speech acts, as the source of participant roles and alignments. This makes her work potentially quite useful for classroom analysis.

From a different perspective, the construct of participant framework may appear to be somewhat similar to the notion of *speech activity*. Gumperz defines speech activity as "a set of social relationships enacted about a set of schemata in relation to some communicative goal"

(Gumperz, 1982, p. 166). The term *speech activity* is typically used to name a temporally extended, conventionally recognized level of activity such as "classroom discussion," "lecturing," "complaining" or "making a speech." (Such activities differ across communities in their particulars but are recognizable on the basis of their recurrent, central participant roles and purposes). In this sense, "he-said–she-said" constitutes a conventional speech activity in the community Goodwin studied. Yet in (1) earlier, Annette's actual utterance does the work of tying current participants to the roles entailed by that conventional speech activity. By virtue of the participant framework introduced through reported speech verbs and their complements in the example utterance, Annette is able to cast Benita as the defendant and thus to actually *make* her a defendant *within* the speech activity.

In our view, then, the construct of participant framework (as elaborated by Goodwin) is distinct from that of speech activity in that it picks out the level of linguistic structure that determines (a) how present participants fill the currently relevant roles and (b) how those participants are situated with respect to current utterances (cf. the previous Goffman quotation). On this view, individual utterances and the participant frameworks they create constitute the infrastructure of any speech activity. But participant frameworks exist outside conventional speech activities as well, as the following example (again from Goodwin) demonstrates. A simple request, taking place outside any conventionally labeled speech activity, introduces roles and rights, and these are taken on by the current participants. Three boys are conversing; one boy, Chopper, is carrying hangers. Tokay wants one.

(3) Tokay: Chopper can I have one?
    Malcolm: No boy. He givin' them to me.
                     (Goodwin, 1990, p. 96)

By issuing a request, Tokay casts himself in the role of supplicant, and Chopper is given the right to grant or deny his request. Before Chopper can do this, Malcolm appropriates Chopper's turn. Moreover, he "animates" Chopper as *his* creature, set to do his bidding. By taking over Chopper's role as the one controlling the resources, Malcolm is also disrupting Tokay's attempt to position himself vis-à-vis Chopper. Malcolm is thus using language strategically, positioning himself socially at the expense of others by manipulating the default participant framework that comes with a request. Of course, this exchange may itself be taken as cuing or framing a larger speech activity. Our point is simply that the two levels of description are distinct.

Participant frameworks and revoicing

As discussed first in O'Connor and Michaels (1993), by *revoicing* we mean a particular kind of reuttering (oral or written) of a student's contribution – by another participant in the discussion. In the following (constructed but typical) example from a graduate seminar, the student makes an assertion and the teacher revoices:

(4) Student: Well, I think that Smith's work is really not relevant here because she only looked at adults.

Teacher: So you agree with Tom then, you're suggesting that Smith is irrelevant to language acquisition of young children?

Student: Yeah.

The defining characteristics of this move will be discussed later. Important points for current purposes include (a) the way the teacher uses the student's utterance in relation to the ongoing academic task, (b) the way the teacher aligns the student with other, previous contributions to the discussion, and (c) the fact that the teacher's revoicing opens up a slot for the student to agree or disagree with the teacher's characterization of the student's contribution, thus ultimately crediting the contents of the *re*formulation to the student. (These three facets are not invariably equally foregrounded; the situated particulars of the activity, the interactants, and the topic will determine the importance of alignment with content, with other participants, and with the speaker in any particular revoicing utterance. We return to this issue later.)

Both Judy Richards and Lynne Godfrey, the teachers we have worked with, play an active role in recasting and reformulating students' contributions in group discussions. Richards often refers to this kind of move as an attempt to "give a bigger voice" to a student's contribution, serving to relay the utterance, originally directed at the teacher, back to the entire group. In the process, the utterance is necessarily transformed (simply by virtue of coming from the teacher, who has a privileged status); in addition, it can be uttered more succinctly, loudly, completely, or in a different register (Halliday, 1988) or social language (Bakhtin, 1986; Wertsch, 1991). Moreover, through revoicing, students can be repositioned with respect to each other *and* with respect to the content of the ideas at hand. We will provide several examples of this conversational move, discussing the participant framework it evokes, suggesting its potential usefulness as a site for students' sociocognitive learning – learning how to externalize reasoning, how to compare views, and how to articulate a position.[4]

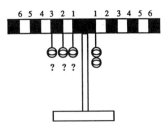

Figure 3.1   Balance scale for the torque unit. Topic question: If you hang the weights shown (cases A, B, and C), do you think the scale will tip to the right, to the left, or balance? Why?

An example of revoicing

In this example, third- and fourth-grade students in Judy Richards's class are working on a science unit on torque, using a balance scale apparatus.[5] A problem is posed with several possible answers, and the students must vote for the answer they think is right. In this case, two weights are placed on the 1 point on the right side of the balance and there are three separate situations to compare on the left side: case A, where one weight is on the 1 point; case B, where one weight is on the 2 point; and case C, where one weight is on the 3 point. In each case, the problem posed to the students is "Will the arm tip to the right, to the left, or balance?"

First, each student casts a vote on whether the scale will balance or tip to the right or left. Cases A, B and C are voted on. The students then discuss the reasons for their choices and may present arguments in an attempt to persuade others of their position. Then another vote is taken to see if any students have changed their minds. Finally, the experiment is tried.

In Richards's classroom, this instructional arrangement carries with it clear participant structures in Philips's sense: rights and responsibilities that each student must come to recognize as part of the classroom culture during that particular activity. Students must present their reasoning to the group and may answer, agree with, or challenge each other. The teacher plays a moderating role, and in this particular instantiation, she controls turn allocation.

At the point we present here, the students have just finished up discussing case A, where two weights are placed on the 1 point on the right side of the balance and one weight is placed on the 1 point on the left side of the balance. Everyone in the class thought the scale would tip to the right because two weights are heavier than one. They are now discussing case B, with one weight on the 2 point to the left of the fulcrum and two weights on the 1 point to the right of the fulcrum. Before this transcript segment, Dorian has said that it will tip to the right but not quite so much because it makes a difference that the single weight on the left has been moved farther out. In turn (1) in the following transcript, Allen agrees with him, emphasizing that case B differs from case A: In case B the scale will tip *less* to the right. Jane asserts a different position. She thinks the scale may tip to the left: The one weight on the 2 point will outweigh the two weights on the other side, although not by much. Allen then announces a discovery: The scale will balance! We have placed Richards's revoicings in boldface in the following transcript.[6]

Transcript excerpt 1: the balance scale[7]

(1) Allen: um/ well/ I think that/ it will/ um/ tip to the right/ like what Dorian said/
              because/ um/ it's just getting a little bit/ like/ when it's farther out it's
              heavier//
(2) Child: me too //
(3) Richards: **'kay so it'll still be/   still to the right but   less so//**
(4) Allen: well it's still/   right but   Yeah//
(5) Child: Judy/ me too/
(6) Allen: and cuz it's getting a little bit farther/ and a little bit farther//
(7) Jane: I sa – / I th – / I think it's a/ a little bit like um/ Dorian and Allen but um/
              it's a little different// I think it will go sort of/ um/ mo:st/ of the way to
              the/ right/ even/ . . . I mean left/ even/ though it like/ well not all the way/
              even/ cuz/ even though these are more/ these are heavier/ they/ double
              the amount/ but/ but/ since this is further out/ it/ it would be/ in/ the um
              weigh more/
(8) Richards: **okay/ so you're suggesting since this is farther out/**
(9) Allen: wait // you know what I discovered?/ that it's/ double the/ I think/ it might balance because/ it's/
              um/ double as far as that is/ and that's double it's weight// so I – that's
              why I might change my vote to balance/
(10) Child: yeah/
(11) Child: yeah/

(12) Child:	yeah/
(many voices)	
(13) Child:	that's what I was gonna say //
(14) Child:	yeah/
(15) Richards:	**'kay so you're gonna predict it balances/ . . . lemme see if I got/ right/ what your theory is// Jane says/ it's not – it's gonna tip/ a little bit to the left/ because this is further out//**
(16) Jane:	but it'll sorta balance/
(17) Richards:	but/
(18) Jane:	sort of/
(19) Richards:	not – / sort of/ but a little bit to the left// and **you're thinking/ that it's going to exactly balance/ because since this is/ twice the dist – / this is twice the weight/ but this is twice the distance//**
(20) Allen:	yeah/

What is accomplished here in terms of creating a participant framework and possibilities for learning? First, we'll describe what Richards does with these revoicing utterances; then we'll review how the actual linguistic content of each creates the participant framework that serves her purposes. Our claims about the possible functions of revoicing are based on many hours of observation in Richards's and Godfrey's classrooms; many more hours of discussion with them about their goals, intentions, and strategies concerning classroom learning; and close scrutiny of particular instances of interaction. We are not claiming that every teacher who uses a conversational move that resembles these examples has in mind the functions we outline here. Nor are we claiming that every possible revoicing utterance found in our transcripts has the same set of functions. Rather, we're attempting to sketch the range of possible purposes and ends that might motivate a teacher to use this discourse strategy.[8]

Functions of revoicing

Revoicing for reformulation

We have found that when the teacher reformulates a student's utterance within a revoicing sequence, she may do so for a variety of reasons, including clarification of content or relevance or the introduction of new terminology for familiar ideas. She may be reformulating it in order to advance her own discussion agenda, changing the contribution slightly so as to drive the discussion in another direction. She may be simply rebroadcasting the student's utterance to reach a wider audience than the student reached. In this example, we see several such functions being served.

When Allen mentions Dorian and reiterates the prediction that the scale will still tip to the right (turn 1), his utterance actually sounds contradictory: paraphrased, he says, "I think it will tip to the *right* because when the weight on the left is farther out, the *left* side is *heavier.*" He leaves out any explicit mention of the important fact that this tip to the right is expected to be *less* than it was in case A. He is correct that when the weight is farther from the fulcrum it contributes a greater force. But we miss the relevance of this fact to his prediction. He has not mentioned the most important fact that links these two statements: The scale will *still* tip to the right, but *less* than it did before, because the weight on the left is now "heavier."

We take one goal of academic socialization practices to be student proficiency in *explication of reasoning.* Explication of one's reasoning for an audience figures in all forms of expository text and in many spoken genres in classrooms at virtually every level. It requires that the speaker make explicit the connection between claims, predictions, or hypotheses and the grounds for these claims. Here Allen seems to have a grasp of the connection between his prediction and the grounds for his prediction, but he fails to make it explicit for the audience in a clear and coherent fashion. When Richards revoices his utterance, she makes this connection clear by filling in the missing element: the link to the previous event, case A: " 'kay, so it'll still be, still to the right but *less* so" (turn 3). By revoicing his utterance, Richards further externalizes and clarifies his reasoning for him, so that it more effectively communicates his explanation to the group. In a sense, she is repairing his utterance for him.

The next student, Jane, begins by explicitly posing her contribution in contrast to the previous speakers. She asserts in turn (7) that she thinks the balance scale will tip to the left. She gives a reason: The single weight on the left side, on the two point, is "further out" and thus provides more force. Even though the *two* weights on the right "double the amount" and are "heavier," the weight on the left is "further out" and would thus "weigh more." Her turn is complete and it fully externalizes her reasoning, but it is full of false starts and hesitations.

Richards begins a revoicing move in (8): "okay, so you're suggesting [that] since this [the weight on the left] is farther out" but is interrupted. What Richards has started to do is to reformulate Jane's turn. She first cites Jane's reason for voting that the scale will tip to the left. What is her purpose here? As mentioned earlier, Richards says she often does this to give "a louder voice" to a student (see also Gray, 1993). The reformulation is done not to add or change content but to strengthen it for purposes of rebroadcasting. More complete examples of this function will be presented later in the chapter.

Finally, in line (15), when Richards finally brings Jane's and Allen's predictions together within one revoicing move, she is, we can infer, at least partially doing this to drive the discussion in the direction she wants it to go. The pedagogy she is using – group discussion of individual predictions about the science experiment – is intended to get students to think about alternative hypotheses and weigh critically the evidence that might support them. She knows that one of the predictions is correct and the other is wrong. By juxtaposing the two contributions as she does in turns (15) to (19), she is furthering the discussion in the direction that serves her larger pedagogical purposes.

In Goffman's terms, the student is the "principal" in each case – the individual who is held responsible for the original content of the utterance on which the revoicing is based. By taking up the student's utterance, Richards is taking on the role of animator, the participant who is casting another as a figure. In these cases, Richards is casting Jane and Allen as theorizers: "lemme see if I got right what your theory is . . . Jane says . . . (etc.)." Thus, although Richards is doing the talking, Jane and Allen retain prominence as the originators of the ideas. As we will see later, this participant framework allows for the splitting up of roles of principal/originator and speaker/animator.[9]

Revoicing to create alignments and oppositions within an argument

The functions just described are achieved primarily through the way the teacher reformulates the propositional content of the student's contribution. By adding material, deleting material, or using different lexicalizations, the teacher may clarify, highlight, or reframe aspects of the student's utterance in relation to the current or desired academic content. In doing this she is positioning the student in relation to that content, conferring on (or attributing to) that student a stance with respect to the topic under discussion, a stance the student may only dimly be aware of.

There is, however, another set of functions served by the revoicing sequence, one that concerns the relationship of the student to other students within the discussion. A discussion entails more than a speaker and a topic; it also entails other interlocutors. These interlocutors are positioned relative to each other vis-à-vis the propositional content –

some are in opposition, some are aligned. This is in the nature of a discussion containing extended reasoning about complex issues. By using the participant frameworks afforded by the revoicing sequence, the teacher places one student in relation to other students as holders of positions. In Goffman's terms, the teacher animates the students as figures of a particular kind: thinkers, hypothesizers, position holders.

In this example, before Richards can finish revoicing Jane in line (8), Allen is struck by a new thought (which may well have been triggered by Jane's words "*double* the amount"): He sees a mathematical relationship between the number of weights and their distance from the fulcrum. He blurts out an utterance that amounts to saying that the force on a side is equal to weight times distance. Paraphrased, Allen says, "Wait. You know what I discovered? . . . . I think it might balance because the weight on the left side is twice as far from the fulcrum as the weight on the right is. And the weights on the right are double the weight on the left." Many students voice their agreement with this, and the cascade of approving comments seems to indicate the group's readiness to see this key relationship.

Richards then steps in and takes Jane's position and Allen's position and creates a contrast at the point of the critical difference between their two positions: She juxtaposes their arguments, thus positioning them in opposition to each other. She addresses Allen and first says, " 'kay, so you're gonna predict it balances." Immediately thereafter she animates Jane, depicting her in opposition to Allen. While directly addressing Allen, she depicts Jane in a contrasting stance with respect to the question at hand. "Lemme see if I got right what your theory is: Jane says it's not . . . it's gonna tip a little bit to the left, because this [the weight on the left] is further out." Jane comes in at this point and tries to clarify, "but it'll sorta balance." Richard accepts this but reemphasizes the difference: "sort of, but a little bit to the left" and continues, addressing Allen. She restates Allen's position, including a more succinct version of his insight about the relationship between weight and distance: "and you're thinking that it's going to exactly balance, because since this is . . . twice the weight, but this is twice the distance." Allen agrees: "Yeah."

In completing these few turns, Richards has created a participant framework and put Allen and Jane into it as central players. She positions Allen's and Jane's competing predictions (the arm will tip to the left slightly or will exactly balance) in terms of two conflicting theories – one that sees distance as the primary explanatory factor (Jane's theory) and the other that sees both distance and weight as relevant and mathematically computable (Allen's theory). In doing this, she has accomplished an alignment that may or may not have been incipient in their contributions. Recall that Jane explicitly placed herself with respect to Allen's and Dorian's positions on the balance question, but her attempt was tentative: "I think it's a little bit like um, Dorian and Allen but um, it's a little different." Allen, on the other hand, did not place himself with respect to any previous turn at the time of his breakthrough. Richards has created a coherent oppositional structure for their two predictions.

This participant framework, then, contains two hypotheses about a future event and entails two originators of those hypotheses. By bringing Allen and Jane into opposition around the balance experiment, Richards has accomplished several things. She has inducted them into public versions of key intellectual roles. These roles – theorizer, predictor, hypothesizer – must be stated in terms of other participants in the ongoing activity and in terms of the actual propositional content under discussion. Here the teacher has created a dramatic landscape for this event, featuring two protagonists. This provides an opportunity for other children (perhaps silently, perhaps vocally) to place themselves in relation to the balance experiment hypotheses, through Jane and Allen as proxies (cf. Hatano & Inagaki, 1991).

In summary, the revoicing sequence may serve a number of functions, several of which are apparent in this example. It allows the teacher to effectively credit a student for his or her contribution while still clarifying or reframing the contribution in terms most useful for group consumption. It may socialize students into particular intellectual and speaking practices by placing them in the roles entailed by the speech activity of group discussion. It may also bring them to see themselves and each other as legitimate participants in the activity of making, analyzing, and evaluating claims, hypotheses, and predictions.

Linguistic concomitants of the revoicing move

How are these functions accomplished? We now examine how the characteristic linguistic elements found in this sequence create the roles and positionings that may support the socializing functions we have previously posited.

The reformulation component

The most obvious component of a revoicing utterance is the reuttering or rephrasing of the student's contribution. In a revoicing move this is

3 Richards:	'kay so it'll still be still to the right but less so
8 Richards:	okay, so you're suggesting since this is farther out...
15 Richards:	'kay so you're gonna predict it balances.. lemme see if I got right what your theory is. Jane says it's not -- it's gonna tip a little bit to the left because this [the weight on the left] is further out.
19 Richards:	and you're thinking that it's going to exactly balance because since this is twice the weight, but this is twice the distance.

Figure 3.2   Revoicing moves in transcript excerpt 1.

often not an exact repetition, but may include a change in the propositional content of the student's formulation or in the language used to frame that contribution. Richards's changes of Allen's initial proposition (turn 3 in transcript excerpt 1) were discussed in terms of their contribution to the relevance and coherence of Allen's statement. In turn (19) (presented again in Figure 3.2), Richards is rephrasing Allen's position again. Her formulation is more succinct than his, but more important, she foregrounds a key aspect of the academic content: the relationship between weight and distance.

In our analysis, one of the most significant aspects of this construction concerns the ultimate disposition of "credit" for the teacher's reformulation: When a student assents to a teacher's revoicing, he or she potentially gets credit for the reformulation.[10] When Richards says to Allen "and you're thinking that it's going to exactly balance because since this is twice the weight, but this is twice the distance," and Allen says "yeah," Richards's reformulation appears not as a correction of Allen's but as an expansion. Allen is getting credit for the reformulated version, which is somewhat more coherent than his own. How does this happen? As we describe later, the linguistic elements in which the reformulation is set contribute to this unusual aspect of the participant framework.

The use of indirect speech

Each of the examples presented earlier, and most others we have found, include the reformulation component within an indirect speech complement. The student is cast as the subject of a verb of speech or cognition ("So you think that . . ." or "So Jane predicts that . . ."). This is a key part of the revoicing utterance. The use of such verbs depicts or animates the student as the originator of the intellectual content of the revoiced utterance, even though the teacher may have reformulated it. These verbs (*laminator* verbs in Goffman's terminology) thus layer the teacher's phrasing onto the contribution of the student.[11] Lamination or layering brings one slice of activity into the participant framework on another, tying the two together. In the context of discussing replayings and reportings, Goffman notes:

> Among the events that an individual may report are utterances themselves, whether self-imputed or imputed to another . . . and this reporting need not be, but commonly is, presented as something to reexperience, to dwell upon, to savor. . . . (1974, pp. 505–506)

We get a fusing of the teacher's words, register, or knowledge with the original intent of the student. Thus, the teacher's revoicing gives added time and space, and heightened clarity or elaboration, to the original student contribution, laminating the teacher's phrasing, register, and information onto the student's contribution. From the teacher, the reasoning is thus rebroadcast back out to the entire group – animating the student as speaking in a broader public sphere.

Goffman is, of course, not the only scholar to have discussed the richness and complexity of indirect discourse in all its varieties. Vološinov (1971), Banfield (1982), and Bakhtin (1986) are three notable works in which the juxtaposition and fusion of multiple points of view through reported speech are explored. Here we are concerned with showing its strategic value for the teacher in her attempt to induct students into a discourse community by getting them to adopt roles in the ongoing thinking practices that she wishes them to develop. The subtleties of this aspect of the move warrant further discussion and are beyond the scope of this chapter. Nevertheless, the use of a laminator predicate and reported speech is a recurrent feature of this particular participant framework.

The use of so and other markers of warranted inference

But we have still not answered the question of how the student is in some sense given credit for the content of the teacher's reformulation. To answer this question, the conversational structure of the revoicing sequence as a whole must be considered. The third salient marker of a revoicing utterance is the discourse marker *so* (or some other analogous item), which marks a warranted inference (Schiffrin, 1987). On Schiffrin's account, this indicates that the speaker is linking her utterance to that of the previous speaker and is making an inference that she believes to be warranted based on that previous utterance. In the following example, an informant Schiffrin is interviewing, Zelda, has been talking about her relatives.

(5) Zelda: They live in the Northeast.
    Debby: Oh okay. *So* you have a lot of family up in the
               Northeast.
                                        (Schiffrin 1987, p. 215)

This meaning of *so* has implications for turn taking and for shifts in participation frameworks. Schriffrin spells out how *so* creates a slot for the addressee's response:

> By marking a response as an inference warranted by one's interlocutor, a respondent assigns to the initial speaker partial responsibility for the accuracy of his/her own inference. However, the division of responsibility for interpretation does not then end: such requests return the floor to the speaker who first warranted the inference – so that the inference may be confirmed. . . . In short, responsibility for the **next** move is shifted back to the one who provided the initial warrant. (pp. 215–216)

When the speaker makes such a warranted inference explicitly marked with *so,* a slot is thus opened up for a turn transition at the end of that utterance. In the preferred sequence, the utterer of the original utterance can give assent or can contradict: "Yes, that's right," or "No, I don't really have that much family in the Northeast. More of them live in the South." Silence is generally construed as assent for the second speaker's inference (Clark & Schaefer, 1985).

For our purposes this aspect of the revoicing move is quite important, as it provides a structuring link between the propositional content of the revoicing, the participant who is animated as the source of the original proposition, and the actual face-to-face interaction between the student and the teacher. The discourse marker *so* or some other indication of a warranted inference (such as Richards's turn 15 in Figure 3.2 – "lemme see if I got right what your theory is") plays a critical role in opening up a new slot in the conversational space, giving the student both an opportunity to respond and a responsibility to ratify or reject the correctness of the revoiced utterance. Notice that both Jane and Allen respond immediately to Richards's revoicings, with Jane modifying Richards's inference and Allen agreeing ("but it'll sorta balance" – line 16 – and "yeah" – line 20).

Beyond the consequences for turn structure, there is another level of significance to this aspect of the move. When the student, the first speaker, is granted the right to affirm or deny the warranted inference, the first speaker (student) and the second speaker (teacher) are for the moment on an equal conversational footing, at least with respect to the implications of the first speaker's utterance.[12] The teacher is thus positioning herself vis-à-vis the first speaker in a way that is quite different in several respects from the positioning she accomplishes within an IRE sequence (see Cazden, 1988; Mehan, 1979). In that type of sequence, the teacher reserves the right to evaluate the student's response, and the turn structure provides no opportunity for the student to negotiate the meaning or significance of his or her contribution after the teacher's evaluation. In the revoicing move, the teacher is accepting the student's response from the start, using it as a base for the warranted inference, and then allowing the student the right to evaluate the correctness of the teacher's inference.

The example given in transcript excerpt 1 thus exemplifies all three ongoing concerns described in the Introduction: the maintenance of smoothly coordinated social participation structures, the coordination of the academic task structure with ongoing social interaction, and the induction of all students into the speech activities associated with intellectual work in the envisioned community of learners. All three of these purposes are aligned through one conversational move, which has a valence that allows all three to proceed at once.

In Figure 3.3, we represent the key elements of the participant framework introduced in a revoicing move, embedded within a group discussion. A characterization of this structure includes the roles of the two central participants, the Inference Maker/Animator and Inference Source/Principal, and the rights and obligations that come with those roles. It must also include a description of the participants (if any) animated in opposition or alignment to the original Inference Source (here, the student who makes the original contribution). Finally, it must specify the content of the third component, the *proposition* that constitutes the reuttered content of the inference. In the revoicing sequence characterized here, the Inference Maker, the teacher, is yoking two contributions together (Allen's and Jane's) to create a pair of opposing positions within the larger discussion question – which way will the balance scale tip?

Revoicing and teachers' goals

The next two examples demonstrate some of the larger purposes for which revoicing can be deployed by the teacher. In the next transcript excerpt, Lynne Godfrey uses this conversational strategy to support a different academic task structure than that described previously, but one that has certain important parallels. In this example, Godfrey's sixth-

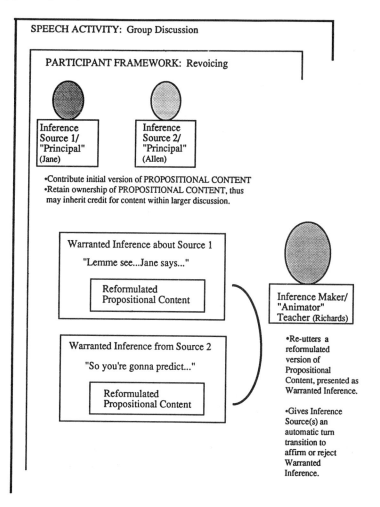

Figure 3.3   Participant framework created by turns 7–20, transcript excerpt 1.

grade students have constructed a set of eighty-seven possible trips on the local mass transit system, specifying these trips by their starting and finishing stations. For example, one trip might start at Alewife and end at Central Station. Each student contributed three different trips to the total sample of trips. Students are now trying to guess what the most frequent or "popular" starting station for a trip is within the sample of eighty-seven trips and to explain the reasons for their guess. The speech activity is thus also group discussion, and the participant structure is similar to that in the example just discussed: Students must present their reasoning to the group and may answer, agree with, or challenge each other. The teacher plays a moderating role and controls turn allocation.

Two of the pedagogical goals to be served in this lesson are getting students (1) to explicate the reasoning supporting their guess and (2) to move from what might be characterized as random guessing to an activity that includes a search for supporting evidence. Godfrey's purpose is to guide them to consider the different bases on which they can refine a random guess into one supported by some sort of evidence. The academic task thus requires a sequence of turns in which students offer their reasons for guessing that one particular station will be most frequently selected as the starting station.

Godfrey raises the question, soliciting bids for the display of students' reasoning about their guess. Notice that after each student contribution, she carries out a modified revoicing of what they have offered, introducing most turns with *so* and linking each participant/addressee with a strategy for refining a guess.

Transcript excerpt 2: guessing the most frequent starting station (turns edited where indicated with ". . .")

(1) Godfrey: so when / when you were making your own <u>personal guesses</u> /
                 <u>how</u> did people do that //

                 . . .
                 did you / just / <u>guess</u>? //
                 did you / use any infor<u>mat</u>ion to help you guess? //
                 um / if you <u>did</u>/ what information did you use to <u>help</u> you
                     guess //
                 (4- to 5-second pause)
                 <u>Marshall</u> / what did <u>you</u> do //

(2) Marshall: <u>I</u> / I started at <u>Ale</u>wife / in the / the beginning //. . .
                 because / um / <u>it's</u> just the be<u>gin</u>ning / <u>um</u> / I think Alewife's a
                     good
                 <u>ter</u>minal // (*students laugh*)
                 and I been to Alewife three times and I liked the way it
                     <u>looked</u> //

(3) Godfrey: okay / so you chose Alewife based on your own personal
                     ex<u>pe</u>rience
                 with Alewife station and liking the way it <u>looks</u> / and /
                 if it's such a <u>ni</u>:ce <u>look</u>ing place why <u>would</u>n't people want to
                     start here? //
                 . . . Michael //

(4) Michael: I/<u>I</u> picked / Alewife <u>too</u> //
                 because / like / alot of people like/ like to ride on the train for
                     a long time //
                 some people might just <u>ride</u> / to Alewife / just for the <u>heck</u>
                     of it //

(5) Godfrey:	so you made your guess based on what you know about hu:man be<u>ha:vi</u>our?

(*students laugh a little*)

(6) Michael:	uhm hmm //
(7) Godfrey:	uhhuh //. . . Cedric //
(8) Cedric:	well / I picked / Alewife / based on the information that was / on the um / tacked up on the <u>boar</u>d / cause I / I looked at it and I saw that // almost fifty per<u>cent</u> of the trips were starting at Alewife //
(9) Godfrey:	so you based it on the information that you got from reading the two <u>charts</u> //

In each of Godfrey's turns, (3), (5), (7), and (9), she subtly reformulates the students' contributions, recasting their guess-refining strategies in language that labels their reasoning as falling within a conventional category of evidence. With each revoicing, Godfrey has placed one student in alignment with one point in the space of possible approaches to fortifying a guess: Marshall based his prediction on "personal experience"; Michael based his on "knowledge of human behavior"; and Cedric consulted the available evidence: posted charts. Although the students' contributions were offered in the language of everyday experience, Godfrey has reformulated them in language that is somewhat more conventional and that points to the normative categories of support for predictions.

In this example, we can see further evidence of the process whereby the teacher lends authority and expertise to the student through the revoicing move. The students laugh when Godfrey revoices Michael's contribution: "so you made your guess based on what you know about hu:man be<u>ha:vi</u>our?" The moment is humorous because Michael's original contribution was stated in untheorized, casual terms, and Godfrey has handed him a more sophisticated reformulation to claim. At once she is gently teasing him while at the same time allowing Michael the next turn, where he assents: Yes, that is what he meant.

Recall that in transcript excerpt 1 Richards yoked together two contributions to create an oppositional structure featuring Jane and Allen. Here Godfrey has linked together a sequence of responses and revoicings that function as a string of examples: examples of alternative ways to reach a solution. She has thereby built up an instance of the highly valued practice of articulating and juxtaposing multiple solution paths (NCTM, 1989). Thus these two examples provide instances of how revoicing sequences work as building blocks of larger classroom discourse structures. In tran-

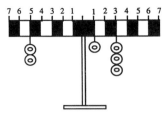

Figure 3.4   Balance scale for the torque unit. Topic question: If you hang
weights on your scale as shown here, do you think the scale will tip to the right,
to the left, or balance? Why?

script excerpt 1 that structure included two opposing "theories" about one
central phenomenon. In transcript excerpt 2 the structure included multiple alternative paths to a solution of a central task. Transcript excerpt 3
will demonstrate that revoicing is not always used to construct one of
these higher-level activity structures. It may be used simply to rebroadcast the contribution of a child who is in danger of being overlooked. Thus
the teacher's purposes served by revoicing may also encompass her goals
for the social organization of the classroom.

This example takes place in Richards's third/fourth-grade classroom
and, like the first transcript, concerns the balance scale experiment, as
shown in Figure 3.4. Students are being asked to voice their prediction
and then to explain their reasoning. First, Richards calls on Renee, a non-
native speaker of English, who has only recently begun to participate.
But she is still too unsure to project her solution strategy with the necessary force. Richards steps in and scaffolds her through the exchange,
then she explicitly revoices Renee's solution. Renee has computed the
torque of the two weights on the left by repeated addition, adding both
weights on the 5 point instead of multiplying 5 times 2. Yet making the
distinction between multiplication and repeated addition is complicated
in this particular case, because the weights on the right of the scale are on
two separate points. Thus, to compute the force of the right side of the
balance, one must both *multiply* (three weights times a distance of three
units from the fulcrum and one weight times a distance of one unit) *and*
add (the totals of those two: 1 plus 9). Renee's contribution, that the
multiplication can be done as repeated addition, is at first not sufficiently
distinct from what the class has already done. Moreover, it is presented
in a quiet and even muffled fashion. It does not come across, so Richards
brings it to the floor again for her, adding her own weight to it.

Transcript excerpt 3: balance and torque discussion

(1) Richards:	Renee / what about you?//	
(2) Renee:	(*Unintelligible*)	
(3) Richards:	We're your audience / we can't hear you// You're doing fine// You think it will balance because . . . //	
(4) Renee:	(*Unintelligible*)	
(5) Richards:	Yes / yuh / three of them at three//	
(6) Annie:	Could you speak up?//	
(7) Renee:	(*Unintelligible*)	
(8) Richards:	So it's ten and ten?//	
(9) Dorian:	Yeah!//	
(10) Richards:	(*Disciplinary interruption*)	
(11) Marta:	Renee / I have a comment for you// Um / I like what you did / I like / cause usually we just / like do what Sadja did on the board / weight times distance // But you added the / the five and the three / and then you added the two// And then you added the other ones and I think that's a neat way//	
(12) Richards:	So instead of / I'm going to give a little louder voice to what I think I hear Renee say// She was saying she wasn't adding five and two / and saying it's seven / she was saying five and five / knowing that if you double something it's like adding it to itself//	
(13) Child2:	Yeah right// Five and five . . . //	
(14) Richards:	Five and five and on this side she was saying three and three and three is . . . / nine /	

As a consequence of Richards's revoicing in turn (12), the students have heard and appreciated Renee's contribution to an extent they would not have had she remained unsupported. In the next two turns, we see Andrea, a mainstream student with great confidence, reach out to align herself with Renee. This is notable because Andrea had recently been explicitly unfriendly and even hostile to Renee. We cannot speculate about Andrea's reasons for the following contribution, nor can we judge whether it is sincere. However, we can assert that if Richards had not revoiced Renee's contribution, Andrea would not have had the opportunity to align herself with it explicitly.

(15) Richards:	Andrea // What d'you wanna . . . //	
(16) Andrea:	Um / I have a comment for Renee// Um / That's very smart// Because I	

was / I wanted to know a different way of how to do it than
    multiplying
and I didn't know how//

Variations and extensions: related participant frameworks

Our exploration of discourse in the classrooms of the exemplary teachers just described has convinced us of the general usefulness of the
participant framework as a unit of analysis in those settings. In this
section we will develop some examples from two other classrooms, also
exemplary in our view, where the most salient sequence of moves differs
in interesting ways from the revoicing sequences discussed earlier.

Douglas, why did Kenny say that?

We have observed the work of Victoria Bill, a teacher who works closely
with Lauren Resnick in an inner-city Pittsburgh parochial school, teaching math to first, second, and third graders (Leer, Bill, & Resnick,
1993). Bill, after becoming thoroughly familiar with current work on
mathematics learning in the cognitive science literature, decided to organize her math classes around a problem of the day – typically a fairly
complex two-step word problem that lends itself to multiple solutions.
(In this classroom, as in Richards's and Godfrey's classrooms, the cognitive merits of deriving multiple solutions are assumed.)

A great deal of talk in this classroom concerns getting students to
reason aloud through their solutions. Although we do find some instances of revoicing in her transcripts similar to those discussed previously, we find another very interesting participant framework that Bill
creates through utterances like those in transcript excerpt 4 that are
underlined. In these cases one student contributes the utterance, and
Bill reutters it and turns to another student, explicitly asking the second
student to evaluate the first student's utterance.

In the example here, the third-grade class has been discussing a problem in which Bill gave each student fifteen Smarties (a candy tablet) to
take home with them. Each child was allowed to eat two-thirds of his or
her Smarties. She has asked them to tell her how many of their Smarties
they got to eat. She has moved on to discuss the fractions two-thirds and
three-thirds, with most questions built around representations on the
board of three groups of five Smarties. Here she discusses what one
student will get when she gets three groups of fifteen.

Transcript excerpt 4: Victoria Bill and two-thirds of fifteen

(1) VB:	She's gonna get three groups// Ok, she's gonna get three out of the three/ Oh, how many does she get//
(2) (*children's voices softly*)	fifteen
(3) VB:	Go ahead and count the whole thing// She [indicates student Marnie] wants to count 'em// Go on up there and point to them// You don't have to count each one if you don't want / you can count however you want// Oh [hears a student and orients to that student] He says, count by *what* //
(4) David:	Five //
(5) VB:	[addressing student Marnie, who is counting the Smarties depicted on the board] **David says you can count by five// Can you//**
(6) Marnie:	Yes /
(7) VB:	Go ahead //
(8) Marnie:	One . . .
(9) Students	(*general sounds of consternation*)
(10) VB:	(to class) She needs you // Do it again Marnie //
(11) Students in unison:	Five / ten / fifteen /

Here Vicki Bill orients the students to each other several times in different ways. In (3) through (5) she picks up on David's comment from his seat, made to no one in particular, that Marnie could count the Smarties by fives; she need not count each Smarty one at a time successively. Thus she is acting as an animator of David, while he retains the role of principal or originator. But she does not mark her utterance with *so* or any other marker of a warranted inference. Thus she does not create a transition relevance point for David to take a turn after she reutters his contribution. Rather, she goes right on and queries Marnie, asking *her* to evaluate the correctness and current relevance of David's comment.

Vicki Bill has accomplished something similar to what Judy Richards has done in example 1, that is, put two students in explicit relation to each other in terms of their current contributions to the problem to be solved. She wanted Marnie to consider David's strategy of counting by fives. But Marnie has not contributed an opposing strategy: She has shown no indication of any strategy at all. Bill jump-starts the process by confronting Marnie with David's suggestion.

Indirect discourse is used here again: It laminates the content of the utterance onto David. "David says you can count by fives. Can you?" is a direct challenge to Marnie to engage with David's idea. It allows Vicki Bill to avoid simply imposing her own suggestion on Marnie. By using David's immediately preceding words in her formulation, she is instead getting Marnie to respond to an idea introduced by one of her peers. Of course, this bridge between the two students would not have existed had Bill not built it out of David's contribution and Marnie's current predicament. But it illustrates again the constant, moment-to-moment thinking and acting that a teacher does in simultaneously aligning students with each other and with the content of the academic moment. At the end of the sequence she again brings Marnie into contact with her peers: As Marnie begins to try to count by fives, Bill looks at the class and uses one of her formulaic utterances: "She needs you." They all begin counting with Marnie.

In the next example, Bill, like Richards and Godfrey in the previous examples, is attempting to get students to explicate their reasoning. But instead of using revoicing moves, as described in the previous sections, she directly draws one student into further explicating the thought of another.

Transcript excerpt 5: Victoria Bill and two-thirds of fifteen

(1) VB: You were allowed to eat two-thirds of them // how many / did you get to eat? //
        (deletion of insertion sequences)

(2) Ken: because / you got to eat ten because there were fifteen / there were fifteen all
        Smarties in that bowl // and then you two-thirds / that make / two out of the
        three groups / two out of the three groups / five plus five plus five is three
        groups //

(3) VB: Okay/
        (deletion of insertion sequences)
        so he said / open your notebooks . . . **you have fifteen Smarties /** and **I**
        said that you could have / two-thirds / of / the fifteen // and I wanna know / how many / you were allowed to eat // **who can explain what /**
        Kenny did? // . . . **he said** / David?

(4) D: He said / five plus five / because / *(long pause)*

(5) VB: How did you know to do five and five though? // Douglas?

At several points Bill appears to be on the verge of revoicing Kenny's attempt to explain his decision about how many Smarties is two-thirds of the total quantity. But by asking a particular student directly to explain

Kenny's decision, she gets the students themselves to repeat, explain, unpack, elaborate, correct, and so on. The strands of reasoning about a particular aspect of the problem are composed together by a number of students over the course of an episode. In Goffman's terms, the teacher first animates Kenny as someone who has accomplished some reasoning. Kenny is the principal, the one who is responsible for his own explicated reasoning. But instead of revoicing his contribution, the teacher then invites the other students to take on the role of animating Kenny themselves. In explaining his reasoning, they will be animating him as a reasoner, but they themselves will be taking on the role of Inference Maker. Making inferences about why an interlocutor said or did something is the converse of externalizing one's own reasoning. Both are necessary activities within collaborative intellectual work, and both are difficult for many children.

Although the structure of these moves is quite different from the revoicing sequence detailed earlier, some of the same purposes are accomplished through different means, different roles, and different stances of the teacher in relation to the student. By looking closely at this level of participant framework, created turn by turn, we see a skillful teacher bringing her students' thinking into contact with each other. As Goodwin remarks, these units of interactional structure "integrate participants, actions, and events, and thus constitute key resources for accomplishing social organization within face-to-face interaction" (1990, p. 10).

Students referencing students

The distinctions and relationships among speech activity, participant structure, and participation framework discussed in the first section become further clarified in some data from a Japanese classroom (Toma, 1991a, 1991b; Toma & Wertsch, 1990; Wertsch & Toma, in press). The curriculum featuring the balance beam unit described previously in Richards's class originated in Japan, and in this example it is being used in a fourth-grade class there. The transcripts from Richards's class and the Japanese class are in some sense instances of the same activity and the same problem space, but at the detailed level of participant framework we can see differences in the discourse context.

This transcript has been analyzed in detail by Chikako Toma, and we will draw on her work here. In the Japanese classroom, the patterning of reported speech and teacher revoicing is strikingly different from that reported in Richards's class, although the activity is the same: Students have been asked to predict whether they think the balance will tip to the right, to the left, or balance, voting for one of the three options. Then they are asked to externalize their reasoning before voting.

In Richards's classroom, there are about 10 times as many teacher revoicings as there are in the Japanese classroom. (We will discuss this in more detail later.) Second, in Richards's classroom, students tend to construct independent turns, without linking their talk explicitly to the talk of other students. The examples we have given in transcript excerpt 1, where Dorian refers to Allen and Jane refers to both Dorian and Allen, are the exceptions to the general pattern. In fact, they are the only occasions in the entire transcript of that session in Richards's classroom where this occurs. More typically, the pattern is that (1) a student says "I think X because Y"; (2) the teacher revoices; (3) the next student says "I think X because P"; and (4) the teacher revoices. Sometimes students will give the same answer as the previous speaker, with the same reason in slightly different words, without any explicit reference to the previous speaker. In the Japanese classroom analyzed by Toma, however, the students frequently cite each other. The following example is a typical turn at talk by a student.

Transcript excerpt 6: Japanese classroom balance problem[13]

Matchan: I am going to address the opinion Mie expressed earlier. (*goes up to the blackboard*)
As Yuko said earlier, something like this is the case (*draws a seesaw*)
and then Yuko was at this side . . . Ummm.
We suppose that Yuko's sister sits here, right?
Then she [Yuko] said it balances to a certain degree, right?
If so, as Mie said . . . for example, Yuko sits here, and then
    Yuko's sister sits here, or here, or here,
      it does not make any difference according to her [Mie's] opinion.
Therefore it is not right, I think.

(Mie's turn occurred 3 turns before this one, and Yuko's turn came 17 turns before Matchan's contribution.) Matchan's turn is strikingly different from what we see in Richards's classroom. Like the other students in her class, Matchan is herself creating the bridges between her contribution and that of her classmates, but in a different fashion than either Vicki Bill, Judy Richards, or Lynne Godfrey. Matchan has presented her argument to the entire group. Her argument against Mei's position uses Yuko's previous argument for support. She animates Mie and Yuko through reported speech, in opposition to each other, and then locates herself in relation to their opposing views.

Table 3.1. *Patterning of reasoning episodes in two classrooms*

Categories	J. Richards session	Japanese session
No. of reasoning episodes	15	21
No. of student utterances making explicit reference to other students' ideas or positions	2	17
No. of reported speeches by students	0	12
No. of teacher revoicings	16	2

This, of course, is activity of a very different sort than that described earlier for Richards, Godfrey, and Bill. Matchan is a student. We can assume that she is not engaged in a purposeful process of socializing her fellow students into intellectual practices. Instead, she is engaging in those practices herself, actively using the discourse strategies that we see Richards, Godfrey, and Bill modeling for their students.

In contrast, Matchan's teacher hardly ever does this for the students. We can see the difference in the above simple table (Table 3.1) that contrasts Richards's class and Matchan's class doing the same activity. Because both transcripts feature individual students taking turns externalizing their reasoning, we have taken each transcript and divided it informally into student-centered episodes of reasoning or expressions of commitment to a particular position. Each episode is centered on one student's reasoning or expression of commitment and may contain one turn or more than one turn. For example, one student may state an opinion about what the balance scale will do next, the teacher may comment, and then another student may comment on the first student's opinion. All three turns would be included in one reasoning episode. The next 'reasoning episode' starts when another student begins to explicate his or her reasoning.

After counting the number of reasoning episodes, we counted the number of teacher revoicings, using as criteria the three characteristics cited in the second section: the reformulation of a previous speaker's utterance, the use of a laminating verb of speech or thought, and the marking of the utterance as a warranted inference, with a concomitant slot for a possible response following it. We found that in the Richards transcript the teacher revoiced student contributions a bit more than once per reasoning episode, whereas in the Japanese transcript analyzed by Toma, the teacher revoiced about once every 10 reasoning episodes. On the other hand, student references to the words and thoughts of other students were far more frequent in the transcript of the Japanese session (Toma, 1991a).

Toma (1991b) suggests that Japanese children are primed from early in their schooling, with the explicit introduction of "speech frames" modeled for them, to refer to others' ideas and use them in constructing their own ideas. It is clear that a variety of influences are at work in the fine structure of classroom discourse. We have just begun the work of characterizing the range of ways that teachers' purposes can be served through participant frameworks and the ways that students' home-based ways of talking enter into this level of classroom talk.

It is important to point out that we are not suggesting that such features are stable and unchanging characteristics of teachers, students, or classrooms, nor are we suggesting that they should be. In fact, we have additional data from Judy Richards's classroom that illustrates this nicely. One week after the first balance session (shown in transcript excerpt 1), Richards instructed her students to sit in a circle facing each other rather than facing her, with the balance apparatus in the center of the circle. She also encouraged them to address their contributions to each other and to select the next speaker themselves. An informal analysis of that session reveals that the students made far more frequent references to each other's previous contributions and used indirect speech to animate each other's contributions, and Richards herself did far less revoicing. Thus the participant frameworks we have described are distributed across activities and participant configurations with great fluidity and flexibility. They are sensitive to a wide range of factors that we have only begun to describe here.

Discussion

It should be clear by now that we are not assuming the effectiveness or the desirability of the discourse moves we have described here. Rather, we are attempting to establish a basis for further analysis. If we wish to begin to understand how particular discourse settings may serve as contexts for socialization and enculturation into complex thinking practices, we must be able to characterize teacher and student participation in group discussion in sufficient detail.

Based on our current analysis, the following preliminary description seems warranted.

1. The teacher's conversational move (utterance) creates a participant framework.
2. The participant framework has roles and responsibilities embedded in it, and these roles articulate with those entailed by the larger speech activity.
3. By directing the utterance to a student, the teacher fits the student into a role given by the participant framework.
4. By taking part in the participant framework embedded in the larger speech activity, the student may incrementally gain access to the discourse practices that are a vehicle for complex thinking and problem solving in groups.

What is the significance of this analysis for the study of classroom discourse more generally? At this point, it may be useful to return to a well-known sequence of conversational moves identified as a recurring pattern, indeed the hallmark of teacher-led classroom discourse – the IRE sequence – referred to by Lemke (1990) as *triadic dialogue* and referred to by some as the IRF sequence – initiation, response, follow-up (cf. Cazden, 1988; Goldenberg, in press; Lemke, 1990; Mehan, 1979; Newman, Griffin, & Cole, 1989; Sinclair & Coulthard, 1975; Wells, 1993). As these and other researchers have discussed, this sequence consists of an initiation move by the teacher, usually a question with a known answer. This is followed by a response from the student, often a simple answer. The third move in the sequence is typically the teacher evaluation (or elaboration, follow-up, or feedback) in reference to the student's response ("What's the capital of Arkansas?" "Little Rock." "Good.").

We can understand this sequence as a creation by the teacher of a participant framework: as the setting up of particular roles and responsibilities through language. As the teacher poses the question, she creates for the students a participant role that one or more may bid for. By some conventional turn-taking mechanism (e.g., raising hands, calling out), a student will take on the role of supplying an answer. But the sequence is such that all participants know that this answer is an attempt to hit a target – the answer the teacher is waiting for. Thus the third move is construed as an evaluation of the student's performance specifically as it relates to the teacher's desired target. If we compare a similar sequence in ordinary face-to-face interaction, the meaning of the third move is quite different: "Do you know the time?" "Four thirty." "Good." Outside the classroom, the third move cannot be construed as an evaluation of the second speaker's performance; rather, it makes sense only as a comment on the usefulness or adequacy of the content ("Good – it's four thirty; I'm not late then").

Many previous discussions of the IRE sequence have called attention to the nature of the expectations that it transmits to students. Edwards and Westgate, for example, see the IRE sequence as creating in students

> . . . [a] perception of the curriculum as sets of facts to be transmitted under pressure of time, and [as having] similar consequences for the shaping of pupils' answers to questions toward predetermined and non-negotiable semantic destinations.
> . . . Transmitting knowledge involves special rights and responsibilities which are evident throughout the organization of normal classroom talk, in the variety of ways we have specified. Receiving knowledge involves a largely subordinate communicative role in which turns are allocated, answers evaluated, and "official" meanings formulated, at the discretion of the teacher. (1987, p. 175)

We would argue that this perception develops by virtue of students' repeated participation in the participant frameworks created by the IRE sequence. Every such sequence is part of the student's socialization through language, and carries with it ways of viewing and experiencing knowledge and oneself as learner.

Of course, the sequence of moves itself is not inherently unproductive. As Edwards and Westgate point out, there are many times that "such direct instruction is necessary and appropriate and indeed unavoidable" (ibid.). Newman et al. (1989) even suggest that the tripartite structure is particularly well suited for the collaborative construction of ideas with "a built-in repair structure in the teacher's last turn so that incorrect information can be replaced with the right answers" (p. 127). The structure of the sequence allows the teacher to maintain the necessary control over the flow of information and advancement of the academic content. Both the topic of the Initiation move (the teacher's questions) and the content of the Evaluation move allow the teacher to advance the intended topic of discussion or learning. In addition, they allow her to check on the status of knowledge, awareness, and attention of students by calling on individuals and posing particular questions. Wells (1993), invoking activity theory, takes the study of the sequence a step further, observing that very different activities and goals can emerge from the same structural sequence.[14]

We would make the same point about the various revoicing participant frameworks described here. They may simultaneously align students with each other and with particular aspects of the academic task, but there may be many other consequences as well. As with any discourse structure or strategy, the context in which such a move originates, the relative positions of the interlocutors, the immediate purposes of the exchange, and the institutional goals and constraints in which the interaction is embedded will all contribute to participants' construal of the meaning of the move and to its consequences.[15] Nonetheless, an analysis at the level of participant framework suggests strongly that the revoicing and IRE sequences encode a different set of meaning potentials. Through the animation of speaking others, the revoicing participant framework makes possible an expanded and more contrapuntal set of voices and participant roles in constructing an idea than does the IRE. Those possibilities may be used well or poorly, but the differences at a basic level of organization can be described.

Unanswered questions

We have largely emphasized the ways this move allows students to take on roles and positions in relation to a proposition that the teacher foregrounds. We have not focused on the nature of that foregrounded proposition. The question of the propositional content of the revoicing move is just as important as the issues of roles and stances. In the hands of a teacher who is not in control of the material, this discourse strategy will provide little if any help. One can scaffold others in building coherent arguments and positions only if one understands what those positions might be. The quality of the teacher's understanding of the student's contribution also limits the effectiveness of this strategy. If the teacher cannot understand what the student is suggesting in terms of the current task, it will be very difficult to incorporate that contribution effectively, with or without the revoicing strategy. Finally, student learning will no doubt depend on the skill and the willingness with which the teacher incorporates student contributions into the ongoing building of new conceptual understandings. Acknowledgment of student positions can quickly become patronizing without a real attempt to link those positions to the academic content. This often involves more elaborate exploration than a teacher is prepared to do under the pressures of classroom life. So, a full understanding of the impact of this strategy cannot be developed without a concomitant account of the relation of the discourse to the cognitive and pedagogical work at hand.

Thus we cannot make any claims about the power of these moves to facilitate learning generally. When used skillfully, such moves allow the teacher to drive the discussion or investigation in a fashion that coordinates individual students, academic content, and intellectual participant roles. The teachers we have studied with are notable for their reflective, intelligent, and thoughtful use of language and their commitment to providing equal access to all students. We think that the students we have observed have probably benefited from these scaffolded discussions. Yet clearly, much empirical work remains to be done before we can evaluate the cumulative consequences of this level of classroom interaction. This empirical work will have a different character than what we have provided here, the microanalysis of a small number of examples. Longitudinal studies of particular students will be necessary, with close attention to the discourse strategies they bring with them to school, and close attention to the ways their thinking and talking develop over time. It will, of course, be very difficult to control for other influences on that development. Thus we, like others who are looking closely at complex classroom interactions (Brown, Ash, Rutherford, Nakagawa, Gordon, & Campione, 1993), are faced with a difficult challenge when trying to discover "what works."

For these reasons, we see the primary value of this work as methodological, rather than as having direct implications for practice. Unlike a structural analysis of conversational turns within a larger speech event, analysis of participant frameworks foregrounds the multiple and shifting roles available to speakers in constructing, coconstructing, and displaying meaning. It thus illuminates a level of strategic, joint activity and gives us tools to say precisely how the use of particular linguistic constructions serves to structure participant alignments and oppositions, as well as relationships between speakers and ideas. As such, it has particular power in fine-grained descriptions and situated explanations of classroom learning, giving us a way to link teacher and student talk to social organization and the social formation of minds.

Notes

1 There is a great deal of current work attempting both to understand the complexities inherent in successful group discussions and to help teachers adopt and develop the skills needed to orchestrate them (cf. Brown et al., 1992; Goldenberg, in press; Wells, 1993; Hatano & Inagaki, 1991; Lampert, 1990; Leer et al., 1993). Much remains to be said, however.

2 Judy Richards and Lynne Godfrey each have over 15 years of experience teaching in elementary classrooms. Both are highly effective. They are cited by other teachers as being highly competent and knowledgeable. Both are involved in professional activities that involve reflection, writing, and content area learning. Both have developed curriculum pieces that combine current research, their own interests, and the needs of their students. More important, our estimations of their effectiveness are based on hundreds of hours of participant observation (O'Connor in Godfrey's classroom, Michaels in Richards's classroom). We have extensive documentation of their ability to

elicit engagement and participation from all students, their dedication to high expectations and high standards, and their commitment to developing their practice.

3 In what follows, we draw on Goffman's notions of *principal, strategist* (or *author*), *figure*, and *animator* (1974, pp. 517–523) in ways that will become apparent.

4 As we discuss in the final section, we have taken a fairly optimistic stance toward this move based on our observations of the two teachers we have worked with. This does not mean that we are unaware of other uses to which this discourse strategy can be put, uses that accomplish the opposite of what we have seen – for example, termination of a discussion through the appropriation and recasting of a student's contribution.

5 This unit comes from a large set of case books that are part of a Japanese science curriculum known as the *Hypothesis–Experiment–Instruction Method (HEI)*. The terminology and actual problems are taken from the case books. Developed by Japanese science educator and historian of science Kiyonobu Itakura, the method has been used in many Japanese classrooms over the past 15 years. We are not promoting or criticizing it as a method for teaching science; rather, we have used it as a research tool. Judy Richards was experimenting with this method in her classroom because she was interested in promoting group discussion and debate; for us as researchers, the method was a good tool to help us study the influence of discussion and students' home-based discourses on children's learning of science.

6 In these transcripts, we indicate nonfinal intonation with a single slash (indicating "more to come") and use double slashes to indicate an utterance-terminating prosodic signal such as terminal pitch, a noticeable pause, a questioning rise in pitch, or some combination (akin to a period or question mark in writing). **Boldface** across an entire turn, as in the current example, is used to identify a particular move, such as revoicing. On individual words, underlining indicates emphasis or stress through prosodic prominence (either amplitude or pitch) on the syllable so marked. Length is marked with a colon following the elongated syllable.

7 In this and all of the transcripts to follow, the children (but not the teachers) are given pseudonyms.

8 Many people have pointed out to us that different teachers might use this strategy for quite different reasons than those we discuss here. We discuss this in the final section of the chapter.

9 Goffman provides extremely complicated examples of such bifurcations (see especially 1974). Here we intend to make the point that such bifurcations can be used purposefully to scaffold novice participation in intellectual discussion. Of course, the splitting of these participant roles among different individuals may serve a huge range of purposes, most far from those discussed here. One analysis of some of these purposes is presented in Schiffrin (1993).

10 In discussions of the IRE sequence several researchers – including Cazden (1988), Lemke (1990), and Goldenberg (personal communication) – have noted that the final move in an IRE sequence provides the teacher with the opportunity for what Lemke calls *retroactive contextualizing*. Cazden calls it *recontextualization*. In this move, the teacher can take a student contribution and recast it within a wider frame or can slightly alter it to accent a different aspect of the lesson topic than the one intended by the student. In our examples the same thing is clearly going on, but there is an additional consequence for the student, not noted by researchers who have focused on IRE sequences. This is the "credit granting" to the principal/originator of the utterance, the student.

11 Goffman's use of the term *laminator verb* is part of a metaphor in which he depicts the speaker (or other participants) as taking a particular "footing" with respect to an utterance. The point of origin is the speaker in a "literal" relation to an utterance – rare in Goffman's discussions. He speaks of layers, or *lamina*, that remove the speaker

incrementally from a literal footing, layers implicating social meanings that are often signaled by linguistic means. For example, "To the best of my recollection, I think that I said I once lived that sort of life" contains at least four layers of removal from a bald assertion, each layer added on through a laminator predicate. See Goffman (1981, pp. 147–153) for further discussion.

12 In fact, Goffman's notion of *footing* is relevant throughout this discussion (Goffman, 1974).

13 This quote is taken from a videotaped session in a Japanese fourth-grade class led by Ms. Kobayashi. We (along with Chikako Toma and Jim Wertsch) gratefully appreciate the chance to see and work with the video. And we are grateful to Giyoo Hatano, who introduced us to the videotape and whose ideas have influenced our thinking about it.

14 In Wells's (1993) examples of IRF sequences undergirding different goal-oriented actions, it might well be the case that the same structural sequence is actually creating different participation frameworks. For example, if the teacher asks a question that is obviously not a known-answer question or does not anticipate one right answer, a different participation framework would be instantiated from that of the prototypical IRE, and the third move would then not have the typical evaluative meaning potential.

15 Several people have asked us whether our revoicing move is not just a variant of the psychotherapeutic "active listening" or a strategy promoted within what is known as the *Parent Effectiveness Training* (PET) program. There are superficial similarities in the structure of the utterances in question. However, the contribution of such an utterance to the ongoing activity will depend on a wide range of contextual factors, as discussed earlier and in the final section of this chapter. We are interested in the ways that the particular properties of this sort of utterance articulate with larger purposes and structures within a particular activity and setting, precisely described. Thus our focus (and our views of this type of utterance) are quite different from those implied by the PET injunction to repeat what the child says.

References

Au, K. (1980). Participation structures in a reading lesson with Hawaiian children: Analysis of a culturally appropriate instructional event. *Anthropology and Education Quarterly, 11,* 91–115.

Bakhtin, M. M. (1981). *The dialogic imagination: Four essays by M. M. Bakhtin* (M. Holquist, Ed.). Austin: University of Texas Press.

Bakhtin, M. M. (1986). *Speech genres and other late essays* (C. Emerson & M. Holquist, Eds.). Austin: University of Texas Press.

Banfield, A. (1982). *Unspeakable sentences.* Boston: Routledge & Kegan Paul.

Bloome, D., & Horowitz, R. (1991). *The writing and rewriting of Yisker Bikher: Continuity and change in the genre of Eastern European Jewish writing.* Paper presented at the annual meeting of the American Anthropological Association, Annual Meeting, November. 1991.

Brown, A., Ash, D., Rutherford, M., Nakagawa, K., Gordon, A., & Campione, J. (1993). Distributed expertise in the classroom. In G. Salomon (Ed.), *Distributed cognitions.* New York: Cambridge University Press.

Cazden, C. (1986). Classroom discourse. In M. E. Wittrock (Ed.), *Handbook of research on teaching* (3rd ed.). New York: Macmillan.

Cazden, C. (1988). *Classroom discourse.* Portsmouth, NH: Heinemann.

Clark, H. H., & Schaefer, E. F. (1985). Contributing to discourse. *Cognitive Science, 13,* 259–294.

Collins, A., Brown, J. S., & Newman, S. E. (1989). Cognitive apprenticeship: Teaching the crafts of reading, writing, and mathematics. In L. B. Resnick (Ed.), *Knowing, learning and instruction: Essays in honor of Robert Glaser.* Hillsdale, NJ: Erlbaum.

Cook-Gumperz, J. (Ed.). (1986). *The social construction of literacy.* Cambridge: Cambridge University Press.

Edwards, A. D., & Westgate, D. P. G. (1987). *Investigating classroom talk.* London: Falmer Press.

Erickson, F. (1982). Classroom discourse as improvisation. In L. C. Wilkinson (Ed.), *Communication in the classroom.* New York: Academic Press.

Gee, J. P. (1990). *What is literacy?* Technical report. Newton, MA: Literacies Institute.

Goffman, E. (1974). *Frame analysis.* Cambridge, MA: Harvard University Press.

Goffman, E. (1981). *Forms of talk.* Philadelphia: University of Pennsylvania Press.

Goldenberg, C. (In press). Instructional conversations. In A. Purves (Ed.), *Encyclopedia of English studies language arts.* National Council of Teachers of English/Scholastic.

Goldenberg, C., & Gallimore, R. (1991). Changing teaching takes more than a one-shot workshop. *Educational Leadership, 49,* 69–72.

Goodwin, M. H. (1990). *He-said–She-said: Talk as social organization among black children.* Bloomington: Indiana University Press.

Gray, L. (1993). *Large group discussion in a 3rd/4th grade classroom: A sociolinguistic case study.* Unpublished doctoral dissertation, Program in Applied Linguistics, Boston University.

Gumperz, J. J. (1981). Conversational inference and classroom learning. In J. Green & C. Wallat (Eds.), *Ethnography and language in educational settings.* Norwood, NJ: Ablex.

Gumperz, J. J. (1982). *Discourse strategies.* Cambridge: Cambridge University Press.

Gumperz, J. J. (1984). The retrieval of sociocultural knowledge in conversation. Reprinted in J. Baugh and J. Sherzer (Eds.), *Language in use: Readings in sociolinguistics.* Englewood Cliffs, NJ: Prentice-Hall. (Originally published in *Poetics Today, 1,* 1979, 273–286.)

Gumperz, J. J. (1990). Speech community in interactional perspective. In H. Parret (Ed.), *La communauté en parole: Communication, consensus, ruptures.* Brussels: Mardarga Publishing House.

Halliday, M. A. K. (1988). On the language of physical science. In M. Ghadessy (Ed.), *Registers of written English: Situational factors and linguistic features.* London: Pinter.

Hatano, G., & Inagaki, K. (1991). Sharing cognition through collective comprehension activity. In L. Resnick, J. Levine, & S. Teasley (Eds.), *Perspectives on socially shared cognition.* Washington, DC: APA Press.

Heath, S. B. (1983). *Ways with words.* Cambridge: Cambridge University Press.

Lampert, M. (1990). When the problem is not the question and the solution is not the answer: Mathematical knowing and teaching. *American Educational Research Journal, 27,* 29–64.

Lave, J., & Wenger, E. (1991). *Situated learning: Legitimate peripheral participation.* New York: Cambridge University Press.

Leer, M., Bill, V., & Resnick, L. (1993). *Mathematical power and responsibility for reasoning: Forms of discourse in elementary mathematics.* Paper presented at the annual meeting of the American Educational Research Association, Atlanta.

Lemke, J. L. (1990). *Talking science: Language, learning, and values.* Norwood, NJ: Ablex.

Martin, J. R. (1989). Technicality and abstraction: Language for the creation of specialized knowledge. In F. Christie (Ed.), *Writing in schools.* Geelong, Victoria, Australia: Deakin University Press.

Mehan, H. (1979). *Learning lessons*. Cambridge, MA: Harvard University Press.

Michaels, S. (1981). "Sharing time": Children's narrative styles and differential access to literacy. *Language in Society, 10*, 423–442.

Michaels, S., O'Connor, M. C., & Richards, J. (1993). Literacy as reasoning within multiple discourses: Implications for restructuring learning. In *Restructuring learning*. 1990 Summer Institute Papers and Recommendations. Washington, DC: Council of Chief State School Officers.

Miller, P. J., Nemoianu, A., & DeJong, J. (1986). Early reading at home: Its practice and meanings in a working-class community. In B. B. Schieffelin & P. Gilmore (Eds.), *The acquisition of literacy: Ethnographic perspectives: Vol. XXI. Advances in discourse processes*. Norwood, NJ: Ablex.

National Council of Teachers of Mathematics (1989). *Curriculum and evaluation standards for school mathematics*. Reston, VA: NCTM.

Newman, D., Griffin, P., & Cole, M. (1989). *The construction zone: Working for cognitive change in school*. Cambridge: Cambridge University Press.

Ochs, E. (1986). Introduction. In B. Schieffelin & E. Ochs (Eds.), *Language socialization across cultures*. Cambridge: Cambridge University Press.

Ochs, E., Taylor, C., Rudolph, D., & Smith, R. (1991). Storytelling as a theory-building activity. *Discourse Processes, 15*, 37–72.

O'Connor, M. C. (1993). *Negotiated defining*. Manuscript, Boston University.

O'Connor, M. C. and Michaels, S. (1993). Aligning academic task and participation status through revoicing: analysis of a classroom discourse strategy. *Anthropology and Education Quarterly, 24*, 318–335.

Philips, S. (1983). *The invisible culture: Communication in classroom and community on the Warm Springs Indian reservation*. New York: Longman.

Resnick, L., Levine, J., & Teasley, S. (Eds.). (1991). *Perspectives on socially shared cognition*. Washington, DC: APA Press.

Rogoff, B., & Lave, J. (Eds.). (1984). *Everyday cognition: Its development in social context*. Cambridge, MA: Harvard University Press.

Saxe, G. (1988). The mathematics of child street vendors. *Child Development, 59*, 1415–1425.

Schieffelin, B. B. (1984). Adε: A sociolinguistic analysis of a relationship. In J. Baugh & J. Sherzer (Eds.), *Language in use: Readings in sociolinguistics*. Englewood Cliffs, NJ: Prentice-Hall.

Schieffelin, B. B., & Gilmore, P. (Eds.). (1986). *The acquisition of literacy: Ethnographic perspectives: Vol. XXI. Advances in discourse processes*. Norwood, NJ: Ablex.

Schieffelin, B. B., & Ochs, E. (Eds.). (1986). *Language socialization across cultures*. Cambridge: Cambridge University Press.

Schiffrin, D. (1987). *Discourse makers*. Cambridge: Cambridge University Press.

Schiffrin, D. (1993). "Speaking for another" in sociolinguistic interviews: Alignments, identities and frames. In D. Tannen (Ed.), *Framing in discourse*. New York: Oxford University Press.

Scribner, S., & Cole, M. (1981). *The psychology of literacy*. Cambridge, MA: Harvard University Press.

Sinclair, J., & Coulthard, R. (1975). *Towards an analysis of discourse: The English used by teachers and pupils*. London: Oxford University Press.

Street, B. V. (1984). *Literacy in theory and practice*. Cambridge Studies in Oral and Literate Culture. Cambridge: Cambridge University Press.

Toma, C. (1991a). *Speech genre and social language of school in the United States and Japan*. Paper presented at the annual meeting of the American Educational Research Association, Chicago.

Toma, C. (1991b). *Explicit use of others' voices for constructing arguments in Japanese classroom discourse: An analysis of the use of reported speech.* Papers presented at a Boston University Conference on Language Development, Boston.

Toma, C., & Wertsch, J. V. (1990). Sociocultural approach to mediated action: An analysis of classroom discourse. *Annual Report of Research and Clinical Center for Child Development,* No. 13, pp. 69–81.

Vološinov, V. N. (1971). Reported speech. In L. Matejka & K. Pomorska (Eds.), *Readings in Russian poetics: Formalist and structuralist views.* Cambridge, MA: MIT Press.

Vygotsky, L. S. (1978). *Mind in society: The development of higher psychological processes* (M. Cole, V. John-Steiner, S. Scribner, & E. Souberman, Eds.). Cambridge, MA: Harvard University Press.

Wells, G. (1986). *The meaning makers: Children learning language and using language to learn.* Portsmouth, NH: Heinemann.

Wells, G. (1993). Reevaluating the IRF sequence: A proposal for the articulation of theories of activity and discourse for the analysis of teaching and learning in the classroom. *Linguistics and Education, 5,* 1–37.

Wertsch, J. V. (1985). *Vygotsky and the social formation of mind.* Cambridge, MA: Harvard University Press.

Wertsch, J. V. (1991). *Voices of the mind: A sociocultural approach.* Cambridge, MA: Harvard University Press.

Wertsch, J. V., & Toma, C. (In press). Discourse and learning in the classroom: A sociocultural approach. In L. Steffe (Ed.), *Social constructionism in education.* New York: Sage.

4   Contextual inquiries: a discourse-oriented study of classroom learning

Deborah Hicks

> The interpretation of meanings cannot be scientific, but it is profoundly cognitive.
>
> M. M. Bakhtin[1]

As Courtney Cazden has stressed in her contribution to this volume, the work of L. S. Vygotsky has profoundly influenced educators' study of classroom learning and teaching, particularly in the area of classroom language use. Cazden points out that different educators, particularly writing researchers, have interpreted Vygotsky's work differently, often drawing quite different conclusions from the "same" pages in the collections of writings entitled *Mind in Society* (1978) and *Thought and Language* (1986) [or *Thinking and Speech* (1987)]. However, regardless of these differences of interpretation, the sociocultural psychology envisioned by Vygotsky has led to new ways of looking at teaching and learning. The sociocultural contexts in which teaching and learning occur are now widely considered critical to learning itself; indeed, learning is viewed as culture and context specific (Moll & Dworin, this volume; Scribner & Cole, 1981). Educational researchers working across a wide range of subdisciplinary areas have begun to take quite seriously an underlying premise in Vygotsky's work: that children's cognitive *work* takes place in a social dimension before this same activity occurs internally. The Piagetian metaphor of the lone child interacting with an objective, logical world, struggling to overcome her initial egocentrism and irrational thought, has given way to an image of a socially responsive

The classroom-based research described in this chapter was conducted during my tenure as a Spencer Fellow under the auspices of the National Academy of Education. I gratefully acknowledge the role of the Academy in making this project possible. I would also like to acknowledge the significant contributions made by Rhoda Kanevsky to the interpretive analyses of the classroom work of Janeen and Mike. Finally, I am grateful to Jim Gee for his many extremely helpful comments on this work at it has emerged.

104

child participating in recurrent joint activity mediated by the uniquely human means of communication: language.

In spite of the profound influence of Vygotsky's work on educational research, I would argue that there are still more profound changes to come. O'Connor and Michaels (this volume) point to this kind of change as they discuss a shift in the overlapping fields of education and psychology (which, in Vygotsky's world, were not necessarily separate domains of study) in terms of how knowledge and learning are being explored. In the work of some sociocognitive theorists like Gee (1990, 1992) and Wertsch (1991), learning is viewed not in terms of the child's construction of mental representations of an objective reality (harking from a cognitive science machine metaphor of cognition) but in terms of the child's appropriation of social discourses. Through the child's participation in culture-specific social events, the child learns how to *be* a student, family member, or church attender. These culture-specific ways of *being* entail the use of socially appropriate discourse genres and, indeed, socially appropriate ways of acting, valuing – and thinking.

The role that discourse, or language used as a social means of communication, plays in this process of learning is crucial. Vygotsky emphasized throughout his work the seminal place of language in the child's learning. Educators working in classroom settings are also acutely aware of how language mediates children's learning in school. Whether the instructional setting is a whole-class discussion, a collaborative journal-writing activity, or an individual school task, sociocognitive theorists and many educators would argue that discourse is a central means through which new understandings are negotiated among participants. It is, in fact, this crucial mediational role of *discourse* in children's learning that is the focal point of the revolutionary changes occurring among educational and developmental theorists.

In this chapter, I begin with a discussion of how the work of L. S. Vygotsky and other theorists, most notably M. M. Bakhtin, has begun to alter the ways in which learning is viewed. I will move from a discussion of two important theoretical constructs, *internalization* (Vygotsky) and *appropriation* (Bakhtin), to a discussion of what one contemporary theorist has termed "thinking as a boundary phenomenon" (Shotter, 1993). In this early section, I set the stage for a discourse-oriented study of children's learning, which will theoretically ground my own work. Then I move to the central goal of this chapter, that of articulating a methodology for such an approach to studying children's learning. This goal stems from my observations that, in spite of the impact of work by Vygotsky and Bakhtin on educational theory, the methodologies appropriate for the contextual study of classroom discourses are still emergent. Thus, I articulate some research questions that might constitute such *contextual inquiries,* and I then explore these questions with respect to the classroom learning of two first graders. I suggest that multilayered forms of interpretive analysis, involving studies of completed texts (both oral and written) as well as emergent discourse and social activity, lend themselves to the theoretical goals of a sociocognitive, discourse-oriented study of learning. I end with a discussion of some societal and ethical issues that are raised by such a study of classroom learning. The study of the classroom discourses of two first graders, Janeen and Mike, calls to mind such critical educational issues as the classroom experiences of children from urban, non-middle-class communities.

Thinking as a boundary phenomenon

One of the central tenets of the theoretical framework developed by Vygotsky is that the means of thinking available to the child are the symbolic resources of her culture. As the child participates in activity structured for her by more mature others, gradually assuming more and more control over her own activity (Wertsch, 1984), she also begins to internalize cultural symbolic systems. According to Vygotsky, language is the most resourceful of the various symbolic tools available within a culture. The gradual movement inward of social speech, or what might also be termed *discourse,* is the means through which the child develops what Vygotsky terms *higher mental processes.* These higher forms of thinking are under the conscious control of the child; she can plan and direct her own actions and those of others around her. This notion is sometimes lost in readings of Vygotsky, since a cursory reading of his work might suggest something more passive: a movement inward of symbolic forms first experienced on a social plane. The now famous dictum from *Mind in Society* – that development occurs on two planes, first the social, then the individual – might suggest such a reading. However, Wertsch and Stone (1985) have expressed a different view of Vygotsky's theory of internalization. Rather than being a rote copying of social symbolic forms, most notably language, internalization implies an active, agentive process of transformation. At the same time that the child assimilates the social speech forms of her culture, she also assumes greater control over them. Thus, her internalization of language (speech, discourse) entails a process whereby she submits to her own purposes the forms of language that mediate social activity in her culture.

The transformative dimension of the child's internalization of social speech forms is even more salient in the work of M. M. Bakhtin, whose writings on the dialogic nature of human communication and cognition have only recently begun to have a wide impact on educational theorists. In comparison to Vygotsky, Bakhtin (1981, 1986) stressed that at the core of human thinking lies *dialogic* speech, speech between oneself and the other. The omnipresent *other,* for Bakhtin, can be an interlocutor with whom one is engaged in active dialogue or a more distal other, a silent audience that exists as a "horizon" when writing or thinking. Thus, even individual thought for Bakhtin entails social activity, since the only means for thought are social speech forms imbued with the utterances of previous speakers. As Bakhtin (1981) writes in *Discourse in the Novel,* "as a living, socio-ideological thing, language for the individual consciousness lies on the borderline between oneself and the other" (p. 293). Whereas in Vygotsky's writing *internalization* emerges as a central theoretical construct, a process by which developmental change occurs, in Bakhtin's work *appropriation* emerges as a similarly important construct. However, appropriation for Bakhtin entails something more along the lines of a conversation, entailing active response. As the individual speaker-thinker engages in activity that involves the discourses of her culture, she also forms a dialogic response to those discourses. Individual thinking, therefore, exists on this rather fluid boundary between the self and the other, between social discourses and one's active response to them. Appropriation engenders a dialogic form of consciousness as the individual speaker develops a response to the utterances in her surround. Moreover, the individual's response to the discourses of others, in turn, reconstructs the social contexts that she inhabits. Thinking, and hence learning, is a creative dynamic; the individual constructs new forms of response at the same time that she appropriates the discourses of her social world.

This emergent quality of the child's interaction in a social world has, I believe, been lost in much of the interpretive research and writing conducted within a social constructivist framework (but see Erickson, this volume, for research on the emergent dimensions of classroom social interaction and learning, and for a discussion of the implications of this kind of research for sociocognitive theory). In many readings of Vygotsky, in particular, the process of learning has been depicted metaphorically as a gradual and steady process of movement inward. The individual learner is depicted as one who *receives* the social symbolic forms of her culture (like language) and then internalizes them verbatim. The now quite familiar construct from Vygotsky's work, the zone of proximal development, is thus similarly depicted as the child performing on her own cognitive tasks that she could once perform only with the help of others. Ironically, this interpretive reading of Vygotsky, and to some extent even of Bakhtin, reinforces the demarcation of "inside" and "out there" that other scholars would argue is not true to the intent of these theorists (see Emerson, 1983, 1993). Rather, as Toulmin (1979) points out in his essay on the "inwardness of mental life," what is inside the individual at any given moment is always a reconstruction of the social activity of her community. The individual thinker is thus fully capable of making choices about what kinds of things go inside and how she will alter what is outside by her dialogic response.

This emergent and somewhat nondeterministic aspect of discursive activity, and hence learning, is for Shotter (1993) and other contemporary theorists (e.g., Billig, 1987) an important dimension of a shift in theory and research occurring within the fields of education and psychology. For example, Erickson, in his contribution to this volume, explores how social activity in classrooms is both reciprocal and complementary. As children and teachers engage in joint activity, they simultaneously construct the social contexts in which they participate. Shotter (1993) (drawing on Vico, 1968) points out that this creative process of joint meaning construction *makes sense* within a particular "providential space":

> It is the socio-cultural, socio-historical nature of this *intralinguistically created* textual context, as it is temporally (and spatially) developed by what is said, that everyone must take into account (when it is their turn to speak, or act) – if, that is, their actions are to be judged as appropriate to it. It is this, the realization that as one speaks, a temporal-spatial network of intralinguistic references is developed into which one's future speech *must* be directed, that I think is the key to the further understanding of the ethical nature of our mental processes. For this network is a "providential space" of joint action with two major properties: first, it carries within it the traces of one's socio-cultural history, and one *ought* to act within it in such a way as to sustain the resources it contains; but second, in *responding* to the "invitations," etc., available to one from one's place or position within it, one acts in one's own unique, creative, novel way. However, if one respects its providential nature, then one's creativity is always intelligible, creativity, because it takes place within the *forms* of the "providential space" in question. (p. 118)

Thus, we have moved from the metaphor of the child as an "appropriater" of an objective, logical world (Piaget) or a symbolic, social world (Vygotsky) to that of the child as actor within emergent and nondeterministic discourse contexts. As the child moves within the social world of the classroom, she appropriates (internalizes) but also reconstructs the discourses that constitute the social world of her classroom. This creative process is what I would term learning. Within this theory of learning, thinking exists as a "boundary phenomenon" (Emerson, 1983; Shotter, 1993) rather than as a property of either the individual child or her culture.

Contextual inquiries of children's discursive activity

I mentioned earlier that the central goal of this chapter is to develop research methodologies that mesh with the theoretical tenets of a discourse-oriented approach to studying children's classroom learning. I termed the approach that I will take *contextual inquiries,* since I mentioned that this approach would entail the use of multilayered interpretive, hence contextual, investigations. Having described the theoretical framework that undergirds my own classroom-based research, I now move to this more methodological discussion. The issue of research methodology is an important one that is often overlooked in educational studies that draw on a social constructivist framework. However, as Ochs (1979) and Mishler (1991) point out, even transcriptions of one's data are theoretical representations. What one chooses to study, how one studies it, and how one decides to represent "reality" in the form of transcriptions, fieldnotes, and interpretive narratives are all methodological issues that draw directly from theory (Geertz, 1973; Rosaldo, 1989). If one's theory of learning is a discourse-oriented one, as described earlier, then research methodologies must reflect this theory. What I want to argue for in this chapter is a methodology that combines the study of children's emergent participation in social and discursive activities with the study of their completed texts, both oral and written. Each of these forms of contextual inquiry (i.e., inquiry grounded in particular social and discursive contexts) can be informative about children's learning. Rather than pursuing further this issue as a rhetorical argument, let me instead provide two examples that will hopefully illustrate my points. Both examples are drawn from my documentation of the classroom discourse of Mike, one of the two first graders whom I have studied.

Example 1: symbolic play[2]
Mike (M), Derek (D), Rasheem (R)

Mike, Derek, and Rasheem are working at the site of a wood blocks construction set atop a desk. Mike and Rasheem both hold plastic vehicles that they have constructed from "Batman parts" (similar to Legos parts). Derek has brought to this activity setting three small plastic dinosaurs. Early in the symbolic play, Mike moves his Batman-parts vehicles inside the wood blocks construction and assumes the "voice" first of a narrator, then of the vehicle (or possibly driver of the vehicle?).

M: and don't touch 'im (.) he'll blow you to pieces you du-
R: -come on
M: I'll blow you to pieces if you touch me

In the earlier moments of the three boys' symbolic play, they negotiate the roles of characters involved in the play.

M: no no # this is the king of dinosaurs
D: UH UH
R: neither one of 'em is the king of dinosaurs (.) is they?
D: NYUH (.) HE the KING of DINOSAURS CAUSE HE the LITTLEST

Later on in the episode, Mike once again moves his vehicle inside the wood blocks construction, assuming the voice of the vehicle (or its driver):

M: I pushed a certain button so I can get in
      cause these robots
      the jewels are doing okay
      let me out (.) you stupid reptiles

Example 2: journal writing

Written: One day a
Teena Mot ninja
Trds But up
BeBpeiand ricsad
Be cos shdr
sn thm to But up
Trds

Gloss: One day Teenage Mutant Ninja Turtles beat up Beebop and Rocksteady because Shredder sent them to beat up Turtles.

   Though both of these examples are narrative discourses that are portrayed here as finished texts, they can also be explored analytically as emergent responses by Mike to the textual contexts of his first-grade classroom and beyond. In Example 1, Mike was a participant in a boisterous episode of symbolic play. Because this episode was videotaped, and because I was also an on-the-spot observer of the play, I was able to produce a very detailed interpretive analysis of it. Repeated analyses of the videotape resulting in transcriptions of one segment of social activity, supplemented by my interpretive fieldnotes and narrative descriptions of this social-interactional moment in the classroom, enabled me to explore the moment-to-moment social construction of meaning between Mike and his peers. Such research methodology has been termed *microethnographic* and is concerned with providing theory-driven descriptions of social meanings constructed in face-to-face interaction (Erickson, 1992).

My transcription of this episode in Example 1 is a central part of my theoretical representation of it (Mishler, 1991; Ochs, 1979). This transcription suggests that the narrative *product* resulting from this episode was constructed in a highly interactive manner, with all three boys making moment-to-moment decisions about the emergence of the story. In part, these decisions were also the result of a friendly bit of power play between the three. What the transcription does not capture (but what my written fieldnotes and videotape do) is the gesture and movement that transpired simultaneously with the boys' verbal narration of events. In the middle section of this episode, for example, Mike and his peers engaged in a brief dispute about the assignment of character roles to the plastic replicas. This verbal dispute was accompanied by facial expressions and gentle nudgings suggesting a power play. Each interactional "moment" in the play was an indeterminate social and discursive space, in which the participants made rapid, coordinated decisions about what form of discourse would occur next. In the latter section of this example, for example, Mike was able to build on both his previous utterances of warning (*I'll blow you to pieces if you touch me*) and the subsequent collaborative decision that the "reptiles" (the dinosaurs) were the guardians of jewels inside the construction [*let me out (.) you stupid reptiles*]. In the midst of this highly interactive episode, Mike's individualistic "slant" on experience emerges from within. For example, his assumption of the voice of one of the characters in the play, both initially and then in the latter section of the example, is an individualistic response to the social interaction of which he is part. And yet, his response also *makes sense* in the context of the interaction. His final "voicing," for example, pushes the narrative forward but also makes reference to the earlier decisions negotiated collaboratively.

The second example that I have included also illustrates a dialectical tension between Mike's interpretive slant on experience and the textual context in which the narrative occurs. However, in Example 2, I portray this tension as one between a prominent cultural text and Mike's unique means of responding to that text. One thing that recent studies in anthropology have highlighted is that cultures are not static entities (Ortner, 1984; Rosaldo, 1989; see also the similar discussion in the introduction to this volume). Participants in "a culture" actually move between various cultures; or, as Gee (1990) might suggest, they engage in various social discourses, at times simultaneously. Like all the children in this first-grade classroom, Mike moved within and between cultures throughout the course of his work and play. In the classroom, Mike was nudged towards the activity of narrative writing by the social participant structure of journal writing. This was one form of textual context that Mike practiced.

Another was his participation in the culture of the Teenage Mutant Ninja Turtles through a variety of social practices. Mike watched the Turtle cartoon series on a daily basis during his first year in school. He also frequently visited a local video arcade, where he played Turtle games with family members and friends. Like most of his peers (if not all), he had been to see the enormously popular film version of the Turtle story. Clearly, the Turtle narrative was a prominent cultural context that he inhabited. Mike was hardly alone in his fascination with the Turtles. Although I did not observe firsthand the episode of social activity that gave rise to the text in Example 2, I observed many similar episodes. Often, groups of children at Mike's desk area wrote Turtle stories. As in Example 1, narrative scenarios were often collaboratively constructed as children drew pictures, engaged in narrative talk, and wrote. However, Mike's response to the textual context of the Turtle story, as well as the social activity of journal writing, represented a reconstruction of social forms of meaning. His written representation of one of the incessant battles between the Turtles and their nemesis, Shredder, was not predetermined by the textual context of journal writing, though it was framed by his movement within this discursive context.

In short, what I am suggesting as a methodology for examining the emergent qualities of social meaning construction, and also the boundary between individual and social meanings, are multiple layers of interpretive analysis. If the theoretical goal is one of articulating the dialectic between what is "inside" the child and what is "out there" in culture, then neither analyses of textual products nor inferential studies of cognitive processes alone are sufficient. Rather, "thick descriptions" (Geertz, 1973) of overlapping textual contexts – including prevailing texts, cultural themes and metaphors, and social activity structures – could be merged with detailed interpretive studies of the individual child's unique means of (re)constructing meaning within these contexts. Such an approach would view learning as a creative, transformative act, though not randomly so.

Let me summarize this discussion by suggesting some focusing questions that might guide the study of children's classroom discursive activity. These questions move from the generalities of the sociocognitive history of particular activity settings (such as journal writing or symbolic play) to the particulars of how the individual child constructs meaning from within those contexts.

1. What are the *shared contexts of meaning* that constitute social activity in a given classroom settings? (That is, what is the shared socio-cognitive history of particular activity settings?)
2. How is the construction of meaning *enacted* within particular activity structures in the classroom? (That is, what is the moment-to-moment course of discursive activity?)
3. What does the *individual child* contribute to this flow of activity? How do her discourses reconstruct the contexts from which they derive?
4. Finally, how does the individual child's reconstruction of social meaning *change* over time? (That is, what developmental changes occur in the way she goes about creating new forms of meaning from within textual contexts?)

Note that the last question is concerned with developmental psychology. However, that question is placed within the interpretive frame of the previous questions, which address the dialogic relationship between social contexts and individual children's discursive activity within those contexts. Such a methodology, I propose, is one that melds with the theoretical goals of a sociocognitive psychology. And, as I hope my more elaborate case studies of Janeen and Mike will illustrate, this methodology is also one that supports certain societal-ethical goals that I believe should be connected with educational research.

Action and conflict in narrative form

I have thus far established that the methodological goal of studies of children's classroom discursive activity should be contextual inquiries of texts and social activity structures, grounded in the question of how children reconstruct social meanings. This type of inquiry conceives learning as an agentive and transformative act, framed by the contexts that give rise to new forms of discourse. I have illustrated forms of contextual inquiry through reference to two examples of the classroom discourse of one first grader, Mike. I would now like to pursue further such contextual inquiries of Mike's discursive activity, with particular focus on how these inquiries can be informative about Mike's *learning* in the classroom. I will move through the four questions just presented, though not necessarily in sequential order, developing interpretive analyses of Mike's discourse in the context of journal writing. Through these analyses, I hope to show how his narrative transformation of the themes of action and conflict, particularly with respect to superhero figures, constitutes an essential piece of the developmental change in his journal writing from January to April.

Journal writing in Mike's classroom was unique in its sociocognitive history, and it is crucial for an understanding of Mike's learning within that setting to consider briefly this history. Mike's (and Janeen's) classroom teacher was an extremely experienced educator who placed high value on children's expression of individualistic themes in their journals. Children wrote every morning in their drawing/writing journals from the beginning of the school year on. Children who earlier in the school year could not yet write independently were encouraged to draw and dictate their stories and ideas. Children were also encouraged to use invented (phonetic) spellings as their understanding of the conventions of print (e.g., sound–letter relationships) developed throughout the year. It was expected that children would write something during the journal writing session, and journal writing was often framed as "writing stories." Typical story beginnings were written in large lettering and posted (*One day* . . .), and in individual conferences children were asked questions like "What's your story about?" During journal writing, children worked at desks that were grouped in short rows facing each other. They chatted freely with their peers, and often journal entries were written on shared topics. For the classroom teacher, whom the children referred to as "Teacher Rhoda," this was a central means through which literacy instruction occurred. An extremely important goal of instruction in first grade generally is to facilitate children's reading and writing development. Journal writing in this first-grade classroom was a context in which children could articulate their emerging interests in narrative form at the same time that they mastered the conventions of written language.

Within this activity framework, Mike, like all his peers in this classroom, participated in recurrent episodes in which narrative themes were explored and articulated through drawing and writing. Earlier in the school year, Mike relied heavily on drawing and dictation as a means of response to this activity framework. By midyear, he was using invented spelling as a means of writing, typically writing short narrative statements linked to his drawings. From the beginning of the school year, Mike drew heavily on superhero themes, often placing superhero figures (e.g., Batman, Superman, Teenage Mutant Ninja Turtles) in narrative frames that involved action and conflict (Hicks & Kanevsky, 1992). The entry from January in Example 3 is illustrative of Mike's response to the demands of journal writing.

Example 3: journal writing

> *Written:* ABt a rodot therodot
> Pnh BtmnandJrkr
>
> *Gloss:* About a robot. The robot punched Batman and Joker.

This particular journal entry can be interpreted as a skeletal form of narrative. A robot figure is introduced, and this main character engages in conflictual action with two other characters, both of whom are super-hero figures. Viewed from within the contextual frame of the socio-cognitive history of journal writing (question 1), this early written text exemplifies Mike's construction of meaning from within that context (question 3). It is a unique response to the mandate of "writing a story," one that undoubtedly draws on Mike's movement in other contexts involving media or cartoon superhero characters. This response is man-dated neither by the context of journal writing nor by Mike's individualis-tic interest in superhero figures. Rather, it is representative of a dialogic process of meaning construction, one in which Mike actively trans-formed the symbolic resources available to him from within the context.

The interpretive analysis of Mike's journal entry from January of the school year is one form of contextual inquiry. Another, equally informa-tive means of inquiry is that of exploring Mike's moment-to-moment enactment of meaning within this activity structure. As the transcription in Example 1 and my accompanying interpretations of it suggested, the microethnographic analysis of particular interactional "moments" of meaning construction can provide contextual detail that cannot be gar-nered from analyses of completed texts. Microethnographic analyses can reveal the interactional processes through which the child's discourse is constructed in moment-to-moment interaction, whether the child is en-gaged in highly collaborative activity or work in an "individual" private space. Such crucial developmental constructs as the zone of proximal development can be viewed as these "zones" are constructed in contex-tual settings (Erickson, this volume). Moving from the first type of contextual inquiry framed earlier, that of the sociocognitive history of a given activity setting, or speech event (Gumperz, 1982), the focusing question then becomes centered on the process of meaning construction.

Example 4, for instance, is extremely revealing of the social-interactional processes through which Mike (re)constructed social mean-ings in the context of journal writing. Recall that a prominent cultural text that Mike drew on for journal writing was that of media-generated superheros such as Batman and the Ninja Turtles. In the transcription shown here, derived from an episode of journal writing that took place in

February, Mike is engaged in journal writing on such superhero themes. He works with his closest friend, Derek, the two boys sprawled on the rug area as their journal drawing and talk emerge. Through their highly interactive activity, Mike and Derek construct parallel narrative discourses. These discourses are action-oriented renditions of the exploits of numerous superhero figures, including Batman, Superman, Spiderman, and some invented figures that Mike refers to as Buster-Dudes.

Example 4: journal writing
Mike (M), Derek (D)

D: I makin all the good guys up
M: I makin all the good guys beat uh # you know uh #
    these good guys gonna beat up X-Man
D: Iˆ makin # do you know who Iˆ makin?
M: who?
D: Superman next
    duh duh duh   M: I makin all (.)
    I makin the uhm # you know these dudes called Bust-dudes?
D: yes
M: he be bustin uhm (.) Batman and everybody up
D: you know what? =
M: = he could bust everybody up
D: there Superman an' Batman   M: (unclear) like this
M: lots of Buster-dudes (.) see?
    the other me::n
    boom boom
    he bus(t)es everything
    M lifts his torso up
D: look # look # at Batman   M: and here go one too
D: and here come Iceˆ man
    du::m du::m du::m   M: here go the biggest Bus(t)er-dudes # see?
    here go the biggest Bus(t)er-dudes # see?
D: doo::ee
M: here the biggest Bus(t)er-dudes (.) see?
D: know who-
M: here go the biggest Bus(t)er-dude
    and he be like (.) ooooh
    pchew pchew
D: Iceman
    you know what?
    Super # and then Spiderman come out   M: AAAAAH!
M: look # then (.) there go Batman
    he gonna get blown to pieces (.) see?
    here go Batman
    he n' get blown to pieces
    aaaaaah =
D: = look
    and here come Spiderman
M: Spiderman # Spiderman can't beat no Buster-dudes up

D: but he can (unclear) Spiderman
M: but he can't beat no <u>dudes</u> up
    that dude be like #<u>ooooh</u>
D: but the # but the # see <u>look</u>
    do:nh do:nh do:nh # spi::derweb [<u>chanting</u>]
    spi::derweb [<u>chanting</u>]
M: but he can't <u>beat</u> no Bust- the biggest Buster-dude up
    cause that Buster-dude be like # he be like # SOLDIERS ATTACK
    <u>dtchu</u> <u>dtchu</u> <u>dtchu</u> <u>dtchu</u>
    M makes a series of bold marks extending from the Buster-dudes
    (see Figure 4.1)

What is revealing about this episode is that it sheds light on some of the social-interactional processes through which the journal entry is constructed. Mike's journal entry itself is a two-dimensional drawing (see Figure 4.1). However, the two-dimensional nature of the drawing shown in Figure 4.1 belies the complexity of the discursive context in which the journal entry was constructed. Obviously, this discourse context was framed in part by the two boys' shared knowledge of various superhero figures. Not only did Mike and Derek share knowledge about the characteristics of media figures like Superman and Batman; they also shared an interpretive frame of "good guys versus bad guys" for situating those figures in an action-based narrative. Over the course of this (approximately) 3-minute episode, they constructed an understanding of which characters were being used in their individual journal entries (D: *you know who I^ makin?*) and of the actions performed by these characters:

M: you know these dudes called <u>Bust</u>-dudes?
D: yes
M: he be bustin uhm (.) <u>Batman</u> and <u>every</u>body up

Since the actions taken by the superhero figures were represented through drawing (as opposed to writing), the two boys' verbal narration related directly to their emerging drawings. Characters were introduced, or later referenced, through deictic reference to journal drawings, sometimes followed by a narration of characters' actions. Mike's verbal highlighting of the Batman figure in his drawing, for example, was followed by his narration of what was in store for this character:

M: look # then (.) there go Batman
    he gonna get blown to pieces (.) see?
    here go Batman
    he n' get blown to pieces
    <u>aaaaaah</u>

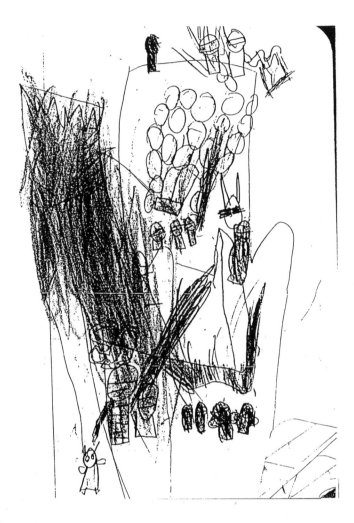

Figure 4.1   Journal entry (Mike): Batman, X-Man, Buster-Dudes.

The emerging drawings themselves were an integral part of the discursive activity in this highly interactive episode. Rather than being an
after-the-fact representation of action-based superhero narratives, the
drawings formed part of the discourse that characterized this moment of
learning. For example, as Mike explains one of the central themes of his
emerging narrative – that of the capacity of the Buster-Dudes to over-

come even the most difficult adversary – he engages in simultaneous action drawing:

M: he [Spiderman] can't beat no Bust- # the biggest Buster-Dude up
     cause that Buster-Dude be like # he be like # SOLDIERS ATTACK
     dtchu dtchu dtchu dtchu
     M makes a series of bold marks extending from the Buster-Dudes

The individualistic voices of Mike and Derek emerge in this episode as unique responses to the discursive context that they also construct. Though responsive to each other, to the point of building on each other's fictitious action scenarios, Mike and Derek construct somewhat divergent narrative worlds. For example, as an individual, Mike displays in this context a narrative strategy similar to that seen in Example 3. He introduces a character and then elaborates on the actions of that character. His narrations are often grounded in conflict, such as characters taking on their adversaries. As in the episode of symbolic play in Example 1, Mike's discursive participation in this episode is individualistic, but it also makes sense within the parameters of this interactional moment in the sociocognitive history of journal writing.

Thus far in my discussions of Mike's classroom learning in the first grade, I have engaged in several kinds of contextual inquiries. I have briefly explored the history of journal writing as a cultural event in this classroom, and I have talked about how Mike typically worked within the discursive parameters of that cultural event. I have noted that Mike frequently drew on superhero figures, incorporated into action-based narrative frames, in response to the demands of journal writing. An early journal text illustrated his conformity to the social demands of journal writing (one must write/draw something, preferably in narrative mode), but also some aspects of his individualistic slant within the discursive framework of this activity. Example 4 shed further light on the sociocognitive processes through which such textual products were constructed. Journal entries such as those shown in Figure 4.1 were constructed through highly interactive discursive activity. Drawing, writing, talk, and gesture occurred simultaneously and were equally important dimensions of the texts that were constructed (Dyson, 1989, 1991). The construction of meaning was a process of social enactment – framed, though not fully determined, by the social history of an activity setting (journal writing), and of the individuals engaged in that activity. Notice that in these discussions of Mike's classroom learning I have not portrayed this sociocognitive process as one of a *movement inward* of social discourse forms (cultural texts, modes of speech, etc.). Rather, I have attempted to portray this process as a complex dialogue. One could assume that Mike has appropriated certain cultural texts and modes of discourse as a means of engaging in journal writing activity (Gee, 1990; Wertsch, 1991). Through microethnographic analyses such as those presented, however, it is apparent that this sociocognitive process is hardly a matter of "copying" external social forms (as an extremely conservative reading of Vygotskian theory might suggest). Rather, this process of meaning construction is more an emergent response to the parameters of particular discursive contexts. The portrait of Mike that emerges from these contextual inquiries is one that emphasizes the agentive and transformative nature of his discursive activity.

Development "from within" discourse contexts

Earlier I presented four questions that might guide contextual inquiries of children's discursive activity in the classroom. In my discussions of these questions, I suggested that an important goal of such inquiries is to document the individual child's *learning,* or developmental changes in her reconstruction of social meanings. Framed in the theory elaborated earlier, that of a developmental psychology grounded in studies of discourse and social activity, the fourth question examines the child's classroom discourses over time. Once again, however, the approach adopted for such examination of developmental change involves multilayered interpretive analyses in which studies of textual products and social processes are given equal weight. In my explorations of Mike's classroom learning over a 4-month period (January–April), I will conclude with a textual analysis of his journal work. Viewed in light of his earlier journal entries and his modes of social interaction during journal writing, a journal entry from late spring in the school year will suggest developmental changes in Mike's journal work.

As I suggested in my very brief discussions of Example 2, the Teenage Mutant Ninja Turtle story, as told in movie versions (*Teenage Mutant Ninja Turtles: The Movie, The Secret of the Ooze*), in a daily cartoon series, and in video arcade games, became a prominent cultural text for Mike in the spring of the school year. By March, Mike had begun writing exclusively about the Turtles, and he filled two journals with Turtle entries from March through June. In an interview about his journal writing, Mike informed me that one of these journals was based on the cartoon series and that the other was based on the movie version of the Turtles story. Using the Turtles as the prominent motif in his journal writing and drawing, Mike created page after page of action-oriented narratives. Typical of his earlier superhero writing, these narratives were often structured around themes of conflict, with the "good guys" (the Turtles) always prevailing over the "bad guys" (Shredder and his band of Foot Soldiers). Coupled with this intense interest in the Turtles was Mike's production of increasingly lengthy entries. By late spring of the school year, the children were expected to compose written journal entries, using invented spellings as well as conventional spellings of words to convey their emerging narratives. Many children in this first-grade classroom, given their literacy-rich environment, had begun to compose lengthy pieces during journal writing. At this point in the school year it was not unusual to see extended *chapter stories* emerge in children's journals, entries written over the course of several days and centered on some unified topic. In late April, the social demands of journal writing had thus shifted somewhat to reflect children's growing technical expertise and literary understanding in composing written narratives. It was in this climate of journal writing activity that Mike composed the following written and dictated entry in late April:

Example 5: journal writing

> *Dictated:* Chapter 1
> *Written:*
> Teen Mot ninja
> teed Bet up
> BeegBpandRvksad
> and did and the Footgj
> *Dictated:* died
> Chapter 2
> But the Foot Soldiers got back up
> *Written:*
> And the ninja Teen
> *Dictated:*
> beat up the Foot Soldiers. The Foot Soldiers keep getting mad
> because they're made out of different kinds of robots.
> *Next page, dictated:*
> Chapter 2
> The Foot Soldiers tried to get back up.
> And Shredder tried to beat Splinter.
> *Written:*
> the foosj wns soa
> ciy to Bet up the and
> the wrar sut
> and the foot sj
> Rshd
>
> *Gloss:*
> Chapter 1. Teenage Mutant Ninja Turtles beat up Beebop and Rock-
> steady, and the Foot Soldiers died. But the Foot Soldiers got back up.

> And the Ninja Turtles beat up the Foot Soldiers. The Foot Soldiers
> keep getting mad because they're made out of different kinds of ro-
> bots. Chapter 2. The Foot Soldiers tried to get back up. And Shredder
> tried to beat Splinter. The Foot Soldiers went [*unclear*] city to beat
> up. . . .

Although some of Mike's invented spellings in the latter part of this
chapter story are unfortunately unclear, what is clear is that this is an
elaborate and complex narrative for him. In my interview with Mike
about this entry, he further explained the paradox presented in this
journal entry: that the Foot Soldiers died but then got back up. From
Mike's verbal explanation, it appeared that even if the Foot Soldiers *fell*
due to their physical attack by the four Turtles, they may have only been
hit. Since the Foot Soldiers were robots made out of different kinds of
material, the different weapons used by the Turtles had varying degrees
of success:

Interview with Mike

D: how did they get back up once they died?
     what happened to them?
M: well # the robots # they strong
     but # but # if the Turtles have their weapons # and they just kick 'em
     # they're not dead yet
     but if they use their weapons they'll die
     but when the Foot Clan # you probably have to hit 'em like # three
     times
D: right # so the Foot Soldiers are robots?
M: *nods yes*
D: [*reading from journal*] and the Ninja Turtles beat up the Foot
     Soldiers
     the Foot Soldiers keep getting mad because they're made out of
     different robots
     [*to Mike*] why did they get mad?
M: sometimes # they're not real strong # cause # they might be made
     out of every kind of material
     but # if Leonardo had sliced 'em # they wouldn't get sliced . . .
     but if Raphael sticked 'em # they would die
     but if Donatello hit 'im (.) he wouldn't die . . .
D: so what kills 'em is the weapons # the Turtles use?
M: *nods yes*

Obviously, the journal entry presented in Example 5, and further elaborated by Mike in a subsequent interview, represents developmental
change compared to the journal entry shown in Example 3 (from January). It is a lengthy and complex entry in which a seeming paradox is
explained through reference to the different materials of the robot adversaries. Mike demonstrates greater facility with the mechanics of writing

and with narrative structure compared with his January entry. He rhetorically frames this entry as a chapter story, and he makes use of invented and conventional spellings to convey the narrative in written form. Things have changed in Mike's journal writing since January, and this change is what is generally referred to as *learning*. However, powerful as this journal text is as evidence of Mike's classroom learning, it is more powerful, in my view, when set within the larger sociocognitive history of Mike's social participation in journal writing. The social history of this event (question 1), Mike's repeated enactment of meaning within this event structure (question 2), and his unique modes of reconstructing social meanings from within (question 3) are all forms of inquiry that lend depth to the question of how his journal work has changed over time (question 4). In other words, these multilayered studies of textual products and social discursive activity allow one to achieve what Bakhtin has referred to as a "depth of understanding" (Bakhtin, 1986). Rather than simply documenting *what* has changed for Mike, one can begin to inquire into the *how* and *why* of this change. Moreover, this discussion of developmental change is deeply contextualized, situated in a particular classroom context in which individual and collective activity occurs.

In these studies of Mike's classroom journal work, I have attempted to develop a research methodology for discourse-oriented studies of classroom learning. All along, I have suggested that the individual child's discourse and learning is somewhat of a "boundary phenomenon." The individual child neither appropriates cultural discourses verbatim nor works within a social vacuum. Rather, her reconstruction of social meanings is always a response to what is available to her "from within" social contexts. This emergent aspect of learning can be further illustrated through reference to the classroom discourse of a second child studied in this first-grade classroom, Janeen. Looking at how a different child reconstructed meanings in this classroom will hopefully shed more light on the methodological approach to the study of learning that orients this chapter. This second set of contextual inquiries will provide further evidence of the utility of multilayered, interpretive analyses of classroom discourse. It will also strengthen the theoretical perspective on learning that grounds such research methodologies: one in which learning is viewed as a dialogic, transformative, and emergent process. Finally, this study of the classroom discourses of Janeen will bring into focus an important facet of the inquiry-guided (Mishler, 1990) research employed here: its implications for the societal and ethical issues associated with educational research. I would in fact maintain that one means of judging the merits of alternative forms of inquiry into classroom learning should be their contributions to pressing societal issues, such as that of equal educational opportunities for all children. The study of Janeen, in particular, highlights such issues through contextual inquiries.

The inner and outer word

One expectation associated with a system of formalized schooling is that individual children will achieve certain developmental milestones within a given time frame. Children in first grade, for example, are expected to become readers of simple literary or basal texts and are expected to be able to perform basic mathematical operations, like simple addition and subtraction. Aside from these generalized expectations about school learning, there are also more specific and local expectations about how children will respond to particular kinds of school tasks. When composing journal entries or other forms of writing, for example, even young children are expected to produce narratives representative of socially appropriate genres – personal accounts, fictionalized stories, or stories that meld fact and fiction. Or, when asked to provide a comment or answer a question during a whole-class discussion, children are generally expected to provide an explanation or a description, often within a certain interlude of "wait time" (see Erickson, this volume, for discussion). Fundamental to the expectations of a system of formalized schooling is the notion that children can engage in socially appropriate kinds of discursive activity, and that they can master certain school tasks within a given time frame.

Both of these school expectations proved to be problematic for Janeen. Janeen entered first grade at a younger age than many of her peers, since her birthday fell just before the school cutoff date of December 31. Perhaps partly for this reason, as the school year progressed it became obvious to Janeen's classroom teacher that she would not be able to meet the school norms for subjects like reading and mathematics. Midway through the school year, for example, Janeen was not yet reading independently, though she was fascinated by books and spent a good deal of time working at the storybook listening center. More important for my explorations here of Janeen's classroom narrative discourses, Janeen's ways of framing her experience through discourse were somewhat divergent from the local practices in the classroom. What was most striking to me and to Rhoda Kanevsky, the children's classroom teacher, was the extraordinary tension that existed for Janeen between inner and outer *discourses* (or, from the Greek *logos, word*): her unique ways of constructing meaning within the social context of the classroom. Throughout this chapter, I have made the point that the dialogic relationship between "inside" and "out there" is emblematic of all discursive activity, and hence thinking. In Janeen's case, however, this dialogic relationship was at times a source of tension. Thus, her discursive activity affords a compelling context in which to explore the individual's thinking (and learning) as it occurs within a particular cultural milieu. I begin this inquiry into Janeen's classroom learning with a discussion of two journal texts composed in the fall and winter of the school year.

Like Mike (Janeen's classmate), Janeen participated daily in the social activity of journal writing. Some of the narrative themes that emerged in Janeen's journal drawings and writings (and, earlier in the school year, in dictations) could be traced to prevalent texts and discussion topics in the classroom. For example, particularly early in the school year, Janeen often copied various written texts found in the classroom, such as poems or lists (e.g., a list of African animals) posted around the room. Also, she sometimes drew on themes that were common to children working at her desk area, such as the widespread practice of drawing/writing about royalty (kings, queens, etc.) and castles. As was the case with Mike, journal writing unquestionably provided a framework of interpretive practices for her own journal texts. At the same time, Janeen's narrative reconstructions from within this discursive framework stood out as highly individualistic. In part, this was because many of her journal entries did not seem to have a textual structure typical of stories. Recall that, in general, journal writing in this classroom was considered a time for children to compose stories representing factual or fictional events. However, consider these two entries, dictated by Janeen in the fall and winter of the school year.

Example 6: journal writing (dictation)

> Star in the sky
> Pumpkin in the sky try to get the stars
> Moon in the sky try to get the triangle
> The cat trying to get the girl
> The two-eyes triangle box try to run to get the girl

Example 7: journal writing (dictation)

> The stars, the moons, and the clouds in the sky were in my dream. I dreamed that I used my chopsticks to move the stars, the moons, and the clouds around. I stirred the sky like I stir a pot of soup and made different designs in the sky with the stars, the moons, and the clouds.

Both journal entries convey a narrative denouement, though not necessarily a plot-sequenced one. In both, Janeen composes a symbolic tableau in which celestial (and some noncelestial) elements are presented in spatial relationships. Narrative events are presented in Example 7 as changes in spatial relationship, as the narrator moves (*stirs*) the elements around as though she were stirring a pot of soup. In Example 6, the narrative events consist of the various elements moving toward (trying to get) one another. Furthermore, these elements are figurative rather than literal. In Example 7, chopsticks are juxtaposed with celestial elements that could (objectively speaking) appear in the sky: moons, stars, clouds. In Example 6, novel characters such as the "two-eyes triangle box" are created, and they are placed in figurative narrative frames with other characters (*the two-eyes triangle box try to run to get the girl*). Finally, Example 6 in particular has a poetic quality in its repetitive phrasing and nonliteral characterization. One might, in fact, term both of these narratives *prose poems*.

When viewed in terms of the many examples of narrative journal entries created by children in this first-grade classroom, these entries stand out as unique interpretive slants on experience. Neither entry would have appeared outside the context of journal writing, since Janeen was nudged toward dictating both entries by her teacher or the teaching assistant. And, inasmuch as both appeared in her journal initially as drawings and later were given textual form through the social intervention of others in the classroom, these entries unquestionably represent a social happening. However, Janeen's entries also pushed the limits of the textual context of journal writing. Furthermore, the difference in interpretive slant represented by these two texts was emblematic of many ways in which the boundary between social meanings and individual meaning (re)construction was a source of tension for Janeen. Within the shared contexts of meaning in journal writing, Janeen's narrative activity represented a unique means of reconstructing social meanings. Her journal narratives made sense within the context of journal writing, but they also were an extremely creative response to that discursive context – a response that in some ways did not "fit" the norm of composing emplotted stories.[3]

The social enactment of narrative

In my explorations of Mike's classroom discourse, I suggested that microethnographic analyses of the moment-to-moment construction of meaning can lend depth to inquiries into children's classroom learning. Such microethnographic analyses are extremely revealing of the processes through which children and their teachers, as Erickson (this volume) suggests, coconstruct zones of learning. I have explored two of the textual products produced by Janeen. I now turn to a contextual analysis of one interactional moment of meaning construction.

The episode that appears as a transcription in Example 8 is typical of the many episodes of journal writing that transpired across the school year. Janeen worked at a desk area (a grouping of desks) and chatted freely with her peers there. Unlike many children working in the classroom, however, Janeen's journal writing activity occurred as a more private textual space. Example 2 (symbolic play) and Example 4 (journal writing) suggested the extremely collaborative nature of Mike's classroom discursive activity. Example 8 illustrates a quite different interactional mode of response to the social activity structure of journal writing. As the transcription unfolds, it becomes apparent that Janeen's movement from talk with her peer, Emma, to work in her journal frequently represents a shift in context (Erickson & Shultz, 1981) marked by changes in posturing and topic. Such fine detail about how Janeen's narrative texts were constructed could not be garnered by the study of completed journal texts. Thus, this detailed examination of the social *enactment* of meaning (question 2) provides an additional layer of interpretive understanding within the study of how Janeen as an individual reconstructed social meaning through discourse.

Example 8: journal writing

> Janeen (J) is drawing a horse figure (see Figure 4.2) in her journal. Emma (E), to Janeen's left, is observing and writing about two silkworms on her desk. Christine (C) and Chen Ju (CJ) are seated across from Janeen.

J: who wanna be in *my* play? [*J looks to E*]
　　holds up journal, smiling
　　wanna be in my play? [*J looks to C, CJ; E looks to J*]
E: lemme see what your (.) what you have [*J looks to E*]
　　what's that?
　　what's that?
J: a horse
E: a horse?
J: *draws in journal*
E: what's this # right here?
J: this his <u>feet</u>(s) [*J draws in journal*]
E: oh [*E leans back*]
J: *draws in journal, with pencil*
　　I made a mistake and put this (unclear) [*she erases*]
　　wanna be in my play? [*J looks to E*]
　　huh?
　　wanna be in my play? [*J turns her torso to E*]
　　draws a single line across bottom of page
　　this gonna be the grass
　　colors the lower part of the drawing, often placing her head very
　　close to the journal page

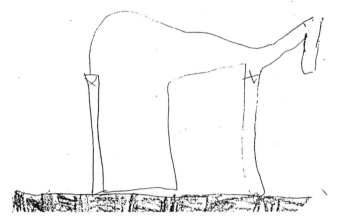

Figure 4.2   Journal entry (Janeen): "The Horse."

Teacher Rhoda (TR) approaches the desk area. She moves to Janeen's desk.

TR: oka:y Aleisha # how you doin? [*J reaches into crayon basket*]
J: *begins to color*
TR: what are you writing about (.) Aleisha?
      I mean Janeen [*TR moves directly behind J*]
      what are you writing about? [*TR scratches J's back*]
J: a horse [*softly*] [*TR leans over J*] TR: huh? what?
J: a horse =
TR: = a horse (.) okay
      I want you to put your crayon down now [*TR places J's pencil on
      journal*]
      I want you to take your pencil and put the title up there [*TR points to
      journal*] # a horse
J: *writes "The"*

Teacher Rhoda leaves Janeen's desk area. Janeen continues to write.

J: ho:::rse [*turns torso toward E*]
      h:: [*articulates as she writes "haerto"*]
      sits back in chair, then resumes writing
E: who you gonna be in my play (.) the queen?
      huh = ?
J: = huh? [*J and E look at one another*]
E: the queen? [*J leans closer to E*]
J: who?
E: the queen of hearts?
      looks at her silkworms
J: *sits upright in her chair*
      I wanna be the baby queen
E: no # there ain't no ba:by queen [*J and E look at one another*]
      you can't be a princess
      a princess is a boy ## of the queen
      so you the <u>queen</u> ## the momma

Teacher Rhoda reapproaches Janeen's desk area.

TR: alright now # okay
      what's it [*the journal entry*] called now?
J: the horse
TR: the horse   J: h:: [*TR slides journal closer to J*]
TR: okay

Teacher Rhoda interrupts her work with Janeen to establish order in the classroom.

TR: now (.) the horse
      what's the story gonna be # tell me
J: *holds pencil poised over journal*
TR: how does it start?
J: the horse =
      = was
TR: the-
TR: go ahead
      the horse was . . .
      J begins to write in her journal, as TR leaves the desk area
J: *leans back in chair*
      the horse was [*softly*]

The "plays" that were the main topic of discussion between Janeen and Emma were rudimentary plays that the girls worked on during Choice, a free-choice activity period. Work on the plays always involved deciding who would appear in whose play, and as such this work often confirmed friendships and other alliances between the children. Although Emma did at one point in this episode refer to Janeen's emerging drawing (*lemme see your (.) what you have*), for the most part the two girls' talk represented a shift in context to the topic of the plays they would work on in the afternoon. Janeen's work in her journal was unquestionably social, though not highly collaborative. In general, this mode of work characterized her journal work and her other forms of classroom activity. Often she became quite absorbed in her own activity, immersed in the work itself.

My interpretations of the episode in Example 8 have thus far focused on the ways in which Janeen negotiated two textual domains or symbolic worlds (Dyson, 1989) – those of work in her journal and talk with her peer(s). However, what strikes me as an additional extremely important aspect of the episode is the social interaction that occurs between Janeen and her teacher, Teacher Rhoda. This interaction is most meaningful if set within the context of the sociocognitive history of the activity setting (journal writing) in which it occurred. Thus, the fact that this episode occurred in May of the school year, after the children had had considerable experience with journal writing; that it occurred during journal writing, when children were expected to produce written texts; and that Janeen had by this time begun to write using invented (phonetic) spellings are all important aspects of the sociocognitive history of this event for Janeen. When viewed in light of this history, the episode in Example 8 represents one "moment" of developmental change, in which Janeen and her teacher negotiated a new understanding of the task at hand (Wertsch, 1984). At this point in the school year, Janeen's teacher had begun to do what Cazden (1983) has referred to as "upping the ante": She had begun to demand that Janeen produce written journal entries, as opposed to drawings along with dictations. Thus, when Teacher Rhoda approached the desk area and noted Janeen's work on her drawing, she gently nudged Janeen toward *writing* a narrative text. At the same time that Teacher Rhoda provided scaffolding for the writing of this text, she provided a "lead" for the production of a particular form of narrative. As I suggested earlier, throughout the school year journal entries had been referred to by participants in the classroom as *stories*. In this interactional moment in time, the form of Janeen's response to the instructional demands of journal writing was molded by Teacher Rhoda. Following both questions (*what's the story gonna be (.) tell me?*) and directives (*I want you to take your pencil and put the title up there*) from Teacher Rhoda, Janeen proceeded to work on a journal entry that assumed *story* form:

Example 9: journal writing
(see also Figure 4.2)

> *Written:*
> The haerto

The haerto WasWakingonThe
graysen AnD aBaBY AnD The BaBy
Jump up AnD htae har hD

Gloss:
The Horse
The horse was walking on the grass. And a baby. And the baby jump
up and hit her head.

In fact, Janeen's narrative journal entries late in the school year reflected ways in which she had appropriated the discourse forms prevalent in the social context of journal writing. For example, in Example 10,
composed just before the end of the school year, Janeen frames her
personal experience in a form reminiscent of the literary, essayist stance
described by Scollon and Scollon (1981). Events are narrated from an
omniscient, authorial perspective, which includes the use of third-person
reference to characters. Furthermore, main events are framed by an
orienting statement (*One day the girls that live in this house were eating
chicken for dinner*) and a conclusion (*After they played for a while they
went home, and took a bath, and went to sleep*). Overall, this narrative
text suggests that Janeen has internalized (or appropriated) the social
meanings that constituted journal writing.

Example 10: journal writing (dictation)

One day the girls that live in this house were eating chicken for dinner.
When they were finish they went outside, and walked to their friends'
house. Their friends' name were Tina and Adrienne. They lived about
five blocks away. After they played for a while they went home, and
took a bath, and went to sleep.

The reconstruction of social meanings

I began this chapter with a discussion of the two parallel constructs of
internalization (Vygotsky) and *appropriation* (Bakhtin), and I would like
to end my interpretive analysis of Janeen's journal narratives with a
return to these constructs. A point made earlier, and one that I will
reiterate here through example, was that internalization was not simply
a process of "taking in." In sociolinguistic terms, internalization does
not entail the simple reproduction of cultural texts; in cognitivist terms,
it does not simply imply the abstraction and representation of what is
"out there" in the real world. Rather, the process of internalization, and
hence the relationship between individualistic and social forms of meaning, is a responsive one. The child is as much a creator of new texts as
she is a reproducer of existing textual forms. Although her own texts

must make sense within the contextual worlds that she inhabits, the child also coconstructs those contexts through her discursive activity. Thus, the forms of meaning constitutive of the classroom as a social setting are not determinant, though they are "providential" in the sense described by Shotter (1993). To examine this issue in a deeper sense, let me turn to a final example of Janeen's discursive activity. With this example, I also move to the fourth methodological focus elaborated earlier: exploring developmental changes in the child's reconstruction of social meanings. The interactional moment of learning explored in Example 8 suggested a sociocognitive process through which particular modalities (such as writing) and narrative forms (stories) were appropriated. Now I consider a narrative journal entry composed by Janeen at a very different point in this evolving sociocognitive history – nearly 1 year later.

Because of the difficulties with school tasks that I noted earlier, Janeen remained in her first-grade class for 2 consecutive years. In spite of the prevailing view that retention is not the best solution to problems of the sort experienced by Janeen, this second year in first grade appeared to be very beneficial for her. By the end of the year, she was reading and writing fluently at a level expected for an incoming second grader. The journal entry shown in Example 11 is representative of the work she did in late spring of this second year. For the entry, Janeen has adopted the narrative form discussed in connection with Mike's Ninja Turtle journal entry in Example 5, that of *chapter stories*. The Turtle Star journal entry in Example 11 was composed by Janeen over several days, and it involved detailed drawings for each successive "chapter."

Example 11: journal writing

> *Written:*
> The adventure Book about turtle and the sares
> Chater 1
> One day They was a TurTle name Micheangelo and he was wake
>   ingTo a Tree
> Chater 2
> Orne uP a Time a TurTle was Bote out her Mather sarme and her
>   name ws The TurTle Sate.
> Chater 3
> One day To TurTle was in The highest castle.
> Chater 4
> One day There was no sares But 15 sares and The sun was out.
> Chater 5
> One day no body was Here But The sares and the sun.

Chater 6
Michelangelo is eating
Chater 7
The in

Gloss:
The Adventure Book about Turtle and the Stars
Chapter 1
One day there was a turtle name Michaelangelo and he was walking
    to a tree.
Chapter 2
Once upon a time a turtle was born (brought?) out her mother stomach
    and her name was the Turtle Star.
Chapter 3
One day two turtles was in the highest castle.
Chapter 4
One day there was no stars but 15 stars and the sun was out.
Chapter 5
One day nobody was here but the stars and the sun.
Chapter 5
Michaelangelo is eating.
Chapter 7
The end.

What is most striking to me about this narrative text is the complex
relationship between inner and outer *word* (discourse) that it suggests.
The entry retains some of the qualities of the prose poetry that Janeen
composed during her first year in this classroom. As in those earlier
entries, shifts in narrative time (Ricoeur, 1985) in this entry are more
representative of shifts in symbolic tableaus. An image appears in drawing and written form of one turtle, Turtle Star, who is enveloped by stars.
The narrative text suggests that this turtle has been born (brought?) out
of her mother's stomach. In the next tableau, two turtles are depicted
visually and textually as immersed in stars. In a subsequent tableau, no
turtles are left, though celestial elements remain. Finally, the coda presents a return to a tableau established at the beginning of the narrative,
one in which Michelangelo (one of the four Teenage Mutant Ninja
Turtles) appears. Thus, rather than a narrative having the plot structure
typical of stories, a denouement in which characters move in a goal-
directed manner toward the solution of some conflict, this narrative text
resembles more a series of snapshot images. Although it threads consistent characters and themes, suggests an authorial stance toward events,
and has temporal movement, this text brings to mind many of the characteristics of the narrative texts seen in Examples 6 and 7: changing sym-

bolic tableaus, celestial elements, and a subtle form of narrative movement through time.

At the same time this text recalls some of the unique qualities of Janeen's narrative journal entries from the previous year, it suggests the merging of socially prevalent discourse forms and cultural texts with Janeen's individualistic interpretations of experience. In Example 11, Janeen has drawn on the Ninja Turtle cultural text, but she has at the same time appropriated this text or creatively reconstructed it. Thus, although she identifies one of the four Ninja Turtles, Michaelangelo, in an opening tableau (Chapter 1), her characterization quickly shifts to a transformation of the Ninjas through her creation of a new character, Turtle Star. In Janeen's drawing, Turtle Star has the form of one of the Ninja Turtles, but she is surrounded by stars. Janeen has also drawn on the discourse organization of stories in this Turtle Star journal entry. Example 8 suggested the social-interactional processes through which social forms of meaning (like the discourse organization of stories) were made available to Janeen. Example 11 as a textual product reveals the enormous developmental change in Janeen's facility with these forms of discourse organization. The entry is titled, and this title (*The Adventure Book about Turtle and the Stars*) projects a story. Phrasing typical of stories (*One day there was, The end*) is used throughout the narrative. New characters are introduced in ways typical of stories, through full nominal specification and often the use of the existential *there* (*One day there was a turtle name Michaelangelo*). Finally, the narrative has both an orientation (Chapter 1) and a coda (Chapter 7), signaled by storybook phrasing and by a common topic, Michaelangelo. Within the interpretive framework of school culture, this narrative text represents an extraordinary amount of *learning* for Janeen.

Viewed in light of the focusing questions that I have posed as a methodological framework for exploring classroom discourses, this text also suggests that the process of learning entails a creative response to the social meanings constitutive of a particular activity setting. Example 8, documenting Janeen's moment-to-moment construction of the "Horse" journal entry, could be interpreted as her cognitive apprenticeship into the social forms of meaning shared by a particular community. At the same time, my interpretive analysis of the Turtle Star journal entry in Example 11 suggests a much more complex picture of this process of learning. Within the shared contexts of meaning that constituted journal writing (question 1), Janeen was a participant in recurrent, socially mediated episodes of social activity that involved consistent kinds of social practices and texts (question 2). Within this framework of social meanings, she reconstructed the cultural texts that were available to her (question 3), merging her individualistic slant on her experience with the forms of narrative that made sense within the activity structure (question 4). I contend that multilayered forms of inquiry such as these are, once again, ones that reflect the theoretical goals of a sociocognitive psychology.

Discourse-oriented inquiries into classroom learning: some concluding issues

I began this chapter by discussing how the sociocognitive theories of Vygotsky, and to a lesser extent the novelistic and discursive theories of Bakhtin, have changed the landscape of research on classroom learning. It is now widely accepted that studying classrooms as particular social contexts in which learning occurs as a situated phenomenon is crucial to understanding children's cognitive development in classrooms (Newman, et al., 1989; Tharp & Gallimore, 1988). Largely due to the significant influence of Vygotskian theory on such studies of classroom learning (see Forman, Minick & Stone, 1993 and Moll, 1990), learning has been reconfigured as a process of social apprenticeship (Brown, Collins, & Duguid, 1989; Rogoff, 1990) into the particular kinds of sociocognitive practices that characterize classrooms. The theoretical focus on the individual child, cognitively constructing mental representations that are abstracted from her encounters with an objective and symbolic world, has begun to shift. Learning has begun to be reconceptualized as a complex dialectic between the individual child and her social world. And yet, this paradigm shift in educational and developmental theory is, in my view, still emergent. As theoretical work within a post-Vygotskian framework continues to emerge (see, e.g., Gee, 1992; Kozulin, this volume), and particularly as educational and developmental researchers begin to draw judiciously on related fields such as literary theory, semiotics, and philosophy (see, e.g., Bruner, 1986, 1990), the process of reconceptualizing classroom learning will continue. From the work that has thus far emerged from this shift, discourse has become a primary topic of inquiry (e.g., Gee, 1990; Wertsch, 1985). From a Vygotskian emphasis on language as a mediator of higher mental functioning has emerged a widespread interest in the complex role that discourse plays in children's learning (Wertsch, 1991; O'Connor & Michaels, this volume).

In my own interpretation of sociocognitive theoretical and research-driven inquiry, I have suggested that discourse does indeed play a unique role in children's learning. As Vygotsky so effectively established in his theory on the origins of higher mental processes, language (i.e., social speech, or discourse) is a primary symbolic mediational tool for the child's cognitive development within her social milieu. Hence, learning could indeed be partly described as a process whereby the social discourses of the child's culture, including her classroom culture, move inward. The social discourses of her community become the child's means of organizing knowledge about the world; moreover, the child's knowledge of the world is constituted by these social speech forms (Gee, 1989, 1990; Heath, 1983). At the same time, I have suggested that this sociocognitive process of movement inward is hardly a process simply of "taking in." I have suggested that, as the child appropriates the social discourses of her community, she also forms an active response to them in the sense described by Bakhtin. Thus, the process of internalization (Vygotsky) or appropriation (Bakhtin) involves active response and agentive transformation. The individual child constructs new discourses at the same time that she appropriates the discourses of her culture. It is this dialogic relationship between social discourses and social activity, and the child's appropriation of those discourses, that I have termed *learning* in this chapter. Following Bakhtin (1981) and Shotter (1993), I have portrayed this dialogic process as both emergent and nondeterministic (or, as Bakhtin would stress, nonsystematic; see the discussion in Morson & Emerson, 1990). Although what Shotter terms *intertextual contexts* do provide an interpretive framework for children's construction of meaning, such contexts do not fully determine children's discursive responses. Learning occurs as the coconstruction (or reconstruction) of social meanings *from within* the parameters of emergent, socially negotiated, and discursive activity.

Finally, the main goal of my work in this chapter has been to articulate a set of research methodologies for exploring the role of discourse in children's classroom learning. I have suggested that, in spite of the existing theories of learning centered on discourse, the forms of inquiry appropriate for such theories have yet to be adequately elaborated. Thus, I have established the central goal of this chapter as a methodological one. Through reference to the classroom discourses of two first graders, Janeen and Mike, I have explored multilayered forms of interpretive analysis in which studies of social-interactional processes and textual products were given equal weight. I termed such forms of interpretive analysis *contextual inquiries,* suggesting the contextually situated nature of such studies. I then framed four research questions that might guide such contextual inquiries, focused on children's discursive activity in classrooms. These four focusing questions moved from more general discussions of the sociocognitive history of particular activity settings (such as journal writing) to discussions of the particular ways in which individual children constructed meaning from within those activity settings.

From these research questions emerged a portrait of Janeen and Mike's classroom learning in the context of journal writing. These portraits emerged as *thick descriptions* (Geertz, 1973) of the children's discursive activity. The study of both finished texts and emergent, moment-to-moment, discursive activity resulted in a deeper understanding of *how* Janeen and Mike constructed meaning in the classroom, not simply *what* developmental changes had occurred. Perhaps most important, these inquiries revealed the transformative nature of Mike's and Janeen's classroom discursive activity. As much as these two children internalized the discourses of their classroom and larger community (such as the Ninja Turtle cultural text), they also creatively transformed those discourses. Janeen's Turtle Star journal entry is particularly revealing in this sense; it suggests the complex relationship between her enculturation into school-based discourses and her response to those discourses.

Having summarized the goals of this chapter, which have been primarily methodological ones, I now turn to the issue of how this work relates to some of the broader issues facing educators (both teachers and researchers) working in classroom settings. I suggested earlier that one of the criteria for judging the relative merits of various theoretical and methodological approaches to the study of classroom learning should be their relevance to pressing social issues. Sociocognitive approaches to education and developmental psychology, I maintain, should not be divorced from societal issues such as the educational experiences of nonwhite or non-middle-class children. Indeed, many sociocognitive researchers have made such connections with social issues a central aspect of their research. Luis Moll and his colleagues, for example, have grounded their studies of social knowledge construction in the particular social and educational issues associated with working-class Latino families (see Moll & Dworin, this volume; Moll, Tapia, & Whitman, 1993). Also, much of the sociolinguistic research on children's "ways with words" has had either the implict or explicit goal of dealing with issues such as equal access to literacy-based school practices (see Gee, 1989; Heath, 1982, 1983; Michaels, 1981).

Such grounding of educational research in issues of wider social importance, in my view, is crucial if one's theory of learning is to be oriented to studies of discourse. From the studies of social discourses and their importance for access to social and educational resources that do exist (see, e.g., Cazden, 1988; Gee, 1990), there is overwhelming evidence that facility in school-based discourses is crucial for educational achievement.

Even primary grade children are expected to participate in literacy-based discourses, such as those involving an essayist presentation of self (Scollon & Scollon, 1981) and a more topic-focused, decontextualized presentation of events (Michaels, 1981). Children in classrooms must be able to "talk science" or engage in literary discussion in ways that represent particular discourse practices (see O'Connor & Michaels and Snow & Kurland, this volume).

Although I recognize such connections between community-based discourses and access to school practices, the contextualized inquiries that I have described are drawn from a theory that situates learning as a dialogical boundary phenomenon. Thus, they avoid the impasse that arises from research suggesting that children from certain communities do not "possess" the discourses of mainstream schooling [such as the Bernstein (1962) study of the "restricted" language repertoires of working-class children]. Rather, such inquiries begin to address the need for deeper understanding of the extraordinary complexity of relationships between the child, her family and community membership, and classroom learning. The case study of Janeen in this chapter is one example of the potential power of such an approach. Janeen is a member of a poor, urban African-American community, and presumably her home-based discourses and literacy-related social practices are not fully consonant with those in her classroom. In the everyday parlance of school systems, Janeen would be considered a child who is "at risk" of failing in school. Indeed, Janeen did experience some difficulties in the crucial areas of reading and math, as I pointed out earlier, and she remained in first grade for 2 consecutive years. However, these generalities of her school experience hardly speak to the richness of her classroom learning (such as the complexity of her Turtle Star journal entry) when explored through multifaceted, contextualized forms of analysis. It is my view, in summary, that such multifaceted forms of inquiry are a means of exploring the classroom learning of children from diverse communities in a way that will be informative – not about their educational advantages or disadvantages, but about the processes through which they actively construct knowledge. These contextual inquiries might be of the sort that could ultimately influence the educational practices of classroom teachers who work with children from different communities. Such is the larger goal of the methodologies that I have described in this chapter.

Notes

1 From "Methodology for the Human Sciences" (p. 160) in *Speech Genres and Other Late Essays*.

2 The following transcription symbols are used in the excerpts from the fieldnotes and in the figures:

(.)	very short pause
#	longer pause (approx. 1 second)
<u>word</u>	stressed word or syllable
CAPS	higher volume
ˆ	rising intonation
vowel::	elongated vowel
word-	speaker turn ends abruptly
= word	speaker turn occurs without notable pause
(unclear)	word not completely clear from videotape

In addition, the transcription of two speakers' utterances on one line indicates overlapping speech.

3 I by no means wish to imply that the children's classroom teacher encouraged only the writing of stories. On the contrary, science writing – observations and explanations – was integral to instruction in this classroom. However, *journal writing*, as opposed to science diary writing, was typically in this classroom, as it is in many primary grade classrooms, a time for composing personal or fictional stories.

References

Bakhtin, M. M. (1981). *The dialogic imagination: Four essays by M. M. Bakhtin* (M. Holquist, Ed.; C. Emerson & M. Holquist, Trans.). Austin: University of Texas Press.

Bakhtin, M. M. (1986). *Speech genres and other late essays* (C. Emerson & M. Holquist, Eds.; V. McGee, Trans.). Austin: University of Texas Press.

Bernstein, B. (1962). Social class, linguistic codes, and grammatical elements. *Language and Speech, 5,* 221–240.

Billig, M. (1987). *Arguing and thinking: A rhetorical approach to social psychology.* Cambridge: Cambridge University Press.

Brown, S. B., Collins, A., & Duguid, P. (1989). Situated cognition and the culture of learning. *Educational Researcher, 18 (1),* 32–42.

Bruner, J. (1986). *Actual minds, possible worlds.* Cambridge, MA: Harvard University Press.

Bruner, J. (1990). *Acts of meaning.* Cambridge, MA: Harvard University Press.

Cazden, C. (1983). Adult assistance to language development: Scaffolds, models, and direct instruction. In R. Parker & F. Davis (Eds.), *Developing literacy: Young children's use of language.* Newark, DE: International Reading Association.

Cazden, C. (1988). *Classroom discourse: The language of teaching and learning.* Portsmouth, NH: Heinemann.

Dyson, A. H. (1989). *Multiple worlds of child writers: Friends learning to write.* New York: Teachers College Press.

Dyson, A. H. (1991). Towards a reconceptualization of written language development. *Linguistics and Education, 3,* 139–161.

Emerson, C. (1983). The outer word and inner speech: Bakhtin, Vygotsky, and the internalization of language. *Critical Inquiry, 10,* 245–264.

Emerson, C. (1993). *Bakhtin and Vygotsky in the context of post-communist education.* Paper presented at the University of Delaware, College of Education Colloquium Series.

Erickson, F. (1992). Ethnographic microanalysis of interaction. In M. LeCompte, W. Millroy, & J. Preissle (Eds.), *The handbook of qualitative research.* New York: Academic Press.

Erickson, F., & Shultz, J. (1981). When is a context?: Some issues and methods in the analysis of social competence. In J. Green & C. Wallat (Eds.), *Ethnography and language in educational settings*. Norwood, NJ: Ablex.

Forman, E., Minick, N., & Stone A. (1993). *Contexts for learning: Sociocultural dynamics in children's development*. New York: Oxford University Press.

Gee, J. P. (1989). What is literacy? *Journal of Education, 171* (1), 18–25.

Gee, J. P. (1990). *Social linguistics and literacies: Ideology in discourse*. Bristol, PA: Falmer Press.

Gee, J. P. (1992). *The social mind: Language, ideology, and social practice*. New York: Bergin and Garvey.

Geertz, C. (1973). *The interpretation of cultures*. New York: Basic Books.

Gumperz, J. (1982). *Discourse strategies*. New York: Cambridge University Press.

Heath, S. B. (1982). What no bedtime story means: Narrative skills at home and at school. *Language in Society, 11* (2), 49–76.

Heath, S. B. (1983). *Ways with words: Language, life, and work in communities and classrooms*. New York: Cambridge University Press.

Hicks, D., & Kanevsky, R. (1992). Ninja Turtles and other superheros: A case study of one literacy learner. *Linguistics and Education, 4* (2), 59–105.

Michaels, S. (1981). "Sharing time": Children's narrative styles and differential access to literacy. *Language in Society, 10,* 423–442.

Mishler, E. (1990). Validation in inquiry-guided research: The role of exemplars in narrative studies. *Harvard Educational Review, 60* (4), 415–442.

Mishler, E. (1991). Representing discourse: The rhetoric of transcription. *Journal of Narrative and Life History, 1* (4), 255–280.

Moll, L. (Ed.). (1990). *Vygotsky and education: Instructional implications and applications of sociohistorical psychology*. New York: Cambridge University Press.

Moll, L., Tapia, J., & Whitmore, K. 1993. Living knowledge: The social distribution of cultural resources for thinking. In G. Salomon (Ed.), *Distributed cognitions: Psychological and educational considerations*. Cambridge: Cambridge University Press.

Morson, G. S., & Emerson, C. (1990). *Mikhail Bakhtin: Creation of a prosaics*. Stanford, CA: Stanford University Press.

Newman, D., Griffin, P., & Cole, M. (1989). *The construction zone: Working for cognitive change in school*. New York: Cambridge University Press.

Ochs, E. (1979). Transcription as theory. In E. Ochs & B. Schieffelin (Eds.). *Developmental pragmatics*. New York: Academic Press.

Ortner, S. (1984). Theory in anthropology since the sixties. *Comparative Studies in Society and History, 26* (1), 126–166.

Ricoeur, P. (1985). *Time and Narrative* (Vol. 2). Chicago: University of Chicago Press.

Rogoff, B. (1990). *Apprenticeship in thinking: Cognitive development in social context*. New York: Oxford University Press.

Rosaldo, R. (1989). *Culture and truth: The remaking of social analysis*. Boston: Beacon Press.

Scollon, R., & Scollon, S. B. (1981). *Narrative, literacy, and face in interethnic communication*. Norwood, NJ: Ablex.

Scribner, S., & Cole, M. (1981). *The psychology of literacy*. Cambridge, MA: Harvard University Press.

Shotter, J. (1993). *Cultural politics of everyday life: Social constructionism, rhetoric, and knowing of the third kind*. Toronto: University of Toronto Press.

Tharp, R., & Gallimore, R. (1988). *Rousing minds to life: Teaching, learning, and schooling in social context*. New York: Cambridge University Press.

Toulmin, S. (1979). The inwardness of mental life. *Critical Inquiry, 6* (1), 1–16.

Vico, G. (1968). *The new science of Giambattista Vico* (T. G. Bergin & M. H. Fisch, Ed. & Trans.). Ithaca, NY: Cornell University Press.

Vygotsky, L. S. (1978). *Mind in society: The development of higher psychological processes* (M. Cole, V. John-Steiner, & E. Souberman, Eds.). Cambridge, MA: Harvard University Press.

Vgyotsky, L. S. (1986). *Thought and language* (A. Kozulin, Ed. & Trans.). Cambridge, MA: MIT Press.

Vygotsky, L. S. (1987). *Thinking and speech* (N. Minick, Trans.). New York: Plenum Press.

Wertsch, J. (1984). The zone of proximal development: Some conceptual issues. In B. Rogoff & J. Wertsch (Eds.), *Children's learning in the zone of proximal development*. New Directions for Child Development. San Francisco: Jossey-Bass.

Wertsch, J. (Ed.). (1985). *Culture, communication, and cognition: Vygotskian perspectives*. New York: Cambridge University Press.

Wertsch, J. (1991). *Voices of the mind: A sociocultural approach to mediated action*. Cambridge, MA: Harvard University Press.

Wertsch, J., & Stone, A. (1985). The concept of internalization in Vygotsky's account of the genesis of higher mental functions. In J. Wertsch (Ed.), *Culture, communication, and cognition: Vygotskian perspectives*. New York: Cambridge University Press.

Part II

Literacy, psychology, and pedagogy

5   A literary model for psychology

Alex Kozulin

In psychology that recognizes itself as a humanistic discipline, culture is considered to be the very fabric of human experience. Accordingly, human activity aimed at the creation and interpretation of culturally significant phenomena should be accepted as paradigmatic. At the beginning of this chapter, I attempt to emphasize this point by contrasting the traditional model of scientific methodology with methodology derived from the humanities. This latter methodology calls for greater attention to human culture. It emphasizes interpretation rather than prediction, and it takes as a guide semiotics rather than physics.

In the literary model for psychology, literature can serve two functions: as a prototype of the most advanced forms of human psychological life and as a concrete psychological tool that mediates human experiences. Humanistic psychology, therefore, has two complementary goals. One of them is to inquire into human psychological life as authoring in potentia. The other is to investigate the role of actually internalized literary modalities as mediators of human experience. These two possibilities are illustrated by the analysis of the relative contributions of decontextualized thinking and intertextually rich discourse for cognitive maturity, and in the possibility of using higher-order "psychological tools" such as the whole literary work as an instrument of cognitive change.

Scientific versus humanistic psychology

For a long time, psychology has been faulted for being an inexact science. Such criticism is provoked by the disparity between psychology's

Portions of this chapter appeared in my (1993) paper, Literature as psychological tool, *Educational Psychologist, 28,* 253–264 (Lawrence Erlbaum Associates, reprinted with permission).

actual performance and its continuing insistence on the scientific character of its methods and findings. Although the poor record of psychology as an exact science is well documented and discussed (Koch, 1981; Sarason, 1981), alternative models of self-identification are in short supply. As soon as the scientific identity of psychology is questioned, the unpleasant ghost of armchair psychology based on introspective self-observation makes its appearance and scares psychologists back into the scientific province.

Only recently and with considerable hesitation have American psychologists begun to entertain the idea of a closer alliance with the humanities (e.g., Bruner, 1986; Polkinghorne, 1988; Sarbin, 1986; Stigler, Shweder, & Herdt, 1990). This still barely visible movement has been triggered, on the negative side, by the limitations of the natural-scientific method as applied to human psychology and, on the positive side, by spectacular strides made in recent decades by philology, linguistics, and cultural anthropology. It should also be mentioned that the cultural psychological approach has been practiced de facto by some professionals and academics who exist on the institutional fringes of establishment psychology (e.g., schools of education, departments of linguistics, reading programs). Their work, however, is not reflected in the standard lore of psychology textbooks and licensing exams.

The pivotal moment in psychology's reorientation toward humanities occurs when it changes its stance toward the categories of nature and culture. Scientific psychology sometimes explicitly, but more often tacitly, assumes that culture is a superstructure of a human existence whose foundations are of a biological character. Culture therefore can be included in the scientific psychological equation as a form of human environment or an external requirement imposed on human behavior. To understand behavior or cognition scientifically means to be able to "bracket" the multiplicity of culturally dependent appearances and to identify underlying natural mechanisms. Only when this has been achieved can one begin the discussion about the so-called ecological validity of the obtained data.

In contrast, in a psychology that is patterned after the humanities, culture is considered to be the very fabric of human experience. It is presumed that the transition from biological evolution to human history has radically changed the psychological equation, so that culture became the true "nature" of the human world. From this point of view the authentic form of human existence is "being in culture." Accordingly, human activity aimed at the creation and interpretation of culturally significant phenomena is accepted as paradigmatic (Geertz, 1973).

An early attempt to reform psychological theory along these lines had been made by Vygotsky (1978, 1986, 1987; Vygotsky & Luria, 1993; see also Kozulin, 1990), who emphasized that higher mental processes emerge out of human activity mediated by psychological tools of semiotic character. Cognitive development therefore appears as dependent on the progressive mastery of ever more complex systems of symbolic mediators. Language, writing, and different literary forms are those cultural–psychological tools that provide the formal mechanism for human mastery of psychological processes. To avoid misunderstanding, it is important to emphasize that semiotic systems and literature in particular are taken here in their formal aspect, as semiotic devices, and not as a body of images or ideas. The word *formal* stands here for such aspects of discourse as its genre specificity, ability to encompass temporary relationships, the hypothetical "as if" possibilities inherent in it, and so on. Thus I am not going to discuss how the *content* of a literary work affects human cognition, but rather how it is affected by the *possibilities inherent in literary form*. Literature may serve both as a prototype of the most advanced forms of human psychological life and as a concrete psychological tool mediating human experiences. Cultural psychology therefore has two complementary goals. One of them is to inquire into human psychological life understood as "authoring" in potentia. The other is to investigate the role of actually internalized literary modalities as mediators of human experience.

The different positions of scientific and humanistic psychologies vis-à-vis nature and culture are translated into different methodological attitudes. The attitude of scientific psychology is derived from the scientific epistemology developed since the seventeenth century. Natural-scientific epistemology reflects a special kind of cognitive and physical practice that allows for the creation of some artificial conditions under which the plane of theoretical representations can be put into correspondence with the plane of physical (or psychological) manipulation with the object of inquiry. This practice, known as a *scientific experiment,* is organized in such a way that the characteristics discovered in the object under study are independent of the procedures involved. Moreover, the laws of the behavior of the object are deemed to be truly objective only if they are not affected either by the method of experimentation or by the fact of experimentation itself.

It has been argued more than once that even the most rigorous psychological experiments cannot comply with the requirements of the scientific model because of the essentially interactive character of any psychological situation (Friedman, 1967). Moreover, the very existence of the processes studied by psychology often depends on irreversible changes occurring in the mental operations of the individual. Learning processes, for example, can often be studied only in the framework of a so-called formative experiment. During such an "experiment," some learning capacities are generated in a child that were absent before and that do not emerge unless the child is engaged in "experimental" activity. In a sense, any study of creative cognition changes the mode of the mind's operation in such a way that it cannot return to its original state. By the same token, any psychotherapeutic encounter is such an "experimental" situation during which the processes in the client's mind can be studied only because they are irreversibly changed.

In humanistic psychology this creative, emergent character of the human mind is accepted as its most important aspect. Consequently, both the subject matter of psychology and its methods are modified. In what concerns the subject matter, culturally intensive processes such as the creation or interpretation of cultural texts should take precedent over purely adaptive, quasi-biological processes. For example, rather than approaching the problem of memory from the point of view of abstractive mechanisms of retention and retrieval of artificial stimuli, it can be approached in terms of integration of disjointed episodes of human life into a coherent narrative whole. The paradigmatic case for this type of memory would be a literary re-creation of the entire life of a given character. In the course of its long history, literature has accumulated a wealth of techniques for creating the aesthetically rounded, completed lives of characters. Some of these techniques are employed, without being recognized, beyond the realm of literature. For example, the child's early autobiographic memory is substantially influenced by the ordering devices supplied by adults in the form of narratives (often resembling short stories) about the child's early years (Halbwachs, 1980). Actually, any culturally meaningful activity can serve as a source of knowledge about human psychological life. Apparently Vygotsky had this in mind when he wrote that "every poem is a little experiment – a snare for psychological functions" (Vygotsky, 1982, p. 406).

A possible solution to the perpetual crisis in twentieth-century psychology would be, therefore, to acknowledge psychology's alliance with the humanities and to conceive it as a systematic form of cultural knowledge. Ontologically, such psychology should be grounded in culture (versus nature), epistemologically it should be concerned with interpretation (versus prediction), and methodologically it should be oriented toward semiotics (versus physics).

At the same time, care should be taken to distinguish the province of humanistic psychology from that of humanities proper. The distinction, however, can be elaborated only in the process of transcending the limits of traditional psychology and trespassing into the field of humanities. Provisionally, the province of humanistic psychology can be defined as a "territory" separating the individual intention toward a culturally mean- ingful act and the objectivized result of such an act that is the proper subject for linguistics, poetics, logic, and so on.

Life as authoring

Psychology following the lead of the humanities has two major direc- tions. One of them can be called a *life as authoring* approach. Within this perspective, the entire range of human conduct is perceived an analo- gous to the process of authoring. Human thoughts, acts, and intentions can be viewed as authoring, and the emerging self can be viewed as an "artifact" analogous to the author of the literary work. As language is potential literature, human conduct can also be conceived of as a poten- tial text. On the other hand, taking into account the supreme position of the production of texts among human psychological processes, its study can be taken as a paradigm for the study of other psychological pro- cesses (Kozulin, 1991). In both cases, the boundary between "artificial" (art and literature) and "natural" (individual psychology) is removed. Literary work becomes a model for the reconstruction of the emergence of the human self, whereas the rules of literary discourse inform our understanding of the narrative thinking of the individual (Bruner, 1986).

The life as authoring approach is based on the ideas of Russian phi- losopher and philologist Mikhail Bakhtin.[1] Whereas in the natural sci- ences the primary given is an object, and what is sought is the causal explanation of its behavior, in the humanities the primary given is the text, and what is sought is its meaning. "The text (written or oral) is the primary given of all those disciplines and of all thought on the human sciences. . . . The text is the unmediated reality (reality of thought and experience), the only one from which those disciplines and this thought can emerge. Where there is no text, there is no object of study, and no object of thought either" (Bakhtin, 1986, p. 103).

The natural-scientific approach to human behavior attempts to derive even the highest forms of human conduct from the elementary, preverbal cognitive and behavioral processes with respect to which language is more or less a passive system of labeling. The principles of humanistic psy- chology, by contrast, suggest that the most trivial of everyday dialogues contain a nucleus of human *language* as a whole, which, in turn, finds its

ultimate embodiment and realization in *literature*. Language therefore is
neither a mere accompaniment of actions nor a simple medium of expression for ideas; rather, it is a tool for turning this reality from "given" into
"developing." Language helps to discern the higher creative potential in
the "lower" forms of psychological life. Language thus offers a paradigm
for any action that involves interaction or interpretation.

From the point of view of the life as authoring paradigm, people, are,
in essence, the creators and consumers of meaning. In the process of
such creation and consumption the human self is emerging. The self
occupies a position analogous to that of the author, whereas the other
occupies a position analogous to that of the literary hero. The author
does not coincide with any of the aspects of his or her life or writing but
reveals the self only in the totality of literary work. In a similar way, the
self cannot be reduced to any of the here-and-now characteristics of the
author's life. Attention therefore should be paid to the issue of the
author–hero relationships as explored in literary theory.

To use this literary paradigm does not mean seeking the answers to the
phenomenon of authoring in the personality of a particular writer, as
psychoanalysis has done more than once (Natoli & Rusch, 1984). Actually, it is quite important to understand that the personality of a particular writer does not coincide with his or her essence as an author. The
author-creator is given only in conjunction with the text and through the
text. Moreover, the distinction should be made between the writer as a
commentator on his life and literary work and the author as he emerges
from the text of this work. The writer's commentaries can be of bio-
graphical but not of cultural-literary interest because they reflect ethical
rather than aesthetic position. Thus the author does not coincide with
the personality of the writer. But the author is not one of his characters
either, even in first-person narratives. The author is present in the text
and emerges only from the text, but at the same time he cannot be
located in this text as a singular figure. "Just as the self can never be
completely imagined as a person like other persons, so the author can
never be fully perceived as another person. The reason for the invisibility of the author is the same as that for the invisibility of the self: The
author is not a single fixed entity so much as a capacity, an energy"
(Clark & Holquist, 1984, p. 88).

One of the primary literary models for construction of a self is that of
an autobiography. Long neglected by psychologists, the genre of autobiography only recently, and not without the influence of Bakhtin,
emerged as a possible venue for the study of narrative thinking. "The
heart of my argument is this," wrote Bruner, "eventually the culturally

shaped cognitive and linguistic processes that guide the self-telling of life narratives achieve the power to structure perceptual experience, to organize memory, to segment and purpose-build the very 'events' of the life. In the end, we become the autobiographic narratives by which we 'tell about' our lives" (Bruner, 1987, p. 15).

The analysis of autobiography as a literary genre not only supplies us with a model of the construction of the self but also helps us to discern the boundary between psychological and aesthetic self-reflection. Relevant to this topic, Bakhtin (1990) made an important observation regarding the "surplus of vision" of the author. When writing from the point of view of one of the characters, the author "lives into" this character's horizon. But then, at a certain moment in the creative process, the author "returns" to his own privileged position and supplements what was visible for the chosen character by other perceptions. Only through this surplus of vision is the author capable of presenting the life of a chosen character as a complete one, as aesthetically finished. In autobiographical writing this "return" is denied because the writer does not have any surplus of vision with respect to the self. Autobiography as an art form compels the author to remain within the horizon of a chosen character through the eyes of whom the writer's life may appear as aesthetically finished. Here we can discern the border between literature as a paradigm for psychological life and literature as an aesthetic phenomenon. In real life (e.g., in the non-literary autobiographic narrative), the individual usually returns to his own privileged position, which dominates the perception of others. And since the self is open to change while alive, the autobiographic narrative remains a personal document rather than a work of art. Aesthetic completeness is not ordinarily the aim of an individual, and thus he sacrifices it in order to have the last word in the tale of his own life.

The author's surplus of vision also allows for the temporal encompassing of the lives of the characters. The individual cannot experience his own life as temporally finished and aesthetically accomplished, if only because the individual does not have the experience of the beginning and the end of his life. The beginning always appears as a story told by others, and the end also, but as a constantly changing story imagined by the individual himself. The life of a character, or a real other, on the contrary, can be seen as an accomplished whole. Our surplus of vision with respect to others allows us to construct a complete story of their lives, to turn these lives from the sequence of disjointed experiences into the whole of memory. Memory about the other is essentially different from reminiscences about and contemplation of one's own life. Only the life of the other taken in its totality can become a subject for the value judgment that goes beyond the aims and meanings held by the person while he was alive. Building my memory of the other is probably the most aesthetically intensive practice available in everyday life.

Thus, the first tentative implication from humanistic psychology to education is that more attention should be paid to the literary creative process as a paradigm of human understanding. Literature should be used not only as a source of information, images, and ideas, but also as a model of representation and thinking.

Literary form as consciousness

The moment one accepts that literature is an important mediator that shapes human cognitive processes, one can no longer be satisfied with such gross dichotomies as "writing versus orality" or "literate mind versus preliterate mind." What is needed is a much more detailed study of the historically changing role of literature as a cognitive psychological tool (Kozulin, 1993).

As a first step in this direction, I attempt to make a distinction between the cognitive role of the classical literature of the nineteenth century and the modernist literature of the twentieth. The ongoing theoretical debates about modernity and postmodernity (Adorno, 1984; Habermas, 1987) have produced convincing evidence that the position of the culture of the highly educated classes in Western society changed dramatically over the course of the nineteenth century. The symptoms of this change have been described in different terms, but in essence, all of them point to the secession of "high culture" from the organic whole of social life. At the beginning of the nineteenth century, the culture of the highly educated was still tied by thousands of strings to the everyday life of the upper classes. Belonging to upper-class society almost automatically presupposed a certain type of education and an acquaintance with a certain class of literary texts. The "high culture" of the educated upper classes was inseparable from an individual's social position and social habits. Of course, there were individuals for whom the production and consumption of such cultural artifacts was of much greater importance than for others. But even their preoccupation with culture was rarely perceived as an existence in a separate realm. Within literature itself, its intertextual aspect was still firmly entangled with this social aspect. "High culture" did not put a wall between itself and the world of everyday experience and did not focus on the task of creating a separate literary universe. Nineteenth-century literature could still speak directly about social reality (thus its "realism"), because its authors and readers shared this reality and its reflections in the universals of the highly educated upper classes in their individual experiences.[2]

The breakdown of traditional social order, which was already apparent in the 1860s but which became accepted as irreversible only in the 1930s, produced, among other things, the radical displacement of "high culture" from its "natural" base in the social universe of the upper classes. This breakdown of the traditional links between the culture of the highly educated and the social order put culture in a new position. It was no longer possible to take for granted the shared cultural and social horizon of the author and his readers. It is not surprising that such a denaturalization of "high culture's" existence prompted it to put forward fundamental questions about its own self-determination and self-definition. The problem was no longer how to write or study poetry, but rather *what is poetry*.[3] At the same time, the displacement of high culture from its "natural" social context created a precondition for the self-conscious "life in culture."

"Life in culture" appeared both as an aesthetic approach and as a social phenomenon. As a social and existential position, "life in culture" became a spiritual (and physical) survival technique of intelligentsia persecuted by Stalinist and other totalitarian regimes.[4] As an aesthetic position, "life in culture" realized itself in a radical intertextuality that presents culture as a chain of signifiers. Probably the best-known author whose writings elevated conscious intertextuality to the level of the universal cultural attitude is Jorge Luis Borges. As a contemporary critic observed: "In his aesthetic elaboration Borges moves in a world of quotations. . . . His stories are allusions to other stories, his characters are allusions to other characters, and their lives are allusions to other lives" (Christ, 1969, pp. 34–35).

Borges achieved in his writing (e.g., his 1962 collection *Labyrinths*) two goals. First, he asserted the primacy of text with respect to life, with life becoming an allusion to the text. In a sense, there is no action in Borges's stories other than *literary* action. Second, Borges collapsed time – or, more precisely, he collapsed the linear time of a unified social-cultural history. The collapse of time allowed him to operate with different cultural epochs as coexistent, copresent. This constitutes the radical shift of literature's method toward that of philology. One would find nothing strange in the copresence, for example, of Humboldt's and Heidegger's views on language on one page of a philological text; at the same time, a literary description of an "actual" dialogue between Humboldt and Heidegger regarding language would be considered a modernist trick. The collapse of time is essential for the implementation of a consciously intertextual cultural position because it liberates culture from its fixed attachments to a specific social and physical reality. In Borges's universe of collapsed time, culture becomes truly a chain of signifiers that have a life of their own.[5]

Although Borges laid bare the device of deliberate intertextuality, it was another modern author, Mikhail Bulgakov, who took a further step and painted a picture of social reality as seen through the lenses of conscious intertextuality.[6] Bulgakov's (1967) novel *The Master and Margarita* is chosen here not only because it represents the very innovative relationships between text and social reality but also because of the enormous influence this novel has had on the mentality of Russian readers. Written in the 1930s by an author who was both shunned and haunted by Stalin's regime, the novel was published for the first time only in the 1960s and immediately became one of the most cherished and widely discussed works of Russian literature. Its influence on public thought is so strong that certain phrases from the book were quickly adopted as new proverbs.

The circumstances under which the novel was written in the 1930s has a direct bearing on the problem of life in culture as a social phenomenon. Bulgakov was aware of the complete rupture between the social order he had to live under and the cultural tradition he belonged to. The only authentic being for an author in such circumstances is the being in the realm of culture rejected by society. Bulgakov's novel is populated by characters who are impossible in the Stalinist social reality: an outcast author (the Master), Mephistophelis (Voland), Jesus (Yehoshua Ha-Nozri). These characters are archetypical figures excluded from the official social-cultural realm of the Stalinist state.

Bulgakov employs many of the devices already mentioned here in conjunction with Borges's work. There is a collapse of time and historical reality in Bulgakov's novel, with Mephistophelis, Pontius Pilate, and the Soviet apparatchiks copresent in the Moscow of the 1920s. There is also a strong assertion of the primacy of text, from the novel's key phrase, "Manuscripts do not burn," to the fact that events in Moscow have a direct relation to the events of Passion Week in Jerusalem, as they are narrated within a novel allegedly written by the Master. Bulgakov, however, did not limit himself to the creation of a separate literary reality into which he and his readers could escape from the hostile social environment. Bulgakov took a truly radical step and turned the tables: In his novel, the perspective of rejected culture becomes a springboard for a comprehensive satirical critique of the official social-cultural reality. It is important to emphasize that Bulgakov's is not the usual literary-social critique. Unlike his nineteenth-century predecessors, he did not pit one set of social ideals against the other while remaining on the plane of the commonly shared social-cultural reality. Society in Bulgakov's novel is denied its status of a given reality; it becomes transposed onto a plane of strictly cultural evaluation where its grotesque essence is masterfully revealed. Bulgakov's is a formal critique in a sense that it is not a critique of social content from the position of shared cultural form, but rather a radical "estrangement" of the critic's cultural position itself.

The dual nature of the literary word, as a "sign for a thing" and as a "sign for a sign," is fully employed in Bulgakov's novel. Each dialogue and each episode can be read at least twice – on the plane of reference to some apparent social and historical event and on the plane of rich allusions to cultural texts unrelated to these events. As a result, a new literary reality is created that has one of its focuses during Passion Week in Jerusalem, where selected pieces from Pushkin and Chekhov are quoted as sacred commandments, and the other in Moscow of the 1920s where, with reference to Dostoevsky, *Roman aktuell* about events in Jerusalem is written (Kaganskaja & Bar-Sella, 1984).

A modernist literary device thus becomes an extremely potent aesthetic weapon in the liberation of the reader's consciousness. This consciousness no longer accepts the official social-cultural horizon as the only real one. For the new consciousness generated by Bulgakov's novel, this official horizon becomes simply irrelevant. Taking into account the enormous influence of Bulgakov's work, which clearly transcended a literary sphere and reached the consciousness of the large mass of Russian readers, one may wonder whether this is not a revealing case for the role of literature as a psychological tool. What we have here is a higher-order psychological tool – the novel – which, because of its formal structure and in a historically specific manner, succeeded in altering the very method of people's comprehension of their social existence.

Thus, the second implication from humanistic psychology to education is that higher-order psychological tools such as a specific literary approach permeating all literary work may serve as potent instruments for changing the consciousness of student readers. To fulfill such a role, this approach should be identified and made available in its "instrumental" capacity to students.

Autonomous text versus intertextuality

As mentioned earlier, the task of humanistic psychology is not only to promote a paradigm of literary action but also to inquire into culturally intensive human activities. One of the issues that the cultural psychological approach might clarify is the problem of the so-called autonomous text. The notion of autonomous text was introduced into psychology and education by Olson (1977). Olson suggested that in *autonomous text,* meaning is explicitly and unambiguously expressed in words and syntactic patterns. In contrast, an *utterance* is contextual and ambiguous. The problem of texts versus utterances has both academic and social implications. As a social problem, it features in the debate regarding power and authority linked with formal literacy and in the opposition between oral and written verbal traditions (Gee, 1986). On the academic side, Olson's thesis about the cultural and developmental superiority of written autonomous text over oral contextual speech has become a standard point of reference. "My argument," Olson wrote, "will be that there is a transition from utterance to text both culturally and developmentally and that this transition can be described as one of increasing explicitness, with language increasingly able to stand as an unambiguous or autonomous representation of meaning" (p. 258).

In this theory, the evolution of human verbal cognition, both historically and ontogenetically, is seen as proceeding from context-dependent oral utterances to autonomous texts, of which scientific papers are the most advanced examples. Scientific text represents the "truth of correspondence" between statements and empirical observations. This truth of correspondence should be distinguished from the "truth of wisdom" that is perpetuated in oral and poetic traditions, and that apparently retains its contextual character (Olson 1977, p. 277).

Although there is much truth in what Olson has said about the cognitive consequences of writing, both his choice of scientific writing as a teleos of language development and his definition of autonomous text are far from convincing. First, the whole issue of decontextualization of verbal thought is not that simple. Although the progression from context-dependent actions and verbal utterances to decontextualized mental operations was established in developmental psychology long ago (Werner, 1948; Werner & Kaplan, 1963), this progression is apparently accompanied by yet another process. This is the process of the ever-increasing role of intralinguistic relations in the child's thinking (Wertsch, 1985, pp. 145–57). Intralinguistic devices can be as simple as reported speech and as complex as sophisticated combinations of different speech genres, allusions, and hidden quotations. In a sufficiently developed verbal system, language serves as a context for itself. The process of cognitive decontextualization, therefore, cannot be accepted as a singular teleos of verbal development. Facility in intralinguistic contextuality is an important goal as well.

Once the importance of contextually rich intralinguistic relations is acknowledged, the dichotomy of orality versus writing appears in a new light (Nystrand, 1986). Many dialogical features often associated with oral speech can be found in literary texts, and not as marginal elements but as responsible for the superior quality of the texts in question. On the other hand, the oral mode itself essentially depends on the mediation provided by written texts. One may conceive of two general types of oral exchanges: one based only on shared referentials pertaining to the extralinguistic world of things, and the other based on the knowledge of texts. In the second case, elements of text known to interlocutors serve as mediators in communication and establish the necessary intersubjective connections. Interlocutors "participate" in the original texts, recognizing the "echo" of these texts in each other's speech. These shared texts provide the necessary base from which any further individual development of the topic of conversation can be started and to which the interlocutor can return, if misunderstood, as to a safe haven.

The alleged "autonomy" of scientific prose is also problematic (Cazden, 1989). The scientific paper is aimed at a specific reader – a professional whose prior knowledge of the language involved is indispensable for the understanding of the paper. Scientific papers rarely contain all required definitions, usually simply referring the reader to an appropriate body of literature. In a sense, the scientific paper represents almost zero autonomy because it remains cryptic to any outsider. It should also be recognized that scientific statements about objective processes in nature are largely indifferent to their mode of expression: They can be made in the form of graphs, formulas, cartoons, oral speech, and so on. The verification of the "truth of correspondence" contained in these statements ultimately depends on the physical replication of the experimental procedures, not on the conformity to the original text. It is, therefore, not only the autonomous but also the textual character of scientific papers that is suspect.

Still, Olson's (1989) claim that "texts have a meaning independent of the authorial intention of their writers and the diverse interpretations of their readers" (p. 119) deserves closer scrutiny. One should, however, abandon the paradigm of scientific paper and focus instead on religious, legal, and poetic texts that are also said to be autonomous or self-sufficient. An appropriate methodology here is that of hermeneutic analysis (Gadamer, 1975; Mueller-Vollmer, 1985).

Autonomous texts are defined as those "which interpret themselves insofar as one needs no additional information about the occasion and the historical circumstances of their composition" (Gadamer, 1980, p. 86). Unlike the scientific paper, which is addressed to a narrow circle of specialists, the religious text addresses the entire community of believers, and the poetic text addresses an even wider and more indeterminate audience. An autonomous text is something which stands by itself, something to which one returns; a text which may be read again and again and which gains more richness when it becomes familiar (Gadamer, 1980, p. 91).

It would be wrong to imagine that the problem of self-sufficiency is of purely academic interest for those engaged in religious exegesis or a study of poetics. The immediate relevance of the issue of self-sufficiency to contemporary social life is underscored by the current debates about the so-called original intent of the framers of the U.S. Constitution. The Constitution is a text whose interpretation poses a clear-cut hermeneutic problem because it has the potential of being relevant to situations which could not be foreseen by its authors.

This peculiar ability of autonomous texts has been noticed in the nineteenth century by Schleirmacher and was brought to our attention more recently by Gadamer: "The printed text should fix the original information (*Kundgabe*) in such a way that its sense is unequivocally understandable. . . . To this extent, reading and understanding mean that information is led back to its original authenticity. . . . However, this 'information' *is not what the speaker or writer originally said, but what he wanted to say indeed even more: what he would have wanted to say to me if I had been his original interlocutor*" (1986, p. 393; italics mine).

Such understanding of autonomous text implies that it must contain an interpretive "free space" that guarantees a meaningful rather than a literal reading of the text, whose content cannot be negotiated with the author. Apparently Plato's dialogues and Shakespeare's tragedies contain just enough of such free space to be able to speak directly to the readers who are separated from the authors of these texts by time and space and who cannot re-create their immediate extralinguistic experiences. The question thus arises: What allows some texts to function as self-sufficient, and what cognitive consequences might this have for those whose psychological life is mediated by the texts?

The perpetual life of autonomous texts can be related to the phenomenon of *effective history* (*Wirkungsgeschichte*) (Gadamer, 1975). The concept of *effective history* denotes – in simple terms – the presence of the past in the present. Our ability to understand the past essentially depends on our awareness of an overarching tradition that encompasses both our point of view and that of the original text situated in the past. The original text, moreover, "lives" in the history and lays its imprint on our language, our concepts, and our understanding of literature. The past text therefore is not only an object that we can approach in a detached manner, but also the source of our own verbal position. One may suggest that eminent autonomous texts, such as those of Plato and Shakespeare, are among the prime agents of the effective history permeating our verbal consciousness and on this basic level linking us to the past. Sometimes such influence is almost palpably obvious. For example, Russian language and Russian literature since the early nineteenth century have had the same source – the poetry of Alexander Pushkin. Not only a great poet, Pushkin was the true reformer of the national literary language and, consequently, everyday speech as well. That is why a contemporary Russian immediately recognizes Pushkin's verses as "natural" because his poetry became the norm of the national language.

The process of effective history can be defined more closely through the notion of intertextuality. Intertextuality denotes, in a general sense, the transposition of one or several sign systems into another, and more specifically the presence of antecedent texts in consequent texts. Intertextuality thus provides a concrete linguistic mechanism for the presence of eminent autonomous texts in the verbal consciousness of people of later epochs. The phenomenon of intertextuality alerts us to at least the double nature of the word: The word is a signifer in respect to some extralinguistic signified, but it is also a signifer in response to the antecedent signifer. "Any text is constructed as a mosaic of quotations; any text is the absorption and transformation of another. The notion of intertextuality replaces that of intersubjectivity, and poetic language is read as at least *double*" (Kristeva, 1986, p. 37).

Though I am not sure that Kristeva's "replacement" of intersubjectivity by intertextuality is not an exercise in deliberate theoretical extremism, it must be admitted that intersubjectivity often realizes itself in intertextuality. For psychology this has far-reaching consequences because it points to the ambivalence of language as an individual/collective tool of thought and expression. Any act of verbal self-expression, for example, has an overtone in the form of intentional or unwitting references to preceding "texts." Moreover, these texts are present as an invisible "third" when any two people are engaged in oral or written conversation. Apart from some special cases, the preceding texts are not present as actual fragments or allusions, but rather as semantic archetypes (e.g., a root metaphor like "man as a machine," or "life as a road").

I suggest that the special importance of eminent autonomous texts is determined by their being a powerful source of such archetypes. Their eminence is based on the ability to cast some fundamental problem in a form that cannot be supplanted. These archetypes become part of our everyday speech and we return to them, for the most part unconsciously, when we attempt to produce novel texts.

Thus, the third implication from humanistic psychology to education is that it is not only decontextualized thinking but also intertextually rich discourse that should become a criterion of cognitive maturity. To achieve this maturity, students should be made aware of the connection between classical autonomous texts and the form of verbal reasoning they employ.

Education and modernity

The phenomenon of modernity has a number of social dimensions such as industrialization, rationalization, breakdown of traditional order, alienation, and so on. I am concerned here with just one of modernity's characteristic features: its sociocultural pluralism. Sociocultural pluralism resulted from the insertion of previously self-contained and self-sufficient groups into one all-embracing sociocultural system. Bakhtin (1973) stated, "Those worlds and those planes – social, cultural and ideological – which collide in Dostoevsky's work were in the past self-sufficient, organically self-enclosed, consolidated, and had inner significance as separate units. Capitalism destroyed the isolation of these worlds and broke down the seclusion and inner ideological self-sufficiency of those social spheres. . . . Their blind co-existence and their blissful and self-assured state of mutual ideological ignorance came to an end; their mutual contradictoriness and, at the same time, their mutual connectedness were exposed with utmost clarity" (p. 15).

For education, sociocultural pluralism and the concomitant democratization of school poses a serious problem. In the premodern period, education was based on a universal model of human experience that usually had religious or mythological foundations. Such a model served as a natural presupposition for both teachers and students. Teachers represented an unambiguous cultural tradition associated with this model, and their task was to transmit and articulate it to students. Thus teachers, who possessed an undeniably authoritative voice, were sup-posed to find didactic means for the transmission of this unambiguous tradition to students. Under new modern conditions, it becomes incumbent on teachers to establish and defend the nonarbitrary character of the chosen cultural position. Because teachers cannot rely on a shared cultural horizon between themselves and their students, they are forced to rediscover this tradition anew.

Traditional education was essentially *retrospective*. The universal model and the cultural tradition were given, and the task of the student was to absorb this tradition and the intellectual tools associated with it. Thus, the student was taught to deal with problems that reproduced these past cultural patterns. Under the dynamic conditions of modernity, the necessity for *prospective* rather than retrospective education became obvious (Silvestrov, 1989). Prospective education implies that students should be capable of approaching problems that do not exist at the moment of their learning. To achieve this capability, students should be oriented to productive rather than reproductive knowledge. Thus, a body of knowledge should appear not in the form of results and solutions but rather as a process of authoring.

Here the model provided by humanities has certain advantages over that of science. The progressivist interpretation of science presents the earlier theories either as fallacies or as approximations to the modern ones. In this context, the process of authoring is obscured by the final result. Something new always appears as better than something old. Humanities suggest an alternative model because it is impossible to say that Tolstoy is better than Shakespeare or that Hegel is better than Plato. Humanities not only focus our attention on the process of authoring but also provide a paradigm for a genuine dialogue of cultures (Bibler, 1989). In the modern mind, Plato, Hegel, Shakespeare, and Tolstoy represent cultural traditions that are irreducible to each other, but that at the same time are mutually complementary – different attempts to solve the same set of fundamental problems.

A study of the classical autonomous texts returns the student to the beginnings of fundamental artistic and scientific problems. These problems appear, therefore, as problems rather than as solutions. Such a "return to the beginning" is characteristic of any genuine authoring, both humanistic and scientific. In this sense, each great poet is writing poetry anew, each great philosopher wrestles with the fundamental enigma of human consciousness, and each great scientist returns to the problem of causality in nature. The just-mentioned return to the beginning, necessitated by the situation of modernity, provides an opportunity for prospective education based on the model of authoring rather than reproduction. Historically, the authoring model is not only derived from humanities but is also used as an educational guideline, mostly in teaching humanities. This guideline, however, can be as readily applied to the work of Newton and Einstein as it has been to Plato and Tolstoy.

Thus, the last implication for education is that a return to the beginning and a dialogical type of learning characteristic of the humanities could be extended to science teaching. Through this, intertextual and decontextualized types of cognition can be successfully combined.

Coda

Literature may serve both as a prototype of the most advanced forms of human psychological life and as a specific psychological tool mediating human experiences. In this chapter, the possibilities of a literary model for psychology have been explored.

First, the life as authoring approach based on the work of Bakhtin helps us to grasp the constructive nature of the self. The self cannot be reduced to its here-and-now characteristics but can be reconstructed through its synchronous and diachronous projections. The relationship between the author and his characters, particularly in such genres as autobiography, provides important clues to how such "reconstruction" is achieved.

Second, the notion of literature as a psychological tool leads us beyond the dichotomy of orality versus writing and poses the question of the historically changing role of literary devices as internalized forms of human verbal consciousness. Modernist literature supplies human cognition with devices that facilitate a critical approach to social reality.

Third, language, as it reveals itself in literary texts, helps us to correct a popular yet misleading view of cognitive development as dependent primarily on decontextualized mental operations. In a sufficiently developed verbal system, language serves as a context for itself. Thus, facility with intertextual relationships is an important aspect of the development of verbal consciousness.

Finally, the modern situation characterized by sociocultural pluralism not only poses a serious problem for education but forces it to see new opportunities. One of them is a return to the beginning associated with prospective education. This education is oriented to re-creation of fundamental problems rather than learning existent solutions. Such re-creation is possible within the authoring model developed in the humanities. This model, however, can also be used for teaching in the sciences.

Notes

1 Bakhtin's life and work is comprehensively discussed in Clark and Holquist (1984). For a synthesis of Vygotsky's and Bakhtin's approaches, see Wertsch (1991).

2 A turning point has been reached in the 1860s, when a new generation of poets and painters deliberately assaulted the organic ties between social and artistic dimensions of culture (See Gaunt, 1967).

3 The problem of literature's self-identification became a centerpiece of the work of Russian Formalists (see Lemon & Reis, 1965).

4 In this respect, the evolution in the views of the poet Osip Mandelstam is quite revealing. In his early post-Revolutionary essays, Mandelstam expressed near-exultation at the idea of a complete breakdown of the old social order, which among other things allegedly maintained false relationships between social and cultural horizons. In the new, post-Revolutionary reality, culture, according to Mandelstam, was completely free – unsupported by the social order but also not bound by it. The idea of living in culture alone seemed very exciting, at least for the poet. Several years later, life in culture acquired a new meaning for Mandelstam, who was persecuted and ultimately exterminated by Stalin's regime. New relationships, and rather nightmarish ones, were established between the new social order and what remained of high culture. For those who were not ready to enter into these new relationships, the only choice was to cultivate life in culture as the last form of personal defense (Mandelstam, 1979).

5 A somewhat similar collapse of linear time is achieved by Mandelstam in his poem "Midnight in Moscow," in which Raphael visits Rembrandt in Moscow and, together with Mozart, they go out to enjoy the city (see Mandelstam, 1973).

6 Bulgakov's dramatic life is discussed in Proffer (1984).

References

Adorno, T. W. (1984). *Aesthetic theory.* London: Routledge & Kegan Paul.

Bakhtin, M. (1973). *Dostoevsky's poetics.* Ann Arbor, MI: Ardis.

Bakhtin, M. (1986). *Speech genres and other late essays.* Austin: University of Texas Press.

Bakhtin, M. (1990). *Art and answerability.* Austin: University of Texas Press.

Bibler, V. (1989). On the philosophical logic of paradox. *Soviet Studies in Philosophy, 28,* 3–15.

Borges, J. L. (1962). *Labyrinths.* New York: New Directions.

Bruner, J. (1986). *Actual minds, possible worlds.* Cambridge, MA: Harvard University Press.

Bruner, J. (1987). Life as narrative. *Social Research, 54,* 11–32.

Bulgakov, M. (1967). *The Master and Margarita* (T. Mirra Ginsburg, Trans.). New York: Grove Press.

Cazden, C. (1989). The myth of autonomous text. In D. M. Topping, D. C. Crowell, & V. N. Kobayashi (Eds.), *Thinking across cultures.* Hillsdale, NJ: Erlbaum.

Christ, R. (1969). *The narrow act: Borges's art of allusion.* New York: New York University Press.

Clark, K., & Holquist, M. (1984). *Mikhail Bakhtin.* Cambridge, MA: Harvard University Press.

Friedman, N. (1967). *The social nature of psychological research.* New York: Basic Books.

Gadamer, H.-G. (1975). *Truth and method.* New York: Continuum.

Gadamer, H.-G. (1980). Religious and poetic speaking. In A. Olson (Ed.), *Myth, symbol and reality*. MI: University of Notre Dame Press.

Gadamer, H.-G. (1986). Text and interpretation. In B. Wachterhauser (Ed.), *Hermeneutics and modern philosophy*. Albany: SUNY Press.

Gee, J. (1986). Orality and literacy. *TESOL Quarterly, 20,* 719–746.

Geertz, C. (1973). *The interpretation of cultures*. New York: Basic Books.

Gaunt, W. (1967). *The aesthetic adventure*. New York: Schocken Books.

Habermas, J. (1987). *The philosophical discourse of modernity*. Cambridge, MA: MIT Press.

Halbwachs, M. (1980). *Collective memory*. New York: Harper & Row.

Kaganskaja, M., & Bar-Sella, Z. (1984). *Master Gambs i Margarita*. Tel-Aviv: Milev.

Koch, S. (1981). The nature and limit of psychological knowledge. *American Psychologist, 36,* 257–269.

Kozulin, A. (1990). *Vygotsky's psychology: A biography of ideas*. Cambridge, MA: Harvard University Press.

Kozulin, A. (1991). Life as authoring: A humanistic tradition in Russian psychology. *New Ideas in Psychology, 9,* 335–351.

Kozulin, A. (1993). Literature as a psychological tool. *Educational Psychologist, 28,* 253–264.

Kristeva, J. (1986). *Kristeva's reader*. New York: Columbia University Press.

Lemon, L., & Reis, M. (1965). *Russian formalist criticism*. Lincoln: University of Nebraska Press.

Mandelstam, O. (1973). *Complete poetry of O. E. Mandelstam* (T. Burton Raffel & Alla Burago, Trans.). Albany: SUNY Press.

Mandelstam, O. (1979). *Complete critical prose and letters*. Ann Arbor, MI: Ardis.

Mueller-Volmer, K. (1985). *The hermeneutic reader*. New York: Continuum.

Natoli, J., & Rusch, F. (1984). *Psycho-criticism*. London: Greenwood Press.

Nystrand, M. (1986). *The structure of written communication*. New York: Academic Press.

Olson, D. (1977). From utterance to text. *Harvard Educational Review, 47,* 257–281.

Olson, D. (1989). Text and talk. *Contemporary Psychology, 34,* 119–121.

Polkinghorne, D. (1988). *Narrative knowing and the human sciences*. Albany: SUNY Press.

Proffer, E. (1984). *Bulgakov: Life and work*. Ann Arbor, MI: Ardis.

Sarason, S. (1981). *Psychology misdirected*. New York: Free Press.

Sarbin, T. R. (1986). *Narrative psychology*. New York: Praeger.

Silvestrov, V. V. (1989). *Filosofskoe obosnovanie teorii i istorii kultury* (*Philosophical foundations of the theory and history of culture*). Moscow: VZPI.

Stigler, J. W., Shweder, R., & Herdt, G. (1990). *Cultural psychology: Essays on comparative human development*. New York: Cambridge University Press.

Vygotsky, L. (1978). *Mind in society*. Cambridge, MA: Harvard University Press.

Vygotsky, L. (1982). Istoricheskii smysl psikhologicheskogo krizisa (Historical meaning of the crisis of psychology). In *Collected papers* (Vol. 1). Moscow: Pedagogika.

Vygotsky, L. (1986). *Thought and language* (rev. ed.). Cambridge, MA: MIT Press.

Vygotsky, L. (1987). *Problems of general psychology*. New York: Plenum.

Vygotsky, L., & Luria, A. (1993). *Studies on the history of behavior*. Hillsdale, NJ: Erlbaum.

Werner, H. (1948). *Comparative psychology of mental development*. New York: International Universities Press.

Werner, H., & Kaplan, B. (1963). *Symbol formation*. New York: Wiley.

Wertsch, J. (1985). *Vygotsky and the social formation of mind*. Cambridge, MA: Harvard University Press.

Wertsch, J. (1991). *Voices of the mind*. Cambridge, MA: Harvard University Press.

6   Selective traditions: readings of Vygotsky in writing pedagogy

Courtney B. Cazden

Selective tradition is Raymond Williams's term for the process by which we select from the legacy of the past to explain, support, and justify actions in the present. In his words, it is

> an intentionally selective version of a shaping past and a pre-shaped present, which is then powerfully operative in the process of social and cultural definition and identification. . . . It is a version of the past which is intended to connect with and ratify the present. What it offers in practice is a sense of *predisposed continuity.* (1977, pp. 115, 116)

Whether conscious or not, selective traditions are influential in societal, professional, and personal life.

I realized this importance anew in discussing the ideas in this chapter with colleagues in South Africa. On the societal level, as an essential contribution to a multi- (or non-)racial South Africa, social scientists are analyzing, challenging, exorcizing, and replacing the selective traditions of Christian Nationalism that have supported apartheid. For example, anthropologists (Boonzaier & Sharp, 1988) have followed Williams in analyzing South African keywords: not only *race* but also seemingly more benign terms such as *culture, ethnicity,* and even *community.*

On a more personal and individual level, a South African colleague explained how she introduces her students to the meaning and importance of *critical literacy* by showing how autobiographical statements she has written for different audiences select more scholarly or more political aspects of her own career.

My purpose in this chapter is at an intermediate level between the

I am grateful to many people for help with this chapter: Michael and Sheila Cole for good talks on Vygotsky (Mike) and writing (Sheila) during early morning walks in Solana Beach, California, 1992; the language educators whose work is discussed here who responded to an earlier version; participants in a staff seminar of the Department of Applied English Language Studies, University of Witwatersrand, Johannesburg, September 1993; and the Spencer Foundation for financial support.

165

societal and the individual, the level of professional theorizing: to explore how different influential writing educators base their ideas on different readings of Vygotsky, citing and quoting different passages from his two most familiar books – *Thought and Language* (1962, hereafter *TL;* retranslated as *Thinking and Speech,* 1987, hereafter *TS*) and *Mind in Society* (1978, hereafter *MS*) – and less frequently from *The Psychology of Art* (1971, hereafter *PA*).

I first set forth briefly my understanding of the cited ideas in *TL* and *MS,* including seeming contradictions within the corpus of Vygotsky's own words. Then I suggest a categorization of readings by prominent K-12 writing educators. In so doing, I have not tried to exhaust either the list of significant educators or the ways in which they have called on Vygotsky for ideas and support. My intent is rather to lay out what seem to me, despite considerable overlap, important differences in focus and emphasis. (Omitted here in the interests of space are references to general discussions of Vygotsky's ideas by other scholars [e.g., Wertsch, 1985, 1991].) In conclusion, I recommend an integration of all three readings and raise questions about three other relevant aspects of Vygtosky's ideas.

Overall, this chapter shows how our conceptions of the content and context of child discourse and of the processes of social learning are influenced by our experiential or theoretical predispositions, even in our reading of a single revered ancestor.[1]

Vygotsky's ideas cited by writing educators

In his preface to *Thought and Language,* Vygotsky gives us his own summary of the "contributions" of his research:

> (1) providing experimental evidence that meanings of words undergo evolution during childhood, and defining the basic steps in that evolution; (2) uncovering the singular way in which the child's "scientific" concepts develop, compared with his spontaneous concepts, and formulating the laws governing their development; (3) demonstrating the specific psychological nature and linguistic function of written speech in its relation to thinking; and (4) clarifying, by way of experiments, the nature of inner speech and its relation to thought. (1962, p. xx)

The last three of these contributions have all become important in writing pedagogy, although, as we see in the next section, differentially appropriated by different educators. In discussing them there, I start where Vygotsky ends, with inner speech; follow with the zone of proximal development; and end with relationships between development and instruction, including spontaneous versus scientific concepts.

Inner speech

Vygotsky's discussion of inner speech has been so frequently invoked in discussions of writing that it is hard for me to think about the act of writing as beginning other than with attempts to hold in mind one's inner speech long enough to transcribe it. Important for the teaching of writing is the set of transformations by which inner speech and thought are generated from social experience; the characteristics of inner speech itself; and the transformations in the opposite direction, by which private thought and speech for oneself become publicly communicable writing.

Probably no idea of Vygotsky's has become as familiar as his assertion that all psychological phenomena occur on two planes – first (temporally as well as logically), on the interpsychological plane of social experience, which is always mediated by means of culturally contingent symbolic systems, notably human language as it is encountered in speech and writing; and second, on the internal plane of individual cognition.

Internalization occurs through a series of transformations, during which inner speech acquires its special characteristics, especially "the preponderance of the sense of a word over its meaning" (*TL,* p. 146). Where meaning is precise, definable in a dictionary, and stable across contexts of use, sense is dynamic and fluid, varying from one individual to another depending on connotations accruing from previous experiences with the word, and shifting within a single individual from one context of occurrence to another. Then through further transformations, inner speech becomes the still more inward thought: "the next plane of verbal thought, the one still more inward than inner speech . . . has its own structure, and the transition from it to speech is no easy matter" (*TL,* p. 149).

When we consider the outward journey, from thought through inner speech to writing, we have to start even further inside, with the affective, volitional tendencies and desires that activate and motivate these inner processes. Then, because thought occurs in simultaneous, whole images that do not necessarily coincide with units of language, it must be partitioned, re-created, and completed as it is transformed into words: "In his [a speaker's] mind the whole thought is present at once, but in speech it has to be developed successively" (*TL,* p. 150). The result is a "rough draft in thought": "Inner speech acts as an internal rough draft in oral as well as in inner speech" (*TS,* p. 272).[2] In Vygotsky's lyrical metaphor for the whole sequence, affect is "the wind that puts into motion the cloud that gushes a shower of words" (combining *TL,* p. 150 and *TS,* pp. 281–282).

Because the initial shower of words is still saturated with idiosyncratic sense, it is transcribable onto a page but must be further revised to be communicable to others. This is Vygotsky's explanation of why writing can seem so difficult: "The change from maximally compact inner speech to maximally detailed written speech requires what might be called deliberate semantics – deliberate structuring of the web of meaning" (*TL*, p. 100).

The zone of proximal development

Any person's experience with the external world is mediated not only by symbolic systems but also by other persons. The zone of proximal development (ZPD) is the difference between what a person can do alone and what he or she can do with assistance. Whereas Vygotsky emphasizes assistance from a more knowledgeable adult, contemporary research has also described assistance among peers.

The metaphorical term *scaffold* was first used to name tutorial interactions between expert and novice by Bruner and his colleagues (Wood, Bruner, & Ross, 1976). Since then, it has become a common name for forms of assistance in a learner's ZPD, whether provided less deliberately by parents or more deliberately by teachers. Because scaffolds are literally temporary, adjustable frameworks for construction-in-progress, their metaphorical sense retains the important Vygotskian meaning of an ever-shifting ZPD.[3]

Within that shifting ZPD, the learner gradually internalizes, and comes to enact alone, new forms of deliberate attention (*MS*, p. 83), new instrumental actions and functional integrations, and new goals – all previously provided by the more expert partner(s). Goals are one expression of the unity of affect and intellect that Vygotsky seeks to reconstitute (*TL*, p. 8). In the spirit of his inner speech metaphor, the acquisition of new goals provides winds from new directions to activate thoughts and actions.

In *TL*'s first chapter, "The Problem and the Approach," Vygotsky contrasts "two essentially different modes of analysis . . . possible in the study of psychological structures": One that fails "analyzes complex psychological wholes into elements," whereas "the right course to follow is to use the other type of analysis, which may be called analysis into units" – since dividing water into the units of rain drops retains such properties, whereas deconstructing water into its elements of hydrogen and oxygen does not (*TL*, pp. 3–5). Vygotsky applies this methodological contrast between units and elements to the researcher's analysis of word meanings. But it can, I believe, also be applied to the expert's or teacher's analysis of a learner's task. Part of the power of the ZPD/ scaffold model of instruction is that such help enables the learner to participate from the beginning in a whole, meaningful unit of functional activity – whether weaving a rug, preparing a meal, performing music, or reading and writing.

When novice and expert act together, their understanding of the meaning of the whole activity, its goals and its instrumental acts, will necessarily overlap only in part. The fact of some overlap makes possible the joint, collaborative activity, and the fact of only partial overlap makes possible continued growth by the learner through that collaboration. This important overlap relationship is clearest in Vygotsky's discussion of the child's development of word meaning: The child and the adult share reference (to some concrete object) before they share meaning (in conceptual terms) (*TL*, p. 60). It is the shared reference that makes communication possible, and it is the accumulated communications, about varied referents in varied contexts, that then become the source of the child's transformations of understanding into increasingly conventional meaning.[4]

Relationships between development and instruction

In *TL*, Vygotsky's discussion of the relationship between development and instruction occurs in the chapter on "The Development of Scientific Concepts in Childhood"; in *MS*, there is a separate chapter on "Interaction Between Learning and Development." His goal for school instruction is the development of higher mental functions, which are characterized by awareness and control, entailing the increasing systematicity of concepts in the child's mind. This systematicity, not the particular domain of their content, is what Vygotsky means by *scientific* or – a less misinterpretable term – *nonspontaneous* (*TL*, p. 85). Nonspontaneous concepts "cannot be absorbed ready-made," and so cannot be taught by direct instruction that would result only in "empty verbalism . . . simulating knowledge . . . but actually covering up a vacuum" (*TL*, p. 83). Instruction can and should build on, reorganize, and transform the spontaneous concepts previously acquired from out-of-school experience.

Included in this discussion of spontaneous/scientific relationships (most detailed in *TS*, pp. 214–222) is one of Vygotsky's two discussions of writing. Here Vygotsky begins with the emphatic statement that "the development of writing does not repeat the development of the history of speaking" (*TL*, p. 98). In other words, three contrasting sets of constructs are here aligned:

development	instruction
spontaneous concepts	scientific concepts
speech	writing

It is not easy to reconcile this emphasis in *TL* on the differences between speech acquired spontaneously and writing learned in school with Vygotsky's other discussion of writing in the final chapter in *MS* on "The Prehistory of Written Language." Here Vygotsky finds the developmental roots of writing in gesture, symbolic play, and drawing. He ends with "three exceptionally important practical conclusions" (*MS*, p. 116): that writing should be taught in the preschool years, that it "should be incorporated into a task that is necessary and relevant for life," and that it should "be *taught* naturally" (emphasis in the original) – that is in play, to whose role in development the penultimate chapter in *MS* is devoted. Included is the statement that "In the same way as children learn to speak, they should be able to learn to read and write" (*MS*, p. 118), which seems to contradict directly the statement quoted previously about the differences between the two processes.

Without understanding the temporal relationship of the two discussions in the development of Vygotsky's ideas, or the context for the original version of the *MS* chapter (remembering that this book, unlike *TL*, was not written as a book by Vygotsky himself, but is rather a collection of Vygotsky's writings put together by the four *MS* editors), it is hard to reconcile the two discussions. We can note that the *MS* chapter is titled "Prehistory," implying perhaps that qualitative changes occur when the "history" of written language begins in school. Supporting this interpretation is Vygotsky's general statement in the *MS* chapter on "Interaction Between Learning and Development" that "Any learning a child encounters in school always has a previous history" (*MS*, p. 84) and his call at the end of that chapter for research that will analyze further what is, at the time of writing, a "hypothesis [of] the unity but not the identity of learning processes and internal developmental processes" (*MS*, pp. 90–91).

A more specific reconciliation that is compatible with the contrast between prehistory and history is suggested by Deborah Hicks:

> I found myself wondering . . . whether Vygotsky [in *MS*] is talking about writing as a modality rather than as a discourse, or mode of thinking [as in *TL*]. Could it be that writing [as a modality] and non-

spontaneous (scientific) thinking are separate processes that later merge, in much the same way that speech and thinking are separate processes that later merge? (Personal communication, April 28, 1993)

As we will see, the seeming contradiction between the discussions of writing in *TL* and *MS* has been one important source of divergent readings of Vygotsky by different writing theorists. Those who cite only *TL* and those who cite only *MS* stand, with respect to recommendations for instruction, on very different foundations.

How writing educators cite Vygotsky's ideas

At the risk of oversimplification, I suggest three clusters of interpretations of Vygotsky's ideas: one centering on inner speech and implicit knowledge, the second on more explicit scaffolded assistance, and the third on cultural and political aspects of writing tasks.[5]

First reading: focus on inner speech and tacit knowledge

For this reading, pride of place belongs to James Britton, now retired from the Institute of Education at the University of London. He began writing about the implications of Vygotsky for English language arts at least as early as 1970 in *Language and Learning,* (reissued 1992). In a recent article on "Vygotsky's Contribution to Pedagogical Theory," he develops his ideas on inner speech:

> By this account, then, we *think* by handling "post-language symbols" – forms that began as speech but which have been successively freed from the constraints of the grammar of the spoken language and from the constraints of conventional public word meanings. It is this freedom that characterizes the fluidity of thought – and accounts for the necessity of *imposing organization* upon our thoughts when we want to communicate them.
>
> It was a brilliant insight on Vygotsky's part to realize that when speech for oneself becomes internalized it is in large part because the child, in handling the freer forms of speech that constitute that mode, begins to be capable of carrying out mental operations more subtle than anything he or she can put into words. (1987, p. 24)

If the source of inner speech is the shared social activity of the child, then classrooms must be language-rich communities. In such communities, according to Britton, teachers should "open up for the learner 'the zone of proximal development' . . . by *lending consciousness* to those learners and enabling them to perform in this relationship tasks they

could not achieve if left to themselves" (1987, p. 25). But, cautions
Britton, such assistance should not attempt to make the implicit explicit:

> [A] learner by taking part in rule-governed social behavior may pick up
> the rules by means hardly distinguishable from the processes by which
> they were first socially derived – and by which they continue to be
> amended. On the other hand, along may come the traditional teacher
> and – with the best of intentions, trying to be helpful – set out to ob-
> serve the behavior, analyse to codify the rules and teach the outcome as
> a recipe. Yes, this may sometimes be helpful, but as consistent peda-
> gogy it is manifestly counter-productive. (1987, p. 26)

Two emphases have been particularly important in Britton's continuing influence. First, drawing on Vygotsky's *Psychology of Art,* especially
in the new addition to *Language and Learning* (1992, pp. 304–316) and
in his latest writing, *Literature in Its Place* (1993), Britton values "literature": "making something of language rather than doing something with
language" (1992, p. 309). This implies a curriculum that emphasizes
writing in what he calls the *spectator* rather than the *participant* role –
that is, poetic genres such as narratives and poetry rather than transactional genres written to inform or persuade. Second, citing Polanyi's
(1958) analysis of tacit learning and subsidiary awareness, Britton (e.g.,
1985) maintains the special importance of out-of-awareness generative
processes controlled by the learner's purpose and the community's feedback and the futility, even destructiveness, of explicit teaching.

Kenneth and Yetta Goodman, leaders of the "whole-language" movement that has been so influential in elementary schools, join Britton in
rejecting explicit teaching. About "Vygotsky in a whole-language perspective" they write:

> The whole language view of literacy development is an immersion
> view. . . . Any attempt by well-meaning adults to make the rules ex-
> plicit can actually inhibit learning. (1990, pp. 225, 233)

In their discussion of Vygotsky's concept of the ZPD (1990, p. 227),
the Goodmans point out the seeming contradiction between two of his
statements, both from the compilation of his writings published as *Mind
in Society.* The first is from the chapter on "Interaction Between Learning and Development":

> School learning introduces something fundamentally new into the
> child's development. In order to elaborate the dimensions of school
> learning we will describe a new and exceptionally important concept
> without which the issue cannot be resolved: the zone of proximal devel-
> opment. (1978, p. 84)

The second is from the chapter on "The Role of Play in Development":

> Play creates a zone of proximal development of the child. In play a child always behaves beyond his average age, above his daily behavior; in play it is as though he were a head taller than himself. As in the focus of a magnifying glass, play contains all the developmental tendencies in a condensed form and is itself a major source of development. (1978, p. 102)

These contrasting quotations about Vygotsky's construct of the ZPD parallel the contrast in his discussion of writing discussed earlier.

The Goodmans agree with the second quotation but not with the first, and they argue against some of the distinctions that Vygotsky discusses at length. For the Goodmans, learning to write follows the same process as learning to speak, whereas Vygotsky emphasizes the more deliberate and self-conscious structuring of the web of meaning that writing entails. For the Goodmans, learning scientific concepts at school is, or should be, no different from learning spontaneous concepts at home, whereas Vygotsky describes them as contrasting relationships between systems of verbal concepts and firsthand experience.[6]

One educator, James Moffett, bridges the first and second groups. Like Britton, his theoretical perspective is grounded in the nature of inner speech; but he has developed a more fully articulated instructional program than that discussed by the educators thus far (Moffett & Wagner, 1992, is the most recent version). In the chronological compilation of his talks and articles produced between 1970 and 1980, Moffett (1981) explains that he "first became interested in inner speech while studying literature [especially Joyce, Woolf, Faulkner, and Eliot] as an undergraduate" (p. 133), "before reading Piaget, Vygotsky or Mead" (p. 62). Although references to Piaget are more frequent than references to Vygotsky throughout these essays, the latest and longest chapter in the book, "Writting, Inner Speech and Meditation," mentions "the enthusiasm of Piaget and Americans for the work of Lev Vygotsky and A. R. Luria, whose school has for decades insisted that the sociohistorical origins of thought have not been adequately emphasized" (p. 137).[7]

Here are some excerpts from Moffett's detailed discussion in this essay on relationships between inner speech and writing.

> Whatever eventuates as a piece of writing can begin only as some focusing on, narrowing of, tapping off of, and editing of that great ongoing inner panorama that William James dubbed the "stream of consciousness." What I will call here "inner speech" is a version of that stream which has been more verbally distilled and which can hence more directly serve as the wellspring of writing. (p. 135)

However personal or impersonal the subject matter, all writing as authoring must be some revision of inner speech for a purpose and an audience. (p. 140)

So much of the dullness, awkwardness, shallowness, and opacity that teachers object to in student writing owes to skimming along in the froth instead of plunging into the current, where intuition lines up with intelligence and particularities of experience correct for cliche. (p. 140)

About the teaching of writing that must follow from "defining writing as revision of inner speech," Moffett adds to the more commonly accepted possibilities of revision "two less familiar teaching issues":

the immediate one of how best to set conditions for tapping and focusing inner speech at the moment of writing down, and the long range one of how best to develop the highest quality of inner speech so that when one sits down to write, the thought that spontaneously presents itself offers the best wherewithal for the more visible and audible composition that will follow. (p. 90)

From these premises, Moffett has worked out detailed suggestions for the K-12 curriculum and for teaching that stress oral language development in the classroom; integrated language arts programs that make reading and writing as mutually reinforcing as listening and speaking are for younger children, and thereby help students experience a variety of genres across "the university of discourse"; and conferences with the teacher and peers to help writers expand ideas and images into explicitness appropriate for the task at hand.

Second reading: focus on scaffolded assistance

Although educators in both the first and second groups incorporate Vygotsky's construct of the ZPD, those in the second group incorporate his discussions of school instruction (in both *TL* and *MS*) more than his discussion of the more child-designed context of play (*MS*). In addition, educators in this second group have grafted onto Vygotsky's ideas Bruner's construct of instructional scaffolds.

In the concluding discussion of their research monograph on *How Writing Shapes Thinking*, Langer and Applebee describe their graft:

This interpretation of the results of our studies has led us to develop an alternative view of effective instruction [alternative to the still dominant curriculum of practice exercises separated from purposive activities]. . . . The view we have adopted grows out of a more general view of language learning, one that has been heavily influenced by the work of both Vygotsky and Bruner . . . [who] see language learning as growing out of a communicative relationship where the adult helps the child understand as well as complete new tasks. . . .

The power of these early language-learning strategies is attested to by the rapid growth of language in the young child, but only recently have we begun to understand these strategies and more recently still to use them as a framework for examining instruction. . . . [W]e have been developing the concept of instructional scaffolding as an important component of effective literacy instruction, functioning much as the adult in adult–child pairs: simplifying the situation, clarifying the structure, helping the child accomplish tasks that would otherwise be too difficult, and providing the framework and rules of procedure that will gradually be internalized until the instructional support is no longer needed. (1987, pp. 139–140)

It is probably not accidental that some of the most detailed analyses of writing instruction in these scaffolding terms describe programs designed for students who need more help than mainstream classrooms usually provide and who must engage in accelerated learning if they are to have any chance to catch up. Clay and Cazden (1990) analyze the writing (as well as the reading) segment of the Reading Recovery program imported from New Zealand for 6-year-olds who have not caught on to reading and writing, and Englert (1992) discusses instruction for "learning disabled" students – both in Vygotskian terms.[8]

In most descriptions, scaffolds are constructed by the teacher for individual students, and the year-long training for Reading Recovery teachers is largely devoted to developing the teacher's ability to fine-tune interactions in the individual child's ZPD in order to set just the right challenge and provide the least possible help. In regular classrooms, brief moments of such individualized help can be given during writing conferences, but more such assistance must necessarily be given in groups.

To my knowledge, Vygotsky does not discuss assistance to learners' ZPDs in a group context, and it is easy to limit one's vision to individual tutorials. But group scaffolds are conceivable, in which ZPDs for individual members will differ but within a range that makes collaboration in a common effort still possible. One Australian educator, Brian Gray, has drawn on analyses of mother–child interactions during book reading (e.g., Goldfield & Snow, 1984) and on Vygotsky in developing teaching strategies, called *concentrated language encounters,* for helping Aboriginal children learn the ways of using oral and written language expected in school. These strategies can be interpreted as a complex coordination of group and individual scaffolds.

Concentrated language encounters depend centrally on repeated firsthand experience with oral and written language use in significant settings – for example, in field trips to observe the doctors, nurses, receptionists, and patients at the local health clinic – and then many opportunities to role-play those activities back at school, with the help of the teacher who participates actively "in role." Some written language forms – transactional genres, as Britton would call them – are integral to social roles, such as telephone messages taken by the receptionist, patients' records kept by the doctor, and instructions on how to bandage a cut. Others are narratives of personal experiences like accidents.

Gray's work (1987; Gray & Cazden, 1992) has become the pedagogical component of what in Australia is called the *genre teaching* of writing, which has been stimulated by perceived limitations of the Australian adoption of ideas from process writing in particular and progressive education in general. Cope and Kalantzis (1993) present various currents within this Australian movement. Rationales for genre teaching combine Basil Bernstein's (1975) warnings about the limitations of implicit pedagogy for many working-class children, Vygotsky's ZPD as interpreted by Gray, and Australian linguist James Martin's development of the construct of genre from the systemic functional linguistics of Michael Halliday.

We are now far from the reliance on tacit learning espoused by Britton and the Goodmans, even though all base their work on a reading of some text from Vygotsky. Arguments between Australian genre educators and Britton and his colleagues in England provide the most direct contrast. One set of these arguments has been collected by Reid (1987). Writing more recently in a chapter on "Recent Perspectives" added to the reissue of Britton's *Language and Learning,* Britton continues the dialogue by taking issue with the discussion of genre in an earlier book by Gunther Kress (1982). Because the new edition of *Language and Learning* is not now readily available in the United States, I provide here an extended quote:

> Gunther Kress's book has a splendid account of the way speaking and writing differ as texts. . . . But it is when he comes to discuss genre that Kress presents a view of writing, mistaken in my opinion, that suggests restrictions under which individual writers work, whether child or adult. The application of predetermined genre rules must inevitably restrict the process familiar to many teachers by which young writers 'rediscover the wheel', or may even unearth alternatives to it. "Society rests," Kress believes, "on a vast network of conventions, and while these conventions are arbitrary when considered in isolation, they are not arbitrary within the context of any specific society" (Kress, 1982, 124). Surely the issue is whether a writer must imitate existing models,

perhaps aware that he is doing so, or whether he is free to write the way he wants, concerned only that a reader can respond with understanding. Earlier in the same chapter Kress seems to be assuming that teachers should teach the rules governing a genre, and are only prevented from doing so because "linguists have only recently begun the task of providing characterizations of genres". (Kress, 1982, 112)

Once again, the linguists' ability to taxonomize language threatens to yield categories that must be taught as an aspect of what school writing requires. (1992, pp. 303–304)

Responding to Britton is easy: "But an author is rarely free to write the way he [sic] wants." Deciding, theoretically and practically, what should be the place of written language conventions in teaching writing is much harder. A further aspect of those decisions comes from the third reading of Vygotsky.

Third reading: focus on the politics of culture

Just as Moffett is the bridge between the first and second readings, Kress is the bridge between the second and third. Kress worked for many years in Australia and now holds the senior position in the English and Media Studies Department at London's Institute of Education once held by Britton. He writes about the Australian work:

From the beginning, genre work has been both a pedagogical and a political project, a pedagogical project motivated by the political project of allowing greater, fairer, possibly equal access to the cultural and social resources and benefits of this kind of society. . . . However, there is a need to keep refining and extending those aims. . . . A language curriculum appropriate for a multi-cultural society . . . will [among other goals] discuss the relations of the various languages in that society in the existing configurations of power, and make available means of analysing that structure, providing means of developing critiques and, via critiques, the possibility of change. (1993, pp. 28–30)

Including this third interpretation as a reading of Vygotsky is suggested by Tony Burgess (1993), a former colleague of Britton's still at the University of London. For Burgess, the important contrast is between the first reading and the third. He characterizes the educators in the first group, especially Britton, as part of "a tradition of thought about the role of symbol in human affairs":

In the first reading, it is the relevance of Vygotskian thought to the individual child which is given the most attention. Readers of this persuasion are interested in learning, development and the role of language in thinking. They are drawn to the account of the symbol and

> symbolizing because this fits well with a stress on creativity and the
> child's active contribution to her learning.
>
>   These readers do not neglect the social, contrary to what opponents
> say. But they tend to treat social considerations in general and benefi-
> cent terms . . . and they tend to illustrate culture without reference to
> power and conflict. Their interest is in processes and practices. . . .
> The points which are underlined are that learning is interactional and
> that culture is socially constructed. (1993, p. 3)

Burgess's contrasting reading foregrounds the "politics of culture" in the
tradition of Gramsci (1971) and Williams (1977). In explaining the need
for this interpretation, Burgess writes:

> An underlying target for me was some confusion around 'cultural' and
> 'social' as terms in the way Vygotsky is taken up. Quite often, here, the
> use slips back into no more than 'interactional'. There is a tendency for
> Vygotskian thought to come to justify a conventional social psychology
> which misses the full import of a 'cultural', 'social', 'historical' position,
> whether or not such a position is without qualification to be attributed
> to Vygotsky in the sense I'm trying to contrast. I believe we want in
> English teaching a strengthened version of development and language
> and learning, one which keeps the focus of (e.g.) Dartmouth but which
> can be connected with theorisations of 'difference', 'variety', ideology
> and power. A fully 'social' view, in other words. (Personal communica-
> tion, April 1993)[9]

In his discussion of this reading, Burgess cites three books by Vygotsky
(1962, 1971, 1978), plus several articles, but gives no direct supporting
quotations.

   He and I agree that issues of variation are compatible with Vygotsky's
ideas, (which is the justification for including these ideas as a "reading"
of Vygotsky). The analysis of "social" can be extended, without contradiction, in just the ways he (and others) suggest. But we also agree that
one has to go to the writings of Bakhtin (1981) and Vološinov (1986) for
explicit attention to these issues.[10]

   For example, in a critique of genre theory and pedagogy Harold
Rosen (like Britton, now retired from the University of London) cites
Bakhtin but not Vygotsky:

> We can see in every act of writing those two forces at work [Bakhtin's
> contrast between authoritative and internally persuasive discourse]. We
> can never totally escape the centripetal pull: we cannot jump out of the
> language system and its practices. On the other hand, we do not have to
> elevate that system into an object which has achieved perfection. On the
> contrary, it is necessary to insist again and again and again on the need to
> disrupt the authoritative voice with the unheard voices of our students,
> to help them engage in the difficult struggles (so difficult for all of us) to
> articulate, develop, refine and advance their meanings as against the

> mere reproduction of words of the textbook, the worksheet, the encyclo-
> pedia and the guides. To insist on this involves squaring up to the oppres-
> sive power of authoritative language. (1992, p. 127)

Whereas Britton criticizes genre pedagogy, included in the second reading, from the perspective of the first, Rosen criticizes it from the perspective of the third.

What this third reading adds to the first two is not simply the dimension of variation in language use and social power in societies heterogeneous in gender, culture, and class, but also how these dimensions of variation affect the individual thinker, learner, and writer. In his answer to the question "What's missing in the metaphor of scaffolding?" Addison Stone argues that "symbolic values attached to ways of seeing and doing" – especially, I would add, to writing – will influence the interpersonal dynamics of scaffolding interactions. "This influence is mediated in part via its effects on the participants' provision [by the teacher] and uptake [by the learner] of appropriate semiotic challenges" (1993, p. 179).

In other words, in this reading, individual development may include resistance as well as internalization (Goodnow, 1993), and text conventions may be contested as well as learned (Diamondstone, 1993, and Dyson, 1993a, analyze interactions from primary and middle school classrooms, respectively, in these terms; see also Hicks, this volume).

In adopting Burgess's adjective "political" only for this last reading, I am not implying that only those who adopt this reading are concerned with the politics of education. On the contrary, Britton, the Goodmans, the Australian genre group, and Burgess – to consider only those I know well enough to characterize in this way – would agree to a great extent on a political analysis of society, regardless of how far apart they may be on what English teaching should be and do. That fact makes their different readings of Vygotsky all the more interesting.

Conclusions

Given the length of this chapter, there is space here only for two brief concluding purposes. First, I want to state my belief that we should work toward an integration of all three readings as a more powerful basis for writing instruction than that provided by any one reading alone.[11] Second, in this integration, we need to extend Vygotsky's ideas about inner speech in two ways – to symbol systems other than words and to sources of creativity – and to consider, at least as a hypothesis, his words in *TL* about transfer.

The fullest discussion of these two extensions of inner speech is by Stephen Witte. In a lengthy article, "Context, Text, and Intertext," Witte (1992) analyzes instances of situated writing – from complex products by horticulture students, lawyers, and corporate managers to grocery lists – that illustrate "boundary problems" between verbal writing and graphic symbols that are too easily dismissed as nonwriting. He probes *TL* for whether Vygotsky's discussion of semiotic mediation encompasses signs other than words, even though his term *inner speech* biases readers' interpretation to words alone, and he argues for the broader interpretation. (See Dyson, especially 1993b, and Smagorinsky & Coppock, in press, for Vygotskian documentations of the importance of drawings for the writing of young children and of a 16-year-old in an alternative program for substance abusers, respectively.)[12] Witte also raises the problem of explaining sources of creativity:

> [A]n adequate theory of writing must be able to account for the fact that writing can be both a process of translating ideas or thoughts into visible language and a process of discovering meaning through language. . . . Innovations are difficult to explain in purely social terms. (1992, p. 263)

To avoid interpreting Vygotsky as advocating a transmission pedagogy, we need not only the critical literacy of the third reading but also a place in our theory for the seemingly miraculous generation of new meanings during the very process of writing that so many writers (including me) have experienced. Perhaps, as Britton's discussion of inner speech's "freer forms" in the first reading suggests, we should think of the sense-saturated quality of inner symbols as a positive, even essential, source of individual creativity, of authoring, and not just a limitation to be overcome.

A third question that might be raised concerns transfer of training, one name for what Vygotsky calls *formal discipline* (*TL,* pp. 96–97), or the specificity of mental abilities (MS). At the end of a memorial issue honoring his long-term colleague and *MS* coeditor, Sylvia Scribner, Michael Cole writes:

> [O]ne of the major intellectual issues we jointly addressed over the years (one not resolved to this day, judging by the diversity of views expressed in the commentaries presented above) was how best to characterize the specificity or generality of the cognitive consequences of participating in different cultural systems mediated by different technologies. (1992, p. 148)

Vygotsky discusses this issue of specificity/generality in both *MS* and *TL* as an aspect of relationships between instruction and development.

In *MS*, he rejects three different theoretical positions, including Thorndike's arguments against "*general* capabilities," which he characterizes as follows:

> Learning is [according to Thorndike] . . . the acquisition of many specialized abilities for thinking about a variety of things. Learning does not alter our overall ability to focus attention but rather develops various abilities to focus attention on a variety of things. . . . [B]ecause each activity depends on the material with which it operates, the development of consciousness is the development of a set of particular, independent capabilities or a set of particular habits. (*MS*, p. 83)

In *TL*, Vygotsky suggests an explanation for Thorndike's research results by differentiating between two kinds of instruction:

> the narrowly specialized training in some skill, such as typing, involving habit formation and exercise and more often found in trade schools for adults, and the kind of instruction given school children, which activates large areas of consciousness. . . . [I]n the higher processes emerging during the cultural development of the child, formal discipline must play a role that it does not play in the elementary processes: All the higher functions have in common awareness, abstraction, and control. (*TL*, p. 97)

As far as I am aware, no writing educators in any of the three readings cite this discussion, perhaps because of the contemporary dominance of the construct of literacies, of writing as constituted in diverse social practices, and of situated cognition more generally – which Vygotsky's characterization of Thorndike's ideas quoted previously fit remarkably well. But especially because Vygotsky's discussion in *TL* of writing in school immediately follows his differentiation between these two kinds of instruction, we should at least consider how the teaching of writing can be more than a "trade school" and how it might contribute to the development of transferable capabilities of "awareness, abstraction, and control."

Notes

1 Only after presenting the original version of this chapter at the University of Delaware did I discover that more than a decade earlier, in October 1981, the Third Delaware Symposium on Language Studies at the same university included a presentation on the same topic: "Soviet Psycholinguistics: Implications for Teaching of Writing," by James Zebrowski. He warned against the limitations of considering Vygotsky's ideas apart from the social context in which they were developed:

> Three qualities, in my mind, distinguish the Soviet theory of activity, and its application to the study of speech activity specifically, from corresponding U.S. alternatives in the field of composition. First, human beings are viewed

as essentially active participants in both their world and in their learning. . . . Second, language and culture are viewed relationally. This means that language processes are always studied not simply in terms of themselves, but also in terms of their use, their history, their connections to the other parts of social life. Third, language and cognitive processes are viewed dynamically, that is, always in change. The focus of study, then, becomes what changes and how it changes both in language and in cognitive processes, rather than what "is." (1982, pp. 53–54)

My discussion is related to Zebroski's in two ways. First, we both focus on Vygotsky's ideas for teaching writing. Second, and less obviously, Zebroski's admonition that "language processes are [and should be] studied . . . in terms of their history, their connections to other parts of social life" can be applied to the study of discourse on more macro, societal and public levels as well as to the more micro, cognitive and individual. One such language process is the formation of "selective traditions."

2 The phrase *rough draft* sounds so contemporary that I wondered if it was a translator's addition. Michael Cole confirmed that a word meaning something like "rough" does appear in the original Russian (personal communication, March 1993).

3 In his chapter in this volume, Erickson analyzes the quality of "shared time" that contributes to the success of scaffolding interactions.

4 Vygotsky's discussion of reference and meaning is in the chapter in *TL* on "An Experimental Study of Concept Formation," a chapter rarely cited in educational citations of his work. In a theoretical introduction to a book on genre teaching in Australia that is part of the second reading, Cope and Kalantzis (1993) point out that "pseudo concepts," which immediately precede the development of true concepts, also involve a coincidence of words and referents that "works pedagogically" (p. 69).

5 An earlier version of this chapter was sent to the colleagues whose work is discussed. I am grateful to them for their thoughtful responses, many of which are incorporated here, but I take responsibility for interpretations in this final version.

6 In a new book on his experience teaching in a South African university for 5 months, Frank Smith (an influential language educator whose views are often similar to those of the Goodmans) has a cryptic comment about Vygotsky. When two Applied English Language Studies students request a lecture on him,

> I rashly say that Vygotsky's contribution, though important, could be summarized in a couple of sentences. The rest is argument, evidence, and applications, which the class as a whole might do well without, even though such matters could be pursued and examined by one or two of them. Of course, I am immediately challenged to summarize Vygotsky's position in a couple of sentences. I say that anything a child can do with help today, the child will be able to do alone tomorrow. There is, therefore, no point in teaching anything that a child does not immediately understand and find useful or relevant. (1993, p. 66)

I discovered this quotation after the completion of this chapter, and so was not able to send it to Smith for his response.

7 Piaget's "enthusiasm" was expressed in an insert he wrote for distribution with early printings of the 1962 edition of *TL*.

8 Differences between educators in the first and second groups on this point have come to have more than theoretical significance. It is currently involved, for example, in the wariness of some whole language advocates in both the United States and the United Kingdom to acknowledge the value – even when well-documented by evaluation research in New Zealand, Australia, the United States and the United Kingdom – of the

accelerated literacy learning in Reading Recovery programs by children who were initially the least successful in their school cohort. Don Holdaway, a South Pacific educator influential in the development of many whole language programs in the United States, has written a very thoughtful article in the hope of lessening the "animosity among the people representing the two sets of ideas" (1992, p. 1).

9 Dartmouth College was the site of the influential 1966 conference that first brought together scholars of English teaching, including Britton and Moffett, from both sides of the Atlantic (Dixon, 1967).

10 One researcher writing on Vygotsky's legacy even suggests that "the contribution of the cultural-historical school is mainly on the epistemological level in the search for the invariance in the psychological processes of humans" (Hedegaard, 1992, p. 122). Could Vygotsky's silence on social variation have been influenced by his involvement in building a new classless society in the Soviet Union of the 1920s and early 1930s and his (at least public) optimism about the possibility of its success?

11 Over the past 25 years, my own work has emphasized each of the readings in turn: the first in *Child Language and Education* (1972) after graduate student socialization in the 1960s into Harvard, where both Vygotsky's *TL* and Chomsky were in the intellectual air; the second since "Peekaboo as an Instructional Model" (1979) written after a trip to the Institute of Defectology in Moscow; and the third only recently, especially in "Vygotsky, Hymes and Bakhtin: From Word to Utterance and Voice" (in Cazden, 1992, and Forman, Minick & Stone, 1993).

12 Vygotsky's seeming bias toward verbal language is not confined to *TL* – as Britton (1993, pp. 8, 83) points out, "The psychology of art is actually about literature" – and it is tempting to speculate about its source. Witte asks whether "the term inner speech might not have been used if the project Vygotsky undertook [in *TL*] had not been to address the inadequacies of Piaget's concept of egocentric speech" (1992, p. 256). Vera John-Steiner, one of the *MS* editors and long interested in what she calls "cognitive pluralism" (1987, 1991), suggests that a bias toward words might be a legacy of Vygotsky's Jewish socialization (personal communication, 1993).

References

Bakhtin, M. (1981). Discourse in the novel. In *The dialogic imagination*. Austin: University of Texas Press.

Bernstein, B. (1975). Class and pedagogies: Visible and invisible. In *Class, codes, and control* (Vol. 3). London: Routledge & Kegan Paul.

Boonzaier, E., & Sharp, J. (Eds.). *South African keywords: The uses and abuses of political concepts*. Capetown and Johannesburg: David Philip.

Britton, J. (1985). Second thoughts on learning. *Language Arts, 62*, 72–77.

Britton, J. (1987). Vygotsky's contribution to pedagogical theory. *English in Education* (UK), *21*, 22–26.

Britton, J. (1992). *Language and learning* (rev. ed.). Harmondsworth, UK: Penguin.

Britton, J. (1993). *Literature in its place*. Portsmouth, NH: Boynton/Cook.

Britton, J., Burgess, T., Martin, N., McLeod, A., & Rosen, H. (1975). *The development of writing abilities (11–18)*. London: Macmillan.

Burgess, T. (1993). Reading Vygotsky: Notes from within English teaching. In H. Daniels (Ed.), *Charting the agenda: Educational activity after Vygotsky*. London and New York: Routledge.

Cazden, C. B. (1972). *Child language and education*. New York: Holt, Reinhart & Winston.

Cazden, C. B. (1979). Peekaboo as an instructional model: Discourse development at home and at school. *Papers and Reports on Child Language Development. No. 17.* Stanford University, Department of Linguistics. Revised version in B. Bain (Ed.), (1983), *The sociogenesis of language and human conduct.* New York: Plenum.

Cazden, C. B. (1988). *Classroom discourse: The language of teaching and learning.* Portsmouth, NH: Heinemann.

Cazden, C. B. (1992). *Whole language plus: Essays on literacy in the United States and New Zealand.* New York: Teachers College Press.

Clay, M., & Cazden, C. B. (1990). A Vygotskian interpretation of Reading Recovery. In Moll (Ed.) (1990). Reprinted in Cazden (1992).

Cole, M. (1992). Sylvia Scribner at LCHC. *Quarterly Newsletter of the Laboratory of Comparative Human Cognition, 14,* 147–151.

Cope, B., & Kalantzis, M. (Eds.). (1993). *The powers of literacy: A genre approach to teaching writing.* Philadelphia: Falmer.

Diamondstone, J. (1993). Register or relevance? Seventh graders write arguments for a mock trial. In J. E. Alatis (Ed.), *Language, communication, and meaning.* Georgetown University Round Table on Languages and Linguistics, 1992. Washington, DC: Georgetown University Press.

Dixon, J. (1967). *Growth through English.* New York: Oxford University Press.

Dyson, A. H. (1993a). *Social worlds of children learning to write in an urban primary school.* New York: Teachers College Press.

Dyson, A. H. (1993b). From prop to mediator: The changing role of written language in children's symbolic repertoires. In B. Spodek & O. Saracho (Eds.), *Yearbook in early childhood education: Vol. 4. Early childhood education and literacy.* New York: Teachers College Press.

Englert, C. S. (1992). Writing instruction from a sociocultural perspective: The holistic, dialogic, and social enterprise of writing. *Journal of Learning Disabilities, 25,* 153–172.

Flower, L. (1979). Writer-based prose: A cognitive basis for problems in writing. *College English, 41,* 19–37.

Forman, E. A., Minick, N., & Stone, C. A. (Eds.). (1993). *Contexts for learning: Sociocultural dynamics in children's development.* New York: Oxford University Press.

Goldfield, B., & Snow, C. (1984). Reading books with children: The mechanics of parental influence on children's reading achievement. In J. Flood (Ed.), *Promoting reading comprehension.* Newark, DE: International Reading Association.

Goodman, Y. M., & Goodman, K. S. (1990). Vygotsky in a whole language perspective. In Moll (Ed.) (1990).

Goodnow, J. (1993). Direction of post-Vygotskian research. In Forman et al. (Eds.) (1993).

Gramsci, A. (1971). *Selections from the prison notebooks.* New York: International Publishers.

Gray, B. (1987). How natural is 'natural' language teaching? Employing wholistic methodology in the classroom. *Australian Journal of Early Childhood, 12.*

Gray, B., & Cazden, C. B. (1992). Concentrated language encounters: The international biography of a curriculum concept. Plenary address to Teachers of English to Speakers of Other Languages (TESOL), Vancouver, March.

Hedegaard, M. (1992). Reflections in honor of Sylvia Scribner's socio-cultural approach. *Quarterly Newsletter of the Laboratory of Comparative Human Cognition, 14,* 122–123.

Holdaway, D. (1992). Reading Recovery in a context of whole language. *Whole Language Teachers Association Newsletter, 7,* 1–4.

John-Steiner, V. (1985). *Notebooks of the mind: Explorations of thinking.* Albuquerque: University of New Mexico Press.

John-Steiner, V. (1991). Cognitive pluralism: A Whorfian analysis. In R. L. Cooper & B. Spolsky (Eds.), *The influence of language on culture and thought: Essays in honor of Joshua A. Fishman's sixty-fifth birthday.* Mouton de Gruyter. Berlin/New York.

Kress, G. (1982). *Learning to write.* London: Routledge & Kegan Paul.

Kress, G. (1993). Genre as social process. In Cope & Kalantzis (1993).

Langer, J. A., & Applebee, A. N. (1987). *How writing shapes thinking: A study of teaching and learning.* Urbana, IL: National Council of Teachers of English.

Moffett, J. (1981). Writing, inner speech, and meditation. In *Coming on center: English education in evolution.* Portsmouth, NH: Boynton/Cook.

Moffett, J., & Wagner, B. J. (1992). *Student-centered language arts and reading K–12* (4th ed.). Portsmouth, NH: Boynton/Cook.

Moll, L. C. (Ed.). (1990). *Vygotsky and education: Implications and applications of sociohistorical psychology.* New York: Cambridge University Press.

Polanyi, M. (1958). *Personal knowledge.* London: Routledge & Kegan Paul.

Reid, I. (Ed.). (1987). *The place of genre in learning: Current debates.* Geelong, Australia: Deakin University, Center for Studies in Literary Education.

Rosen, H. (1992). The politics of writing. In K. Kimberley, M. Meek, & J. Miller (Eds.), *New readings: Contributions to an understanding of literacy.* London: A&C Black.

Smagorinsky, P., & Coppock, J. (in press). Cultural tools and the classroom context: An exploration of an artistic response to literature. *Written Communication.*

Smagorinsky, P., & Smith, M. W. (1992). The nature of knowledge in composition and literary understanding: The question of specificity. *Review of Educational Research 62,* 279–305.

Smith, F. (1993). *Whose language? What power? A universal conflict in a South African setting.* New York: Teachers College Press.

Stone, C. A. (1993). What's missing in the metaphor of scaffolding? In E. Forman, N. Minick, & A. Stone (Eds.), *Contexts for learning: Sociocultural dynamics in children's development.* New York: Oxford University Press.

Vološinov, V. N. (1986). *Marxism and the philosophy of language.* Cambridge, MA: Harvard University Press.

Vygotsky, L. S. (1962). *Thought and language.* Cambridge, MA: MIT Press.

Vygotsky, L. S. (1971). *The psychology of art.* Cambridge, MA: MIT Press.

Vygotsky, L. S. (1978). *Mind in society.* Cambridge, MA: Harvard University Press.

Vygotsky, L. S. (1987). *The collected works of L. S. Vygotsky: Vol. 1. Problems of general psychology.* Including the volume *Thinking and speech.* New York and London: Plenum.

Wertsch, J. (1985). *Vygotsky and the formation of mind.* Cambridge, MA: Harvard University Press.

Wertsch, J. (1991). *Voices of the mind.* Cambridge, MA: Harvard University Press.

Williams, R. (1977). *Marxism and literature.* Oxford: Oxford University Press.

Witte, S. P. (1992). Context, text, and intertext: Toward a constructivist semiotic of writing. *Written Communication, 9,* 237–308.

Wood, D., Bruner, J. S. & Ross, G. (1976). The role of tutoring in problem solving. *Journal of Child Psychology and Psychiatry, 17,* 89–100.

Zebroski, J. T. (1982). Soviet psycholinguistics: Implications for teaching of writing. In W. Frawley (Ed.), *Linguistics and literacy.* New York: Plenum.

Part III

Discourse and literacies

7   Sticking to the point: talk about magnets as a context for engaging in scientific discourse

Catherine E. Snow and Brenda F. Kurland

Introduction

This chapter presents data on how children and their mothers talk about magnets. We wanted to know whether discussion between mothers and 5-year-old children on the topic of magnets would be an occasion for scientific discourse, and whether such discourse would be characterized by explanations that differed in form from the more commonly studied narrative talk. Our curiosity about scientific discourse has a number of sources: (1) less interest in children's ability to coconstruct with adults stretches of discourse on a particular topic, on the assumption that such extended discourses require knowledge of rules that go beyond the grammatical rules that govern utterance production; (2) interest in testing the hypothesis that experience with such extended discourse contexts is a good predictor of children's literacy skills and school achievement as they enter the middle grades of elementary school; and (3) interest in seeing whether mother–child discourse about science topics might have some features that could prepare children for classroom discourse on topics of science, social studies, and math. In this chapter, we focus first on the relationship of oral language extended discourse to literacy, and in the discussion we turn to the question of the features of science talk, both at home and in the classroom.

Oral language skills relate to literacy

It has been widely observed that children's oral language skills relate to their literacy skills. For example, the best simple predictor of reading

The authors would like to express their appreciation to the Spencer Foundation and the Ford Foundation, which have funded the Home School Study of Language and Literacy Development; to Patton Tabors, David Dickinson, Diane Beals, Jeanne De Temple, Petra Nicholson, Ellen O'Connell, and all the home visitors and transcribers who have worked on the project; and to Rob Traver, Donald Morrison, and Kay Merseth for insights concerning science education.

189

skills is children's vocabularies (Anderson & Freebody, 1981). Children with language problems typically also show reading problems (Snow, 1993). Children's sophistication in oral language tasks like telling stories and giving definitions relates to their literacy achievement (Snow, 1991). And children who engage at home in oral language interactions that have "literate" features are likely to do well on school literacy tasks (e.g., Heath, 1983, among many others).

One issue of central interest in work at the Harvard Projects in Language Development over the last few years is to find an explanation for the empirical relation between oral language skills and literacy (see Snow, 1993; Snow & Dickinson, 1991, for overviews). What is the mechanism by which oral language accomplishments promote or underlie literacy achievement? Although it is easy to find correlations between aspects of oral language and literacy, it is much harder to find evidence that would provide an unambiguous explanatory link between oral and literate accomplishments. Are oral language skills of a certain type a prerequisite for literacy achievement? Do the factors that promote high levels of oral language also promote literacy? Or does achieving some level of skill in literacy then feed back into higher-level oral language skills?

We have argued that one part of the answer to the question of how oral language skills relate to literacy centers on the crucial problem in literacy of producing and understanding extended discourse (Beals & Tabors, 1993; De Temple & Beals, 1991; De Temple, Wu, & Snow, 1991; Rodino & Snow, in press; Snow, 1983, 1991, 1993; Velasco & Snow, 1993). Extended discourse – a sequence of sentences or even paragraphs on the same topic – is the norm in literacy but may not be very common in many children's oral language experiences. Extended discourse has its own rules and its own "grammar," as complex as the rules that govern the production of correct and grammatical sentences. These rules, we argue, are acquired most readily through participation in the production of extended oral discourse – for example, stories, explanations, or discussions that focus on a single topic over several turns. Of course, oral extended discourse is likely to be conversational – that is, two or more participants coconstruct the discourse – whereas literate extended discourse is typically produced by one writer for a distant, perhaps unknown, reader. Thus, literate extended discourse forms are different from oral conversations on two dimensions: They violate the pragmatics of face-to-face conversation, and they require adjustments in order to make explicit connections across utterances.

Our work has focused on variation in children's access to extended discourse, on the argument that practice in producing and understanding extended discourses of various sorts is likely to promote the skills required to analyze the extended and distanced discourse of classrooms and of literacy.[1] The skills of dealing with extended discourse designed for a distant audience are tapped directly by oral language tasks like telling stories and giving definitions. These are tasks that children who are having problems in literacy acquisition also find very difficult. There is, furthermore, evidence that a large and sophisticated vocabulary, although not itself a discourse skill, is a skill acquired in the context of exposure to extended discourse (Beals & Tabors, 1993; Dickinson, Cote, & Smith, 1993). Extended discourse provides the context needed to learn vocabulary without explicit teaching.

What are the crucial properties of extended discourse that might explain its relation to literacy?

1. *Planning.* One feature of the successful production of extended discourse is that it must be planned, so that interutterance connections are made clear. In oral language, such planning is often indicated by dysfluencies (pauses or *ums*) occurring just before important words. Many of the linguistic devices encountered in literacy are a product of the planning for explicit cohesion; one example is the use of connectives like *because, moreover,* and *however* to mark explicitly the relation of subsequent utterances to previous ones.

2. *Audience needs.* Effective communication requires understanding how much one's audience needs to be told. When talking to strangers, one may need to explain a lot even to tell a simple anecdote, whereas in describing the same incident to a friend, one can assume that the characters, the places, and perhaps even the personality traits that help motivate the anecdote are already known. In conversational exchanges where turns are brief, the audience has considerable opportunity to make it known if their needs are not being met – for example, by asking questions, looking puzzled, or interrupting. On the other hand, the speaker who continues for several utterances, providing no chance for the audience to give feedback, must anticipate what the audience already knows or does not know, whether the discourse is comprehensible or not, and what impact the discourse is having. Analyzing the needs of the audience is, of course, a task that poses great difficulty to new (and even to experienced) writers, and many of the devices one encounters in written text are, again, explicit responses to the perceived needs of the envisioned audience.

3. *Self-monitoring.* To ensure that one's text is responding effectively to the audience's needs and is correctly representing one's intended meaning, producers of extended discourse must engage in self-monitoring and revision. This task is considerably more difficult in the oral mode because it must be done "on line," whereas writers typically have both time and opportunity to return to their texts, reread them with a bit of distance, and revise extensively.

4. *Hierarchical structuring.* Extended discourses occur within particular

genres and with particular purposes. These genres – narratives, for example – have a culturally agreed-on macrostructure that makes the discourse more comprehensible if it is adhered to (Peterson & McCabe, 1983). For middle-class American children, for example, personal experience narratives typically start with some sort of orientation ("We were at the mall, Mom and me"), then relate a problem ("and we couldn't remember where we parked the car"), a series of actions or events ("and we looked everywhere"), a high point ("and Mom decided to call the police because she thought it must have been stolen"), and a resolution ("but just then I saw it parked between two huge school buses. It was right there all along, and we couldn't see it."). This hierarchical structure is less likely to be present in conversational exchanges, even those that may cover the same information content as the extended discourse version of the narrative. And literate presentations are even more tightly macrostructured – in fact, these macrostructures are part of what is taught in writing courses.

Children learn extended discourse skills from family interactions

Under what circumstances are children exposed to and do they have the opportunity to engage in extended discourse in natural settings? Perhaps most widely cited in this regard is the role of reading books: When being read to, or when looking at and discussing picture books, children hear talk that is focused on a single topic over many successive utterances. Particularly in storybooks, the hierarchical structure imposed by the narrative genre is displayed. Furthermore, repeated readings of favorite books enable children and their parents to elaborate on their previous conversations, generating ever more complex and sophisticated discourses around the topic (see, e.g., Snow, 1983; Snow & Goldfield, 1983).

In addition to book reading, perhaps the most intensively studied context for extended discourse, children have opportunities to engage in extended discourse during fantasy play (at least if the play is organized around more complex themes than just chase-and-shoot scenarios). "Playing house," for example, involves assigning roles, planning actions, and engaging in dialogue all centered on a particular plot or scenario, and can be an occasion for many successive utterances that are thematically related to each other (e.g., Galda, 1984; Pellegrini, 1985; Yawkey & Miller, 1984; see also Hicks, this volume, for a translation of such fantasy themes directly into writing).

Most of the analyses and discussions of children's extended discourse skills and experiences have focused on the narrative genre, the one most often encountered in picture books and in fantasy play. The presumption of narrative may serve as one of the contextual factors influencing how children's early encounters with literacy are managed (see Hicks, this volume, for a discussion of contextual influences). It is striking that in the classroom Hicks studied, the teacher often presented journal writing as an opportunity to write "stories" – perhaps presupposing that children prefer writing stories or that stories would elicit their most sophisticated writing. It is not exactly clear why narrative has achieved this status of the default genre, though many explanations seem plausible. Bruner (1986) argues that narrative is the most central, natural way of relating bits of information to each other; that it represents a more accessible way of thinking than the paradigmatic, nonnarrative mode of thought. On the other hand, young children show considerable interest in procedures, in classification, in construction, and in information organized in lists or in taxonomies, and show facility with forms of thinking that are not strictly narrative. Perhaps narratives represent the first noticeable attempts to connected discourse in very young children's language (e.g., Nelson, 1986). But children also evince an early interest in explanations (Beals, 1991; Beals & Snow, 1994), as well as some capacity to participate in producing explanations as early as age 3 (Barbieri, Colavita, & Scheuer, 1990; Beals, 1991). The presupposed primacy of narrative is certainly reflected in children's literature, in which the vast dominance of narrative texts seems to proceed from the assumption that preschool children prefer or most easily understand narrative forms (see, e.g., Egan, 1993). But if offered nonnarrative picture books, many children might just as readily choose them, and children of age 5 have been shown to process as much information from expository as from narrative texts (Pappas, 1993).

The unquestioned focus on the narrative mode as the default for young children's participation in extended discourse may have obscured the importance of another domain of children's discourse, namely explanatory talk about how the world works. The purpose of this chapter is to explore the kinds of talk engaged in by a group of low-income mothers with their 5-year-old children in a situation that made a certain kind of explanatory talk, namely "science talk," a reasonable option; the mothers and children were asked to play with a powerful magnet and a collection of disparate objects that were or were not attracted to the magnet. No instructions were given other than "Play with these toys," leaving open the possibility that these dyads would use the magnet as a focus for fantasy play or kinds of talk other than explanation. We were interested, first, simply in describing the kinds of talk that occurred in this situation. Second, we sought relationships between the ways the mothers structured the talk during the magnet task and their approach to other opportunities for extended discourse – book reading, play with toys that evoked fantasy, and unstructured dinner table conversations. Finally, we were interested in whether children's opportunities for participation in extended scientific discourse related to their literacy skills in the same way as has already been shown for their participation in extended narrative discourse. We also speculate in the Discussion section about the relation between mother–child explanatory talk in the sessions we observed and the nature of classroom discourse on science topics in the elementary grades.

The study

The mother–child conversations discussed here were collected as part of a larger study of the determinants of literacy achievement in children from low-income families (Snow, 1991). We report here on a group of 68 children[2] we have followed from age 3 through the early school years. During the preschool period, we carried out yearly observations in the children's homes, each including an interview and a series of structured interactions with their mothers, and in their preschool or kindergarten classrooms. The magnet talk was collected during the home observation at age 5. Starting when the children were 5, we have also administered at yearly intervals a battery of oral language and (pre)literacy tasks designed to tap the extended discourse skills we consider particularly relevant to literacy, as well as more standard, school-recognized measures of reading and writing skills. A brief description of the subjects, the home observation procedures, and the outcome measures is provided here; for more information about analyses of the home data, see De Temple and Beals (1991); for information about the classroom observations, see Dickinson and Smith (1991); and for information about the outcome measures, see Dickinson and Tabors (1991).

Subjects

The children in the study come from a range of backgrounds, though all the families were low-income and English-speaking. Forty-four of the children (64.7%) were white, 18 (26.5%) were African-American, and 6(8.8%) were of Hispanic heritage. Thirty-one were males, and 37 females. Potential subjects were contacted when the children were 3 through Head Start centers or other day-care centers serving a high proportion of low-income children. Since the purpose of the study is to explore the predictors of literacy success in children at risk for school failure, we chose to concentrate on children whose parents had relatively little education and who would mostly be attending urban schools.

Although all the families in the study were considered to be low-income on the basis of the child's eligibility for Head Start or state subsidies for preschool, they actually represented a fairly wide range of social and economic circumstances, and those circumstances, of course, changed (occasionally for the better) over the course of the study. Twenty-eight of the mothers (41.2%) reported that they had graduated from high school and did not pursue further education. Twenty-three of the mothers (33.8%) reported that they did not finish high school, and the remaining 17 (25.0%) reported that they received some post–high school education. Most of the families (57.4%) cite a resident parent's earnings as their primary source of income, but 41.2% of the families depend primarily on Aid to Families with Dependent Children (AFDC) or other welfare programs. (The one remaining mother gave child support as a primary source of income.)

Family configurations also varied widely. At the time the magnet task was administered, a total of 36 families consisted of one parent (the mother) and her child or children. In 29 families there were two adults, usually the father, stepfather, or another adult male, as well as the mother, in the household. The remaining three families reported more than two adults living in the home – for instance, in cases where a single mother lived with her family of origin.

In order to illustrate the range of families included in the study, and the variety of interactions we observed, we present here background on two children, George and Tammy, whom we will also include among the examples in our discussion of the findings.

George

George was a white boy who lived alone with his mother in a former mill town north of Boston. George and his mother had a close relationship, and the interactions observed in the study were characterized by observers as affectionate and rich. However, George has not been very successful in school. He was described as having behavioral problems in his Head Start class and kindergarten, perhaps because he was one of the youngest children in the classroom. By first grade, after being held back because of his age, George was diagnosed as having Attention Deficit Disorder (a frequent diagnosis in his school system). Despite these problems, George's mother remained convinced that his intelligence was high, and she expected him to go to college and get a doctorate. George was characterized by project researchers as confident and competent but often restless.

During the course of the study, George's mother earned a bachelor's degree in psychology and music education from a public, open-access university. While she was in school, her only income source was AFDC. During maternal interviews, she cited reading books as one of the primary activities they engaged in together. George's mother often referred to child development literature when talking about George's school experiences; she reported reading many books on psychology and education, as well as magazines such as *Psychology Today*. The family profile, replicated by many families in the study, was one of a relatively rich and literate home environment accompanied by considerable parental cynicism about the quality or effectiveness of the public schools. George's mother had had an unhappy school experience herself, and found herself unable to communicate effectively to teachers about her conviction that George was misbehaving because of boredom, not because of Attention Deficit Disorder.

Tammy

Tammy was a white girl who lived with her mother, father, older sister (by 2 years), and younger brother (by 1 year) in a housing project in a large working-class town outside of Boston. Tammy was very quiet, both at home and at school. Home visitors attributed this in part to her somewhat overbearing father, who was the dominant figure in the family. When she entered elementary school, Tammy was placed in a remedial reading program (Chapter I).

Tammy's mother was a high school graduate; she did not work outside the home, citing the cost of day care as making it not worthwhile. She was in poor health during the years of the study, with a heart problem. In interviews with researchers, Tammy's mother appeared confident that Tammy would show normal school achievement, expecting her to graduate from high school but doubting that she would go on to college. She did, however, mention nursing as a possible occupation for Tammy. Tammy's mother reported that the family enjoyed various types of family outings, including trips to nearby parks and beaches, puppet shows, the zoo, and the library.

Home observation procedures

The home visits carried out when the children were 3, 4, and 5 years old included a maternal interview, a toy play session, and an elicited report. We focus here on interactions collected in the context of book reading and during mealtimes, as well as from the magnet task administered only at age 5.

Book reading

The mother was asked to sit down with the child and read or look at two books: *The Very Hungry Caterpillar* (Carle, 1969, 1987) and a book selected by the child from among those present in the home. If the child was unable or unwilling to select, we provided a second book. When the children were 4 and 5, we always provided the second book, *What Next, Baby Bear!* (Murphy, 1983). When the children were 5, we asked them to read as the third book an expository book about elephants (Hoffman, 1983). *Animals in the Wild: Elephant* was included for much the same reason as the magnet task: to elicit explanatory, scientific talk in addition to narrative. However, it generated very little discussion, and most dyads simply read it until the child got bored. In analyzing the talk that occurs during book reading, our purpose has been to identify talk that goes beyond the information presented in the pictures and the text; we have identified a category of talk we call *nonimmediate*, which includes questions or predictions about what might happen next in the story, questions or comments about reactions to the story, speculation about the characters in the story, making connections between events or items in the story and experiences the child has had, and discussions of print or language (see De Temple & Beals, 1991).

George and Tammy during book reading

In reading *The Very Hungry Caterpillar* when George was 5, George's mother used the book as an opportunity to discuss cause and effect. She made observations about the sequence of events ("one week later" in the following excerpt refers to the fact that the caterpillar had hatched from the egg on a Sunday) and asked George an inferential question about the consequences of eating a leaf. George paid close attention to the book (making comments such as "wow") and answered all his mother's questions.

Example 1: George at 5 years, book reading[3]

```
MOT:    "that night he had a stomachache"
MOT:    he ate all those things
CHI:    wow
MOT:    "the next day was Sunday again"
MOT:    one week later
```

MOT: "the caterpillar ate through one nice green leaf # and after that he
         felt much better"
MOT: why do you think he felt much better?
CHI: because he ate <all those things>[?]
MOT: (be)cause that's his real food right?
MOT: and all this other junk # is for *us* not for caterpillars right?
CHI: right

Tammy at 5 had read *The Very Hungry Caterpillar* with her mother
twice previously in our observations; nonetheless, interaction around
the book was mostly restricted to labeling the pictures, without any
attention to explaining the caterpillar's stomachache or giving reasons
for the caterpillar's actions.

Example 2: Tammy at 5 years, book reading
MOT: "that night [>] he had a stomachache"
CHI: hmm [<].
MOT: "the next day he // was Sunday again # the caterpillar ate through
         one nice green leaf and after that he felt much better"
MOT: where's the green leaf?
MOT: an(d) this
MOT: okay right
CHI: [*points*]
MOT: where's the caterpillar?

Mealtimes

At each home visit, we left a tape and tape recorder and asked the
mother to record a family mealtime when everyone was present. The
mealtime tapes represent the closest approximation to natural family
interaction available to us, since we have little idea how typical of daily
interactions are the behaviors displayed during the interactions we structured. The mealtime tapes were transcribed and analyzed for the presence of narratives and explanations, two types of talk that involved
extending a discourse topic over many successive turns. See Beals
(1991), De Temple and Beals (1991), and Beals and Snow (1994) for
more information about the mealtime talk.

George and Tammy during mealtimes

George and his mother typically ate meals alone together, so the opportunities for quiet conversation were abundant. In fact, their second mealtime (when George was 4) had the highest percentage of explanatory talk
in the entire sample. We present here an example of an explanation
jointly constructed by George and his mother about why one must wait

after a meal before swimming. George's mother stated a rule and explained it, and George asked a further question because he did not understand her explanation. In addition to the explanation, the example includes some explicit teaching of vocabulary (cramps) initiated by George.

Example 3: George at 4 years, mealtime

MOT: okay well we still have to wait
CHI: wait <for what> [>]?
MOT: <<can't go>> [<] / # can't go swimmin(g) right after you eat
MOT: you have to wait a little while so you won't get cramps
CHI: huh?
MOT: you have to wait a little while so you don't get cramps
CHI: what's cramps?
MOT: cramps are when your stomach # feels all tight # [*clears throat*] and it hurts (be)cause you have food in it
MOT: and you're in the water

Tammy's excerpt is from the first year of the study, when the tape recording of mealtime conversation was not yet familiar to the families. Her parents felt she should "perform" for the tape recorder, so they encouraged her to recite the alphabet and explained to her why she should talk louder. Although this is a rather rudimentary explanation, it is not atypical; in fact, only 5.6% of Tammy's family mealtime talk was explanatory when she was 3 (the mean for all 3-year-old mealtimes was 12.9% explanatory), and her family did not return mealtime tapes after that time.

Example 4: Tammy at 3 years, mealtime (parents are trying to get Tammy to sing the alphabet)

FAT: you gotta open you mouth
MOT: open your mouth an(d) say it louder
MOT: 'A' go (a)head
MOT: we're only listenin(g) to you that's all

Outcome measures

The outcome measures derived from an individually administered battery we call the *SHELL: School-home early language and literacy battery*. It includes a variety of standardized and nonstandardized tasks designed to give a broad assessment of children's abilities with age-appropriate emergent literacy and print skills and with the oral language skills that our earlier work has shown relate strongly to literacy outcomes.

Definitions

The child is asked, for each of the first 10 words on the Wechsler Intelligence Scale for Children (Wechsler, 1958), to tell what it means (e.g.,

"Tell me what *hat* means" or "What's a *hat*?"). The child's answers are transcribed and then coded to reflect the choice of a formal definitional syntactic form, as well as the amount and quality of information provided. The codings are composited into two scores; the Formal Definition score reflects the use of formal definitional syntax, quality of superordinate provided, and sophistication of the restrictive relative clause. The Communicative Adequacy score reflects the amount of correct information provided and the length of the definition, without taking form into account.

The range of sophistication in the definitions is suggested by the performance of George and Tammy on the definitions task at age 6. We present here two formal definitions given by George; both contain a superordinate (though relatively unsophisticated – *car* and *something*) and relevant information restricting the class identified by the superordinate:

Example 5: George at 6, giving definitions during the SHELL

EXP:	truck
CHI:	it's a car that's big
EXP:	mmhm
CHI:	and it has four wheels
EXP:	mmhm okay
CHI:	and it runs real fast
EXP:	what's a hat?
CHI:	a hat is something you wear on top of your head

Tammy gave a nonformal definition for "truck" – in fact, an association rather than a definition – and although she provided the superordinate *something* for "hat," she failed to restrict the category sufficiently:

Example 6: Tammy at 6, giving definitions during the SHELL

EXP:	what is truck?
CHI:	dump truck
EXP:	what is a hat?
CHI:	something that you wear

Peabody Picture Vocabulary Test (PPVT)

This is a standardized receptive vocabulary test (Dunn & Dunn, 1981) for which we used the standardized age-specific percentile score as our measure.

Comprehensive Assessment Program (CAP)

This set of assessments of preliteracy skills (ability to recognize letters, to read environmental print, to write one's name, to do rhyming and phoneme segmentation tasks), developed by Jana Mason and Jana Stewart, was administered as part of the kindergarten SHELL. It is comparable to a readiness battery widely used in schools for decisions about placement in kindergarten or first grade.

Bear story

The child is shown three pictures depicting a bear picnic and an adventure recovering a kite from a tree. The pictures are then put away, and the child is asked to retell the story. Scores are based on the presence of story structure elements and on the number of event clauses produced.

The examples of bear stories produced by George and Tammy are typical of 6-year-olds' performance on this task. Their stories included at least a few event clauses and George's included orienting information, but neither child did a very good job with the plot line; neither provided a high point (the bear falls from the tree while trying to recover a kite) or a resolution. Both children were showing signs of on-line self-monitoring, manifested in their retracings (marked as (/) and (//) in the transcription) and self-interruptions, though Tammy seemed to tell the story under the assumption that background information was shared with the listener (starting with "the bear," for example).

Example 7: George at age 6 telling the Bear Story during the SHELL

CHI:	um . . .
CHI:	<there was three> / # there was three bears one was on a tree and one was not on a tree
EXP:	yeah
CHI:	<and they> / and they were playing around with each other
EXP:	mmhm
CHI:	and the other bear with the little bear in the wagon # he was tolding [*holding*] his teddy bear in the wagon
EXP:	he was towing his teddy bear in the wagon?
CHI:	he was *holding*
EXP:	holding his teddy bear in the wagon
CHI:	he was holding his teddy bear in the wagon
EXP:	mmhm
CHI:	and while his big brother was pushing him
EXP:	mmhm
CHI:	the end

Example 8: Tammy at age 6 telling the Bear story during the SHELL

CHI:	the bear <he went up> // he got caught up on the tree with his kite
CHI:	one of the bears # he had that kind of cart . . .
CHI:	with eggs in it
CHI:	and the bear <he had> // he rolled a ball

Picture description

A complex circus scene is shown to the child through a slide viewer; the child is asked to describe it so that the experimenter "knows which picture you have." Length of description and presence of specific statements of relation among the items pictured are coded to generate the total score.

Snowy Day

The familiar children's book *The Snowy Day* (Keats, 1962) is read to the child, and 10 comprehension questions, both literal and inferential, are inserted at regular intervals. The child's score is the number of questions answered correctly. Some of the questions require understanding and talking about physical processes (e.g., "What happened to the snowball?").

The magnet task

At the end of the home visit conducted when the children were 5, the observer offered the child a set of toys, including a powerful magnet encased in a black plastic covering, and an assortment of small metal and plastic objects (ball bearings, colored hard plastic balls with centers that were magnets, pennies and nickels, washers, paper clips, a tiny battery, small sponge sea animals, a plastic lobster, etc.). The child was told, "You and your mother can look at these things together while I clean up the other toys." A tape recorder was left near the mother–child pair during the interaction.

The resulting interactions were transcribed using CHAT (MacWhinney, 1991; MacWhinney & Snow, 1990), a set of transcription guidelines that make possible automated analysis and electronic archiving of language data (see note 3). After transcription and verification by an independent transcriber, the transcripts were coded using a set of codes designed to show whether or not talk focused on the phenomenon of magnetism, and whether talk focused on processes and procedures for understanding magnetism, or merely on the objects and phenomena as they were observed. In particular, talk about magnetism was distinguished from talk about objects, and talk about processes was distinguished from contextualized descriptions of objects or actions.

Analyzing the magnet task

Once the task had started (and the experimenter was no longer involved in the conversation), each utterance of both the mother and the child was coded for membership in one (or occasionally two) of five categories. One category concerned task orientation and was excluded from further analysis. The other categories reflected the two dimensions mentioned previously: magnetism versus nonmagnetism and process versus object.

1. *Task orientation talk.* Task orientation (ORIENT) consists of talk that mediates the interaction but does not deal directly with the objects. This includes evaluations ("are you having fun?"), nonspecific talk about the task ("I know what to do"), and exclamations made during object play ("wow!"). About half of the talk during the magnet task was *orientative*. The mean percentage of utterances coded as orientation was 42.07% (s.d. 14.40) for the mothers and 56.35% (s.d. 16.77) for the children. This talk occurred both as blocks of conversation and as conversational outbursts during task talk. Orientation talk may serve to enhance scientific aspects of the task ("let's do something interesting"), may detract from the task ("let's get this over with"), or may show involvement without adding content ("wow!"). Because the majority of these utterances guided the activity but did not affect the content of the discourse, the "task talk" described later does not include orientation talk; we also excluded unintelligible utterances from the total reported.

2. *Science process talk.* Science talk centered on magnetism (the magnets and their properties) rather than nonmagnetic qualities of the objects. Process talk involved talk about some process or goal governing the interaction. Process science talk (PRO:SCI) centered on scientific aspects of magnetization rather than objective phenomena. This was manifested mostly in explanations or attempted explanations of magnetic properties or generalization of the properties (such as saying that all metals will stick together). Another type of process science talk organized the task for systematic discovery of the magnet's properties ("let's see which ones stick and which ones don't"). Example 9 shows a mother and her son exploring (however superficially) the question of how magnets work (this example is fully coded, using some coding categories (e.g., OBJ:SCI) that are elaborated later).

Example 9: Kurt

MOT:	those keep sticking to it huh?
%cod:	$OBJ:SCI
CHI:	mmhm
%cod:	$OBJ:SCI
MOT:	you know why?
%cod:	$PRO:SCI
CHI:	why?
%cod:	$PRO:SCI
MOT:	think
%cod:	$ORIENT
MOT:	what do you think is inside that black box?
%cod:	$PRO:SCI
CHI:	metal?
%cod:	$PRO:SCI $OBJ:SCI

MOT:	what?
%cod:	$ORIENT
MOT:	we've talked about this before
%cod:	$ORIENT
MOT:	what's inside?
%cod:	$PRO:SCI
MOT:	that makes everything stick like that [*laughs*]?
%cod:	$PRO:SCI
MOT:	like on our refrigerator?
%cod:	$OBJ:SUP
CHI:	magnets
%cod:	$PRO:SCI
MOT:	very good
%cod:	$ORIENT

3. *Science object talk.* In addition to the science process talk, a good proportion of talk about the magnets focused on observable properties rather than processes. We coded as "object science" (OBJ:SCI) utterances that objectively described magnetic properties ("these stick together"), made predictions about attraction and repulsion of objects, and referred to the materials of which the objects were made. In the following example, Rosalyn describes objective properties of the magnets:

Example 10: Rosalyn

CHI:	Mom this is real fun [*dangling ball magnet from donut magnet*]
%cod:	$ORIENT
CHI:	oh!
%cod:	$ORIENT
CHI:	[*giggles*]
MOT:	it jumped
%cod:	$OBJ:SCI
MOT:	watch this
%cod:	$OBJ:SUP
MOT:	it jumps
%cod:	$OBJ:SCI

These descriptive utterances call attention to magnetic properties of objects without evaluation of the phenomenon.

4. *Artistic process talk.* Some process talk focused not on magnetization but on other interesting aspects of the magnet, such as the possibility of using the objects in conjunction with the magnet to construct a sculpture, a tower, stairs, or a face; or transforming the small objects into figures in a fantasy. This "artistic process" talk (PRO:ART) also includes alluding to magnetic properties as "magic." The following conversation does not discuss the scientific properties of the base magnet and colored ball magnets but rather uses them creatively:

Example 11: Rosa

CHI:	and we put these . . .
%cod:	$ORIENT

```
MOT:    oh that's a good idea
%cod:   $ORIENT
MOT:    hmm
%cod:   $ORIENT
CHI:    all around it [colored balls around circles]
%cod:   $ORIENT
MOT:    oh like a cake?
%cod:   $PRO:ART
MOT:    hmm?
%cod:   $PRO:ART
MOT:    are you # baking a cake?
%cod:   $PRO:ART
CHI:    yup
%cod:   $PRO:ART
MOT:    you're decorating the cake
%cod:   $PRO:ART
```

5. *Superficial object talk.* The category "superficial object" (OBJ:SUP) was used for talk that dealt with the assorted objects, focusing on their names and/or visual physical attributes (e.g., labeling the objects, identifying their color or shape). Directives to manipulate the objects were incorporated into this category. An example of an interaction dominated by object talk of this sort follows.

Example 12: Tammy

```
MOT:    what are these called?
%cod:   $OBJ:SUP
MOT:    know what <those are> [>]?
%cod:   $OBJ:SUP
CHI:    <marbles> [<]
%cod:   $OBJ:SUP
MOT:    yeah
%cod:   $OBJ:SUP
MOT:    did you know what these are called here?
%cod:   $OBJ:SUP
MOT:    oh do you know what <this is> [>] called?
%cod:   $OBJ:SUP
CHI:    <what> [<]?
%cod:   $OBJ:SUP
MOT:    do you know what that is?
%cod:   $OBJ:SUP
CHI:    pen [?]?
%cod:   $OBJ:SUP
MOT:    paperclip
%cod:   $OBJ:SUP
MOT:    <do you know what # do you know what this> // do you know what
        this big thing is called?
%cod:   $OBJ:SUP
CHI:    hmm
%cod:   $OBJ:SUP
```

```
MOT:    when things stick to somethin(g)?
%cod:   $OBJ:SUP
MOT:    they're called a magnet when things stick to somethin(g)
%cod:   $PRO:SCI
MOT:    is that called a magnet?
%cod:   $OBJ:SUP
MOT:    say magnet
%cod:   $OBJ:SUP
CHI:    magnet
%cod:   $OBJ:SUP
```

Segments that emphasize labeling may reinforce vocabulary development, but do not focus the child's attention on concepts such as uses for magnets and why magnets work.

Ten percent of the transcripts were coded by a second researcher, and reliability of coding for the five major categories was computed using Cohen's Kappa, a measure of reliability corrected for chance occurrence. A Kappa of 0.79 was found, indicating substantial reliability between coders.

Results

Kinds of talk

Our first question was: How did the mothers and children talk during the magnet session? Did they interpret this situation, as we had hoped, as one in which an investigation of the properties of magnets could be carried out or at least discussed? Perhaps not unpredictably, some did and some didn't. Table 7.1 gives an overview of the mean occurrence of each of the major types of talk we identified and the percentage of dyads in which this type of talk occurred.

The greatest proportion of the task talk centered on the small objects – naming them and discussing their visible physical attributes (size, shape, color, function) or involving directives about what to do with them: this "superficial object" talk accounted for about 49% of the children's and 55% of the mothers' utterances, on average, and only one of the dyads produced no such talk. Some talk about the objects, the science object talk, focused on their property of "stickiness," on the materials of which they were made, or on making and testing predictions about their magnetizability. Just 25% of child utterances and 22% of maternal utterances were classified as science object talk. A smaller percentage, 13% for the children and 14% for the mothers, of the task talk was coded as science process talk, that is, focused on discussions of

Table 7.1. *Types of task-oriented talk during the Magnet Task*
(n = 68)

	Mother		Child		% of dyads
	Mean %	S.D.	Mean %	S.D.	
PRO:SCI	14.28	10.70	12.53	10.44	94.1
PRO:ART	7.79	8.05	14.02	17.20	86.8
OBJ:SCI	21.78	13.62	24.89	16.89	97.1
OBJ:SUP	54.67	22.00	48.55	22.51	98.5

PRO:SCI, science process; PRO:ART, artistic process; OBJ:SCI, science object; OBJ:SUP superficial object.

the magnet and how it worked. Only 4 of the 68 of the dyads never engaged in science talk of this sort; in an additional two dyads, only one member produced science talk (one mother and one child). This means that 62 of 68 dyads engaged in collaborative talk about the scientific process of magnetization. Some dyads engaged in building structures with the magnets and the small objects, or used them to play (14% of child utterances and 8% of maternal utterances; 87% of the dyads engaged in at least some artistic process talk).

How do these various types of talk relate to each other? In other words, were there certain types of dyads who focused on object talk, others who focused on science, and still others who engaged primarily in fantasy or building? First, it should be noted that mothers and children were very well matched: In every case, the mother's use of a particular category of talk correlated extremely highly with the child's use of it (see Table 7.2). Second, children who engaged in larger proportions of superficial object talk (OBJ:SUP) participated in relatively little discussion of the objects in terms of their materials, density, or magnetizability (OBJ:SCI, $r = -.57$), little building and fantasy talk (PRO:ART, $r = -.43$), and little science talk (PRO:SCI, $r = -.31$). Much the same picture emerged for the mothers.

Children who produced a large percentage of science process talk, on the other hand, showed no particular pattern with regard to the other categories. The same is true for children who engaged in relatively large amounts of talk in the artistic process category. It seems as if talking about the objects in a concrete and/or directive way (superficial object talk) was negatively associated with extended talk of any type about science or about alternative ways of using the magnets, but talk about

Table 7.2. *Correlations among types of talk (percentages of task talk), n = 68*

	PRO:SCI mother	PRO:SCI child	PRO:ART mother	PRO:ART child	OBJ:SCI mother	OBJ:SCI child	OBJ:SUP mother	OBJ:SUP child
PRO:SCI mother	1.00	0.59***	0.05	−0.07	0.30*	0.11	−0.55***	−0.35**
PRO:SCI child		1.00	0.02	−0.18	0.23	−0.03	−0.34**	−0.31**
PRO:ART mother			1.00	0.66***	0.27*	−0.05	−0.47***	−0.30*
PRO:ART child				1.00	0.09	−0.10	−0.42***	−0.43***
OBJ:SCI mother					1.00	0.63***	−0.72***	−0.55***
OBJ:SCI child						1.00	−0.31*	−0.57***
OBJ:SUP mother							1.00	0.76***
OBJ:SUP child								1.00

*$p < 0.05$.
**$p < 0.001$.
***$p < 0.001$.

scientific aspects of magnets did not preclude building and fantasy, and vice versa.

As might be expected from their performance on other tasks, George and his mother engaged in a high proportion of science process talk.

Example 13: George

MOT:	<how come> / ## how come all # the silver colored ones stick but the money doesn't stick? [*puts nuts and a nickel on the base*]
%cod:	$PRO:SCI
MOT:	hmm?
%cod:	$PRO:SCI
MOT:	you know why?
%cod:	$PRO:SCI
CHI:	<I don't know how it does> [?]
%cod:	$ORIENT
MOT:	you think money has // # is a magnet?
%cod:	$PRO:SCI
CHI:	no
%cod:	$PRO:SCI
MOT:	(be)cause it's a different metal?
%cod:	$PRO:SCI $OBJ:SCI
CHI:	yeah
%cod:	$PRO:SCI
MOT:	but it's the same color
%cod:	$OBJ:SUP
CHI:	yeah
%cod:	$OBJ:SUP

Relation of science process talk to other types of extended discourse

How did dyads who produced a lot of process talk, like George and his mother, function in other settings where extended discourse was possible? Table 7.3 gives the correlations between magnet task talk and the types of talk observed during book reading and at mealtimes when the children were 5. It can be seen that mothers who produced more science process (PRO:SCI) talk also engaged in more *nonimmediate* talk during book reading (Mother, Nonimm) when the children were 3 years old, and that the mealtime talk in those families when the children were 3 included a higher percentage of explanations. As would be expected, given the negative correlation between science process talk and superficial object talk, percent of mealtime talk that was explanatory correlated negatively with superficial object talk for mothers and positively with children's science process talk. There were no significant correlations between mealtime narratives and any characteristic of talk during the magnet task, supporting our contention that science

Table 7.3. *Correlations of categories of talk during the magnet task with nonimmediate talk during book reading and explanations and narratives during mealtimes when children were 3.*

	PRO:SCI mother	PRO:SCI child	PRO:ART mother	PRO:ART child	OBJ:SCI mother	OBJ:SCI child	OBJ:SUP mother	OBJ:SUP child
Mother nonimm[a]	0.31*	0.12	-.05	-.15	0.17	-0.03	-0.12	0.02
Child nonimm[a]	0.17	0.01	0.10	0.08	0.15	-0.15	-0.12	0.09
Explanations[b]	0.35**	0.31**	0.17	0.13	0.18	-0.17	-0.32*	-0.10
Narratives[b]	0.13	0.21	0.13	0.03	-.02	-.05	-0.11	-0.03

*$p < 0.05$.   [a]n = 68
**$p < 0.01$.   [b]n = 55

talk might be a context for exposure to extended discourse that is independent of narrative.

One interesting specific connection between extended talk in the magnet task and in the other contexts can be made. During the same session as the magnet task, the children had read the book *Elephant* with their mothers, then played with a set of toys that included a realistic plastic elephant. In only 12 dyads did the mothers or children comment on the elephant in a way that recalled the book. George and his mother were one of the dyads that did exploit the information just acquired about elephants.

Example 14: George and his mother playing with toys

CHI: elephant[?]
MOT: that's what we just read about isn't it?
CHI: yeah <an elephant> [>]
MOT: <elephant> [<]?
CHI: dinosaurs
MOT: dinosaurs yeah
MOT: hippopotamuses
MOT: what kind of an elephant do you think that is?
CHI: African el- // elephant
MOT: African elephant
MOT: how come?
CHI: <(be)cause it has little> // (be)cause it has huge ears

Of the 12 mothers who made a connection during free play to the book they had just read, 5 scored among the top quartile (8 in the top half) in percentage of science process talk they produced during the magnet task. Tammy and her mother did not refer to *Elephant* when playing with the animal toys. They had the following conversation while reading the book:

Example 15: Tammy at 5 and her mother reading *Elephant*

MOT: "African elephants live in the plains as well as forests"
MOT: "this African elephant lives in the open grassland"
MOT: "it flaps its huge ears to help keep cool in the hot African sunshine"
MOT: okay
MOT: an(d) what are those?
MOT: more of what?
MOT: what are they called?
MOT: what are those?
CHI: don't know
MOT: are they elephants [>]?
CHI: elephants [<]
MOT: yeah

Another opportunity for explanatory talk occurred during the reading of *What's Next, Baby Bear!* (Murphy, 1983). The book tells the story of a bear who takes an imaginary journey to the moon in a cardboard box. Although the text never acknowledges that the trip was only in Baby Bear's imagination, several mothers mentioned this explicitly during the book reading. Interestingly, introduction of the clarification that the trip was "just in Baby Bear's head" was typically triggered by Baby Bear's selecting a colander for use as a space helmet. For some reason, this particular juxtaposition of reality and fantasy was more salient than many other excursions into fantasy – the fact that the bears were wearing clothes, living in a house, and talking, that Baby Bear made plans to go to the moon, or even that Baby Bear found a "rocket" in the closet. The following is another excerpt from George and his mother:

Example 16: George at age 4 reading with his mother

MOT: "he found a space helmet on the drainboard in the kitchen"
MOT: "and a pair of space boots on the mat by the front door"
MOT: is that a space helmet really?
CHI: no [*softly*]
MOT: what is it really?
CHI: the thing that you wash
MOT: that you wash right
MOT: you / you # put spaghetti in it when you're getting the water out
           right?
CHI: <mmhm> [>]
MOT: <a colander> [<]
CHI: colander

Did the dyads that engaged in science talk during the magnet task also engage in such extended talk about the reality–fantasy distinction while discussing the space helmet page in *What's Next, Baby Bear?* Of the dyads in the top quartile on percent of science talk in the magnet task, 11 out of 17 engaged in extended explanatory talk while reading about the space helmet, and only 2 dyads read through the passage with no talk at all. In one of these cases, there was no extended talk in part because the 5-year-old child was reading the book himself!

Relation of science process talk to children's performance on other language and literacy tasks

We were interested in science process talk because of our presumption that opportunities to engage in that sort of talk would help children develop sophisticated language and literacy skills. Did participation in science process talk relate to skill in other forms of extended discourse or to literacy outcomes? Table 7.4 presents correlations between the magnet task categories of talk and the outcome measures from the

Table 7.4. *Correlations between types of talk on magnet task and preliteracy outcome measures, n = 68.*

	PRO:SCI mother	PRO:SCI child	PRO:ART mother	PRO:ART child	OBJ:SCI mother	OBJ:SCI child	OBJ:SUP mother	OBJ:SUP child
Formal def.	0.31*	0.25*	0.06	0.20~	0.17	0.02	−0.37**	−0.29*
Commun. def.	0.39**	0.35**	0.03	0.12	0.40***	0.23~	−0.47***	−0.42***
PPVT	0.33**	0.32**	0.14	0.12	0.36**	0.16	−0.38**	−0.36***
CAP	0.24~	0.23~	0.01	0.10	0.17	0.02	−0.25*	−0.19
Bear story	0.38**	0.30*	0.00	0.04	0.07	−0.02	−0.20~	−0.16
Picture desc.	0.04	0.18	0.14	0.16	0.17	0.00	−0.15	−0.20~
Snowy Day	0.32**	0.29*	0.23~	0.10	0.42***	0.08	−0.43***	−0.27*

~ $p < 0.10$.
* $p < 0.05$.
** $p < 0.01$.
*** $p < 0.001$.

SHELL. We see that maternal use of superficial object talk relates negatively to all outcomes, with substantial negative correlations to skill in defining words, to vocabulary, and to story comprehension. In contrast, maternal and child engagement in science process talk relates positively to the children's definitions, to their vocabularies, to their story comprehension, and to the quality of the stories the children tell in the bear story task. Maternal use of science object talk shows a similar pattern. Although the analysis presented here certainly cannot rule out the possibility that these correlations are an artifact of child sophistication, the fact that in every case the correlation with the maternal behavior is as high as or higher than with the child behavior reduces the plausibility of that explanation. In further analyses of these data, we will have the opportunity to fit regression models in which the effect of child language sophistication is removed.

Discussion

Our findings suggest that there are families where children as young as 5 are engaged in extensive talk about the physical world and in explanations of both physical and psychological phenomena. These opportunities for science talk do not exclude considerable exposure to narrative in these children's lives, but the science talk experiences by themselves correlate with outcomes at age 5 that are known to predict later literacy achievement.

We have argued elsewhere that an important mechanism mediating such relationships is the opportunity children have to hear, engage in, and practice extended discourse. Science talk about the magnet typically consisted of several successive turns of talk about a single topic – why some objects stuck and others didn't, how magnets work, or what different kinds of materials were represented among the small objects. The object talk that some dyads engaged in did not have the same degree of topic structuring; typically, only one or two successive utterances were devoted to each object before the next one was selected.

The talk we have observed may well prepare children for school in ways not directly related to literacy as well. Some dyads were engaging in what might be described as good classroom-style scientific discourse (asking questions, collecting data, hypothesizing, weighing evidence), and those children might be expected to understand the discourse structure of science lessons better than children without such experience.

In recent years, science educators have emphasized the value of hands-on science curricula, based on the assumption that children learn best from action and personal observation rather than from reading texts or hearing lectures (e.g., Harty, Kloosterman, & Matkin, 1989). One science educator we know says, for example, "In science classes there is altogether too much talking. Students aren't learning when teachers are talking." Perhaps this downgrading of talk in science classes reflects the type of talk that typically occurs – a lot of lecturing and individual student–teacher exchanges (Cazden, 1988; Lemke, 1990) – rather than collaborative group conversations that can model the process of scientific discovery for the students (Morrison, Newman, Crowder, & Théberge, 1993). Science educators who work with younger elementary school children emphasize the need for scaffolding conversations in which adults ask questions that help children organize their observations, give information that might otherwise require tiresome detours into printed sources, and remind children of what they know and what questions they have not yet answered (e.g., Butts & Hoffman, 1993). Some school systems emphasize that parents, even those with little background in science (like the mothers in our study), can help their children explore, observe, and question in a scientific way (Gennaro & Lawrenz, 1992; Williams-Norton, Reisdorf, & Spees, 1990). It is also worth mentioning that classroom activities in the notably effective Japanese elementary math classes involve far fewer separate problems than those in American classes but much more discussion of each problem and its various possible solutions (see O'Connor & Michaels, this volume). There, conversation about math problems is assumed to generate more learning than practice in solving the problems.

Recent work by Grotzer (1993) gives a clear example of the value of adult scaffolding and provision of linguistic and other symbol-based supports to children learning about science. Grotzer was trying to teach children about alternatives to linear causal relationships, using food webs and homeostatic systems as examples of circular and branching causal links. She found a powerful effect of an intervention that included a lot of one-on-one talking about the various causal links in complex systems, and better performance from children who had been talked to about models a few steps more complex than their own. Providing fairly abstract charts of various causal models (e.g., arrows linking to each other in a circle or arrows branching from a single central "cause") also helped the children to articulate more complex interrelationships than they had spontaneously. Grotzer's work is one example of the power of adult conversation to help children produce extended discourse about complex topics and also to develop a more sophisticated understanding of those topics.

The mothers in this study were not, in general, well informed about the nature of magnetism, and none of the dyads observed emerged from their interactions with a fully formulated or correct notion of how magnets work.[4] We were not assuming, though, that children needed good explanations of magnetism from their mothers; rather, we were seeking the kind of extended discourse that emerges from focus on one topic and exploration of a series of questions about it. We were seeking evidence that some families would promote activities like classifying, questioning, formulating hypotheses, and predicting consequences more than others. Indeed, we found that some dyads did this quite a lot and others not at all. Furthermore, we found the expected relationships to literacy outcomes, mediated, we argue, by the practice with extended discourse that such discussions offer. We cannot, of course, rule out the impact of exposure to more sophisticated vocabulary or greater world knowledge that some children enjoyed, but the fact that none of the dyads actually came up with much information about magnets and how they work makes this last explanation somewhat less credible.

If we were to analyze the science talk we observed from the point of view of science educators, we might worry about some of the ways of talking that the mothers and children slipped into. The most common way of talking about what happened to the objects involved the word "stick" – "Will this stick?" "Why doesn't that one stick?" It is possible that "stickiness" is too limited a metaphor for the effects of magnets to help stimulate insights about the nature of magnetism. For one thing, it may seduce the dyads into overlooking the repulsion effects produced when like poles are brought into contact. Commonsense stickiness is produced by glue, and its opposite involves failure to stick rather than repulsion. Similar problems with the use of folk terms in a scientific sense have been noted by Roth and Anderson (1987) with regard to children's understanding of the meaning of "food" in photosynthesis. Although such metaphorical uses can help learners relate unfamiliar to familiar phenomena, they can also promote the generalization of many aspects of the familiar phenomenon that are simply wrong in the novel context.

Conclusion

We have viewed "science talk" in this chapter primarily as an opportunity for the construction of extended discourse. This is, of course, only one of several lenses through which science talk can be viewed. O'Connor and Michaels (this volume) refer to the externalization of reasoning as a function of teacher–student science talk; teachers *revoice* often tentative student comments in order to encourage the entire class to consider alternatives, generate hypotheses, and weigh evidence. Morrison et al. (1993) distinguished three modes of talk during the science lessons they observed: *correct answering, story-telling,* and *sense-making.* Correct answering, indexed by the presence of test questions and the all too frequent initiation–response–evaluation sequence, is often critiqued as less than optimal teaching – and we saw that Tammy's mother engaged in much of this type of discourse, asking narrowly focused questions, each of which had a single correct answer, and evaluating Tammy's responses. George's mother, on the other hand, set up talk at mealtimes, during the book readings, and during the magnet task in a way that promoted sense making – trying to figure things out by asking genuine questions and providing crucial novel information that could help George make better sense of what he already knew.

Clearly, sense-making is what we hope will occur in more classrooms, and the kind of talk with which children whose home interactions emphasize correct answering might have great difficulty. Explanatory talk is not the only way of making sense; narratives are a way of making sense that is particularly well adapted to the psychological realm, and narratives have been analyzed as problem-solving devices. We would agree with Morrison et al. (1993), though, that sense-making is the most productive kind of talk for teaching and learning science. Its importance suggests, among other things, that those of us studying and facilitating children's discourse should not limit ourselves or them to narrative forms.

Notes

1 Sociolinguistic variation, of course, further complicates the relation between oral language skills and literacy. Consider, for example, how the wide social variation in oral narrative style can make understanding standard written narratives much harder for some children than for others. We have not, however, focused on variation in type as much as on variation in amount of extended discourse children have access to.

2 A total of 84 families started the study. A few families were lost to follow-up because they moved or withdrew from the study. The 68 focused on here include all those families in which the 5-year-old visit including the magnet task was completed and the child outcome measures were available at age 5. Mealtimes at age 5 were available for 53 families.

3 Examples 1–16 are simplified versions of the more elaborate CHAT transcript format (MacWhinney, 1991). For updated information about the CHAT transcription system, which is prescribed for use in the CHILDES database, contact Brian MacWhinney at brian+@andrew.cmu.edu. The following utterance-level phenomena have been noted in these examples: pausing (#), repetition (/), correction (///), overlaps ([>], [<]), transcriber uncertainty, and stress (italics). In Examples 9–13, additional lines from the

CHAT transcript are introduced with a percent sign, and are distinguished as coding lines. Codes begin with a $ symbol and are capitalized, to distinguish them from the text.
4 In fact, the writers of this chapter had to study several volumes in a children's science series to construct the reasons why iron and steel are easily magnetizable but copper and aluminum are not, why magnets have two poles, and why the earth functions as a magnet.

References

Anderson, R. C., & Freebody, P. (1981). Vocabulary knowledge. In J. T. Guthrie (Ed.), *Comprehension and teaching: Research reviews.* (pp. 77–117). Newark, DE: International Reading Association.

Barbieri, M. S., Colavita, F., & Scheuer, N. (1990). The beginning of the explaining capacity. In G. Conti-Ramsden & C. E. Snow (Eds.), *Children's language* (Vol. 7). Hillsdale, NJ: Erlbaum.

Beals, D. E. (1991). *"I know who makes ice cream": Explanations in mealtime conversations of low-income families of preschoolers.* Unpublished doctoral dissertation, Harvard University Graduate School of Education.

Beals, D. E., & Snow, C. E. (1994) "Thunder is when the angels are upstairs bowling": Narratives and explanations at the dinner table. *Journal of Narrative and Life History*, Vol. 4, 331–352.

Beals, D. E., & Tabors, P. O. (1993, March). *Arboretum, bureaucratic, and carbohydrates: Preschoolers' exposure to rare vocabulary at home.* Paper presented at the biennial meetings of the Society for Research in Child Development, New Orleans.

Bruner, J. (1986). *Actual minds, possible worlds.* Cambridge, MA: Harvard University Press.

Butts, D., & Hoffman, H. (1993, February). Hands-on, brains-on. *Science and Children*, 15–16.

Carle, E. (1969, 1987). *The very hungry caterpillar.* New York: Philomel.

Cazden, C. (1988). *Classroom discourse: The language of teaching and learning.* Portsmouth, NH: Heinemann.

De Temple, J. M., & Beals, D. E. (1991). Family talk: Sources of support for the development of decontextualized language skills. *Journal of Research in Childhood Education, 6*, 11–19.

De Temple, J. M., Wu, H. F., & Snow, C. E. (1991). Papa Pig just left for Pigtown: Children's oral and written picture descriptions under varying instructions. *Discourse Processes, 14*, 469–495.

Dickinson, D. K., Cote, L., & Smith, M. W. (1993, April). Preschools as lexical environments. In C. Genishi (Chair), *Word learning research for literacy theory and early childhood practice.* Symposium presented at the annual conference of the American Educational Research Association, Austin, TX.

Dickinson, D. K., & Smith, M. W. (1991). Preschool talk: Patterns of teacher–child interaction in early childhood classrooms. *Journal of Research in Childhood Education, 6*, 20–29.

Dickinson, D. K., & Tabors, P. O. (1991). Early literacy: Linkages between home, school, and literacy achievement at age five. *Journal of Research in Childhood Education, 6*, 30–42.

Dunn, L. M., & Dunn, L. M. (1981). *Peabody picture vocabulary test – revised.* Circle Pines, MN: American Guidance Service.

Egan, K. (1993). Narrative and learning: A voyage of implications. *Linguistics and Education, 5*, 119–126.

Galda, L. (1984). Narrative competence: Play, storytelling, and story comprehension. In A. D. Pellegrini & T. Yawkey (Eds.), *The development of oral and written language in social contexts*. Norwood, NJ: Ablex.

Gennaro, E., & Lawrenz, F. (1992). The effectiveness of take-home science kits at the elementary level. *Journal of Research in Science Teaching, 29*, 985–994.

Grotzer, T. (1993). *Children's understanding of complex causal relationships in natural systems: A research study*. Doctoral dissertation, Harvard Graduate School of Education.

Harty, H., Kloosterman, P., & Matkin, J. (1989). Science hands-on teaching-learning activities of elementary school teachers. *School Science and Mathematics, 89*, 456–467.

Heath, S. B. (1983). *Ways with words: Language, life, and work in communities and classrooms*. Cambridge: Cambridge University Press.

Hoffman, M. (1983). *Animals in the wild: Elephant*. London: Belitha Press.

Keats, E. J. (1962). *The snowy day*. New York: Puffin Books.

Lemke, J. L. (1990). *Talking science*. Norwood, NJ: Ablex.

MacWhinney, B. (1991). *The CHILDES project: Tools for analyzing talk*. Hillsdale, NJ: Erlbaum.

MacWhinney, B., & Snow, C. E. (1990). The Child Language Data Exchange System: An update. *Journal of Child Language, 17*, 457–472.

Morrison, D., Newman, D., Crowder, E., & Théberge, C. (1993, April). *Sense-making conversations and student epistemologies*. Paper presented at the meeting of the American Educational Research Association, Atlanta.

Murphy, J. (1983). *What next, Baby Bear!* New York: Dial Books for Young Readers.

Nelson, K. (1986). *Event knowledge: Structure and function in development*. Hillsdale, NJ: Erlbaum.

Pappas, C. C. (1993). Is narrative "primary"? Some insights from kindergartners' pretend readings of stories and information books. *Journal of Reading Behavior: A Journal of Literacy, 25*, 97–129.

Pellegrini, A. D. (1985). Relations between preschool children's symbolic play and literate behavior. In L. Galda & A. D. Pellegrini (Eds.), *Play, language, and stories: The development of children's literate behavior*. Norwood, NJ: Ablex.

Peterson, C., & McCabe, A. (1983). *Development psycholinguistics: Three ways of looking at a child's narrative*. New York: Plenum.

Rodino, A. M., & Snow, C. E. (in press). "Y . . . no puedo decir mas nada:" Distanced communication skills of Puerto Rican children. In G. Kasper & E. Kellerman (Eds.), *Advances in communication strategy research*. New York: Longman.

Roth, K. J., & Anderson, C. W. (1987, November). The power plant: Teacher's guide to photosynthesis. *Occasional Paper No. 112*, Institute for Research on Teaching. East Lansing: Michigan State University.

Snow, C. E. (1983). Literacy and language: Relationships during the preschool years. *Harvard Educational Review, 53*, 165–189.

Snow, C. E. (1991). The theoretical basis for relationships between language and literacy development. *Journal of Research in Childhood Education, 6*, 5–10.

Snow, C. E. (1993). What is so hard about learning to read?: A pragmatic analysis. In J. Duchan, R. Sonnenmeier, & L. Hewitt (Eds.), *Pragmatics: From theory to practice*. New York: Prentice-Hall.

Snow, C. E., & Dickinson, D. K. (1991). Skills that aren't basic in a new conception of literacy. In A. Purves & T. Jennings (Eds.), *Literate systems and individual lives: Perspectives on literacy and schooling*. Albany: SUNY Press.

Snow, C. E., & Goldfield, B. (1983). Turn the page please: Situation-specific language learning. *Journal of Child Language, 10*, 551–570.

Velasco, P., & Snow, C. E. (1993). *Cross-language relationships in oral language skills of bilingual children*. Manuscript, Harvard Graduate School of Education.

Wechsler, D. (1958). *The measurement and appraisal of adult intelligence* (4th ed.). New York: Wilkins & Wilkins.

Williams-Norton, M., Reisdorf, M., & Spees, S. (1990). Home is where the science is. *Science and Children, 27*, 12–15.

Yawkey, T. D., & Miller, T. J. (1984). The language of social play in young children. In A. D. Pellegrini & T. Yawkey (Eds.), *The development of oral and written language in social contexts*. Norwood, NJ: Ablex.

8   Biliteracy development in classrooms: social dynamics and cultural possibilities

Luis C. Moll and Joel E. Dworin

The study of literacy has achieved prominence during the past three decades, including analyses of its social and intellectual consequences (e.g., Goody, 1987; Olson, Torrance, & Hildard, 1985; Street, 1984). Indeed, literacy has become one of the truly interdisciplinary areas of study, involving historians, linguists, anthropologists, psychologists, and educators, among others. Particularly revealing have been studies of people's ways with literacy, that is, the nature and uses of written language within specific and varied social conditions and practices (e.g., Heath, 1983; Scribner & Cole, 1981). These studies have shown that literacy is not a unitary phenomenon; that it is varied and complex; and that its possible consequences for thinking must be understood in relation to specific, diverse sociocultural practices, that is, to what people do with literacy within their circumstances of life. As Cole and Nicolopoulou (1992) put it, the emphasis of these studies is "on the actual 'morphology' of different kinds of literate practice; their analysis requires the investigator to take into account the structural, political, and ideological features of the society in question" (p. 345).

In addition, the theoretical emphasis on the "practices" of literacy has brought a fresh perspective to the study of literacy in schools. What has changed, as Olson (1987) points out,

> is the recognition that literacy skills are not merely the "abilities" of children. Rather, literate competencies reflect a broad range of factors including the forms of oral discourse that children have mastered before they even enter schools, the mastery of a particular form of discourse for talking about text, sets of assumptions about the fixidity and interpretability of texts, metalinguistic terms for referring to texts and their structures, and habits of using texts for a variety of purposes. (p. 2)

This recognition leads to a focus on children's actions with literacy within the social contexts that constitute classroom life; that is, what

221

goes on in classrooms, and why and how it takes place, count. The formation of "habits of using texts" is of both theoretical and practical interest.

In this chapter, we describe some of our work with a special aspect of literacy: that of biliteracy, the development of literacy in two languages. Curiously, the general phenomenon of biliteracy has been neglected in the literature (but see Goodman, Goodman, & Flores, 1979; Hornberger, 1989), despite its seeming ubiquitousness, given the propensity for bilingualism in the world, and although its study could shed new light not only on the varieties of literacy but also on the study of its intellectual consequences.[1]

Consider, for example, the work by Scribner and Cole (1981) among the Vai of West Africa. These authors concluded that the consequences of literacy were intimately bound up with the nature of the specific social practices of its users. They contrasted different types of literacy, each tied to a language (English/school, Vai script, and Arabic language) and to a variety of (sometimes overlapping) practices. An additional implication of their work, one that is rarely addressed, is that the biliterate person (e.g., in English and Vai script) may experience a range and variety of literacy practices (through, for example, their participation in social networks different from the monoliterate) that could "amplify" the potential intellectual consequences of literacy beyond what can be accomplished by the monolingual person in one language or the other. In addition, there are the potential metalinguistic benefits, intuitive or conscious, of reflecting on two languages in reading and producing text.[2]

One of the few settings in which to study biliteracy in the United States is with Latino, working-class children in bilingual programs.[3] We are especially interested in those situations in which these children attempt to become literate in two languages *simultaneously*, a phenomenon that occurs primarily, at least in this country, in bilingual classrooms.[4] In line with our interdisciplinary emphasis, we study biliteracy from what we call a *sociocultural* approach. Our version of this approach combines anthropological fieldwork and analysis (see, e.g., Moll, Tapia, & Whitmore, 1993; Vélez-Ibáñez, 1988) with a psychology (Cole, 1990, 1992; LCHC, 1983, 1986) inspired by the work of Vygotsky (1978), among others (Luria, 1976; Scribner, 1986). Most of our research is conducted in close collaboration with classroom teachers (Moll, Amanti, Neff, & González, 1992; Moll & Greenberg, 1990) in order to address our applied goal of developing a pedagogy that fosters an interdependence between academic tasks, and knowledge and resources found outside the classroom (Moll, 1992a; Moll et al., 1992).

For present purposes, however, a sociocultural approach is meant to include at least three aspects or levels of study. First is the broader social and institutional context. In the next section we address some of the important social factors that form part of the study of biliteracy. We find that these factors, usually neglected in the analysis of bilingualism or literacy, help define and control the experience of schooling for the students and teachers in our studies (Moll, 1992a).

Second, we study biliteracy in relation to the social organization of classroom activities. Although we are interested in issues that are usually studied by isolating aspects of language and literacy or under experimental conditions – for example, the influence of text structures on children's reading – or issues of bilingualism and cognition, we focus mostly on how children use literacy in activities that constitute the sociocultural systems we call classrooms (e.g., Moll & Díaz, 1987; Moll & Whitmore, 1993). Our first case study example focuses on the progress of a first-grade student learning to write in both Spanish and English. We highlight how the child himself functions as a "cultural agent" as he tries to integrate the sociolinguistic and literate experiences he brings into the classroom with what constitutes learning to write within this setting, as mediated through his growing control of the conventions of writing in both languages.

Finally, we are particularly interested in how literacy is used as a tool for communication and thinking. Following Vygotsky (e.g., 1978), we are interested in the *mediational* potential of biliteracy, especially in facilitating multiple and flexible ways of promoting and supporting the academic development of the students (Moll, 1992a). Our second case study example concentrates on those special aspects of literacy that Wells (1989), among others, has labelled *literate thinking*: those uses of language in which its symbolic potential is deliberately exploited as a tool for thinking (p. 253). In working-class classrooms, where instruction is often reduced to "basic" levels (Moll, 1992a, 1994), we are particularly concerned with developing an approach in which, as Wallace (1989) puts it, one moves "beyond minimal interpretations of literacy as the ability to read and write to a view of literacy as a resource which offers possibilities of access to what has been said and thought about the world, of the kind which day-to-day spoken interactions can less readily offer" (p. 7).

Constraints and possibilities

Most bilingual instruction in the United States occurs in working-class and poor neighborhoods. Schools in these neighborhoods have been shown to differ systematically from schools in wealthier areas. Particularly important to consider is that instruction in these classrooms is usually rotelike and characterized by a low intellectual emphasis on the so-called basic skills. This emphasis usually denotes limited uses of literacy as the instructional (and learning) means and what we could call a "dogmatic" relationship to knowledge as something given to the students and teachers by others, especially through a mandated text or curriculum (Moll, 1994).

It is also important to consider that most bilingual education programs in the United States have as their overall goal the development of English proficiency for their students. In these programs, literacy development in the first language of "language minority" students is not a priority. In fact, Spanish retains its status as a "marked" language within these programs, and they lack any serious commitment to develop their students' Spanish literacy. Instead, Spanish is used mostly as a "bridge" to learning English. That is, Spanish is used as the predominant language of learning temporarily (and sporadically) while the students are learning English. Once students have "transitioned" into all-English instruction, there is no longer any instruction in the students' first language (Kjolseth, 1973; Lambert & Taylor, 1987). In arguing against this approach, Kjolseth (1973) has written:

> The school's policy is essentially a burnt bridges' approach: the ethnic language is seen only as a bridge to the non-ethnic language – one to be crossed as rapidly as possible and then destroyed, at least as a legitimate medium of instruction, although some voluntary classes in it as a foreign language may be maintained. (p. 13)

In short, the development of dual literacy or biliteracy is not a major policy concern of bilingual education programs (however, see Crawford, 1989, pp. 163–174; Dolson & Mayer, 1991, pp. 146–150).[5] Therefore, it is not unusual to visit a bilingual classroom and not encounter any Spanish literacy for any purpose.

We should also mention that some children internalize the negative societal attitudes toward Spanish, toward bilingualism, and toward their ethnic groups, regardless of the teachers' efforts. This is a pressure unknown to middle-class Anglo children in monolingual schools. This attitudinal issue is not addressed very well in the research literature (however, see Commins, 1989; Griego Jones, 1993), but teachers report to us its prevalence.[6] For example, most of the teachers we have worked with have told us about (and we have observed) children who are ashamed or refuse to speak Spanish or who are ridiculed by their peers for their accented English. Several teachers have also reported discovering children in their classes who know how to read and write in Spanish but have concealed it, the stigma about spoken Spanish having generalized to its written forms. The point is that these attitudes, a reflection of broader societal attitudes, help create the context for the learning of literacy in classrooms, and shape the motivation of children and teachers to develop literacy in one language or the other (see Valdés, 1991).

Nevertheless, bilingual classrooms are diverse settings. In our classroom observations, for example, we have found considerable variety in the specific literacy activities that make up classroom life (also see Edelsky, 1989; Moll, 1988). Most of the classrooms use basal readers, often in two languages, and rely primarily on worksheets and similar artificial exercises for writing, regardless of language. Still, we have also observed classrooms that emphasize student inquiry, where students actively use reading and writing in studying a broad number of topics, although most of the activities may be in English. In short, being in a bilingual classroom does not guarantee certain types of experiences or engagement with print, and biliteracy is not necessarily fostered, especially as part of a systematic program that lasts for several years,[7] but this does not mean that biliteracy does not occur.

In our studies, we have identified a large number of elementary school children who are biliterate. For example, using our collection of writing samples (in both languages) from approximately 200 students in 10 classrooms (fourth and sixth grade) in working-class communities as an indication of biliteracy, we found that about 20% of the children were already proficient writers in two languages, and about 40% were "fair" writers in both languages. The potential for widespread and proficient biliteracy clearly exists. Of the remaining students, only about a dozen could not write with minimal proficiency in both languages.[8]

As an example of proficient bilingual writing, consider the writing sample in Figure 8.1 from one student, Delia, a fifth grader, collected during the research.[9] As can be seen, this girl is a very good writer in Spanish. She communicates clearly, has developed her topic well, elaborating on the differences between wild and domesticated animals, and has even included personal information to embellish the story. She displays a good sense of audience (and of humor) and her writing is highly readable, with clear punctuation (some misplaced accents, notoriously difficult for children learning Spanish in this country) and conventional spelling.

Delia's English (second language) writing sample was collected about a week after the Spanish sample. She chose the same topic used for the Spanish sample and developed it, elaborating also on the difference be-

clases de gatos   'Oct 30, 195?

marta
3pm

A mí me han dicho que
los gatos son los animales
más limpios que hay. Yo
tengo un gatito y le
he enseñado muchas cosas
diferentes. Yo le he enseñado
a cazar, subirse a los árboles,
comer lo que le doy y le enseñé
a jugar.
    En este mundo hay gatos
de toda la clase.
    En selvas, bosques, zoo y
en tu propia casa o barrios hay
gatos. En las selvas y en
los bosques hay toda clase
de animales salvajes que
corren o atacan a la gente y
a los animales.
    En la casa o barrios
algunos gatos son domésticos
porque la gente los cría y
los cuidan. Los gatos
que no son domésticos o
no están domesticados por
la gente so salvajes y
si los tratas de agarrar
te rasguñan la cara o
manos.

They have told me that
cats are the cleanest animals
there is.
    There many kinds of cats,
there tigers, lions, mountain lions
cheetas, panters and cats that you
take care at home.
    The cats that you
take care at home are
domestics, and tigers, lions,
mountain lions, cheetas and panters
are wild. Others wild because
they kill people, eat other animal
and they are not domesticated
by people.
    If you play around
with a kitten the kitten smite
bite you, run away or
keep on playing.
    Wild cats like to hunt
other wild animals.
    Domestic cats are
little and, wild cats are
big and strong

They have told me that cats are the cleanest animals there are.
I have a little cat and have taught him many different things.
I taught him how to hunt, climb trees, eat what I give him, and
I taught him how to play.
    In this world there are all kinds of cats.
    In jungles, forests, zoo and in your own house or neighborhoods
there are cats. In the jungles and in the forests there are all kinds
of wild animals that eat or attack people and the animals.
    In the house or neighborhood some cats are domestics because
people raise them and take care of them. The cats that are not
domestics or domesticated by people are wild and if you try to grab
them they will scratch your face or hands.

Figure 8.1   Delia's writing samples in English and Spanish.

tween domesticated and wild animals but providing different supporting details. This sample is probably not as good as her Spanish sample, but it is coherent and clearly communicates her thinking. It would be safe to conclude that this student is already a proficient writer in both languages and will become even better, given the opportunity and support.

Early biliteracy: the case of George

George was 6 years old and a first-grade student in a bilingual classroom. There were 28 students in the class, which at the beginning of the school year included 7 monolingual Spanish speakers, 2 monolingual English speakers, and 19 Spanish-dominant bilingual students. According to the teacher, by the end of the school year all of her students were bilingual to varying degrees.

Of all the students in the class, the teacher reported that only one, Natalia, was able to read when she began first grade. By June, however when school ended, eight of her students were reading and writing in both languages: Denise, Sergio, Natalia, Daniel, José, Javier, Rafael, and George.

The writing of letters was the most common genre in this classroom, and there was some story writing. The teacher often conducted brainstorming writing sessions in which the students in the class offered topics and she wrote them all on the chalkboard at the front of the classroom. On one of the walls she put up "starter sentences," in both English and Spanish, for the students to use during their writing (e.g., "Today I am going to write about/Hoy voy a escribir de"). In addition, the students learned that the writing process involved preparing drafts, editing, rewriting drafts, and finally publishing. In response to a question about how many drafts students usually wrote, George replied, "They write three or four. I only write two."

During writing, the children often talked about their work (or other areas of interest) with each other, moving freely about the room and providing assistance and support with the writing process. The teacher usually worked with a small group of students in the reading corner, sat at her desk with paperwork or made herself available to students by request. A part-time teacher aide was also available to work with students and their writing several times each week.

After writing a second draft of their work, the students would get individual assistance from the teacher with editing. This editing usually included a reading aloud of the piece by the students and then a discussion of the writing. The teacher would then write corrections in red ink on the draft, primarily correcting punctuation, spelling, format, spacing of letters/words, and so on. The students would then return to their desks to begin writing a third draft, incorporating the corrections from the second draft. A similar process would take place for the third draft. Finally, the students would publish their work, using the class's computer to print out the final copy.

George was among the best students in the class, according to his teacher. He was born in Mexico but raised in this country. His mother, also born in Mexico, works part-time as an early childhood educator at her church and as a homemaker. His father, also from Mexico, graduated as an electrical engineer in that country, but he is currently employed as a carpet layer and attends English classes at a local community college. The family moved to Arizona 2 years ago from California because the fundamentalist church to which they belong, which forms an important part of their lives, is located in Tucson. The family attends church all day on Sundays and on Tuesday evenings. All of the church activities are conducted in Spanish. George plays softball in a church-sponsored program.

George has two sisters: Dania, who is 5 years old and attended a Head Start program this past year, and Rubi, who is 1. George also attended a Head Start program, but in California, and last year he attended the bilingual kindergarten at his current school. Although George's parents encourage him to speak English to develop his abilities in that language, his mother "pushed Spanish," according to the teacher: "She wanted him to be in Spanish reading and wanted him to be bilingual. For academic and economic reasons, both his parents speak some English." During "Love of Reading Week," when adults from the community are invited to read books to children in classrooms, George's mother told the teacher that she would read to the class in Spanish because her English "wasn't good enough to read in English."

George's family has a library at home, and George has his own collection of books in English and Spanish. He is allowed to "read" some of the books that belong to his father, and his father reads to him in both English and Spanish. George also has a library card from the public library that he uses about once a week. His family also reads the Bible in Spanish at home on a daily basis.

George's given name is Jorge, like his father's, and the family calls him Jorgito. He "became" George last year in kindergarten, where there was another boy named Jorge, so the teacher decided to call him George. In his first-grade class, he asked to be known as George. George's oral proficiency in Spanish was very advanced when he started

I learned to write Tolson

Figure 8.2   George's first writing sample (August 21, 1992).

first grade, and "that helped him to become bilingual – he transferred what he knew in Spanish into English," according to the teacher. However, in a language assessment test administered by the school at the beginning of first grade, George scored a 5 in verbal ability in both English and Spanish, the highest score on a scale that ranged from 1 to 5. That is, George may have been more fluent in English than even the teacher recognized at the beginning of the year.

According to the teacher, George was not reading or writing at the beginning of first grade. His development, however, was very rapid. On a reading test administered by the Reading Recovery (Clay, 1985) teacher at the end of the school year, George was assessed as reading at the fourth-grade level in Spanish, and could have read at the fifth-grade level, according to this teacher, had she brought any fifth-grade books with her when she administered the test. Natalia, George's classmate, had a similar score on this test.

George, then, along with some of his classmates, is a developing bilingual writer (and reader), someone who is learning two literate systems simultaneously. As such, we should understand his writings in Spanish and English together, and not just through the prism of what is known about single-language literacy (Valdés, 1991).

George's portfolio (as of this writing) included 12 papers, dating from August 1992 to March 1993; 7 were in Spanish, 4 were in English, and 1 was written using both languages. Four different genres of writing were represented among the 12 papers: 5 letters, 3 narratives, 3 worksheets, and 1 caption. The writings in English were two letters and two narratives. We present five samples of his writing that illustrate his development of biliteracy within an 8-month period. We should reiterate that at least seven other students in this class (or 29%) displayed a similar level of proficiency in both languages.

Figure 8.2 shows one of the earliest writing samples of the school year. This sample is significant because it is written mostly in English, showing

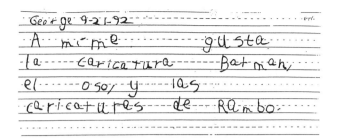

I like the Batman cartoon [caricature], the bear, and the Rambo cartoons [caricatures].

Figure 8.3   George's second writing sample (September 21, 1992).

George's willingness to write in that language, and because it reveals some of George's knowledge about writing in both English and Spanish early in the year. George wrote a sentence in English (*I learned to write Tolson* [the name of the school]), followed on the next line by part of a word in Spanish (*Apren[dí]*), which appears to be the beginning of the same sentence in Spanish. Note that he begins both sentences with a capital letter, showing knowledge of that grammatical rule. The "L" in "learned" is capitalized, and a vertical line was inserted between the large case letters "I" and "L" to indicate word spacing. The second "e" is omitted, indicating perhaps an invented spelling based on phonetics. The next word is "write," with the "t" and "e" omitted, possibly because the next word, "Tolson," begins with the same phoneme as the "te" in "write." Note that "Tolson," the name of the school, is capitalized appropriately. George has added a period at the end of the sentence, displaying knowledge of punctuation conventions. We should mention that he wrote the sentence with the page upside down, and wrote his name in orange crayon with a period in pencil after it.

The next piece of writing (Figure 8.3), displaying proficiency in Spanish, was written exactly one month after the sample shown in Figure 8.2. It shows well-developed knowledge of conventions: George's name ("George") and the date appear at the top of the page, on the left-hand side, and he began the sentence with a capital letter ("A"), used the accent mark correctly on the pronoun ("mí"), used commas conventionally, and capitalized proper names (Batman, Rambo). Also, note the correspondence between the articles and the singular and plural feminine nouns ("la caricatura"; "las caricaturas"). The spacing between words is generally conventional, although somewhat far apart. The hand-

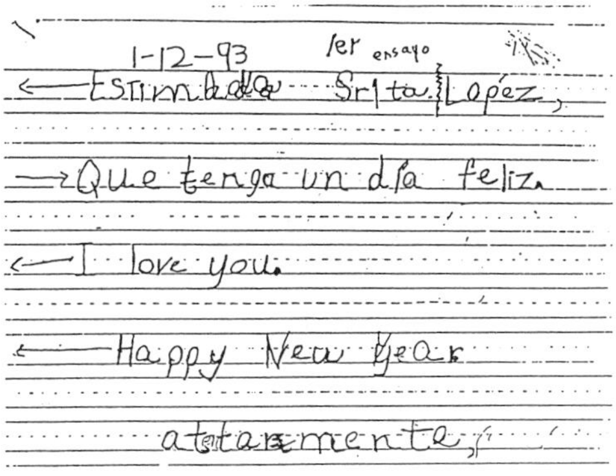

Dear Miss Lopez Have a happy day. I love you. Happy new year.
Attentively George A.

Figure 8.4   George's letter to a student teacher (January 12, 1993).

writing is very good and clear, although the letters sometimes "float" above the lines on the page. This sample indicates that George's writing in Spanish is quite well developed, especially in contrast to the English sample presented earlier. He has good control over the writing system and is able to write about popular American cultural characters (Batman, Rambo) in Spanish.

The writing sample shown in Figure 8.4 is a note written to an adult, wishing her a happy new year. Note that George uses both languages to create his note, a genre the class has practiced often. However, he does not mix the languages, instead relying on intersentential code switching, a common switch among bilinguals, and a marker of developing bilingual fluency. There is little difference between the first and second drafts: The teacher wrote over some of his words (e.g., the "ada" in "Estimada" to align the words to the line on the paper), and inserted a period after "Srita." (an abbreviation of "Señorita" [Miss]), and a comma after the addressee's surname (Lopez,) to abide by the salutary conventions. She also placed the accent on the first vowel of ("día" [day]; George had included both a period and an accent mark over the letter "i"), corrected the spelling of "atetanmente" (to "atentamente" [attentively or thoughtfully], a common letter closing in Spanish), and placed a comma after the closing, again abiding by the conventions. Again, George demonstrates that he is appropriating the sociocultural (graphophonic) conventions of written language in Spanish, an important achievement, and using the genre as a context to communicate in English as well.

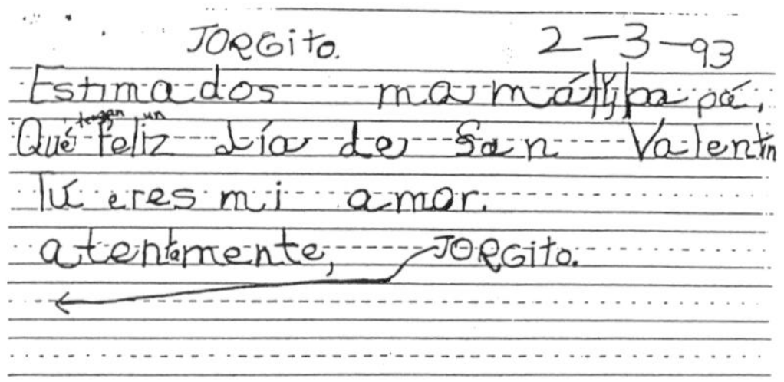

Dear Mom and Dad, I hope you have a happy St. Valentine's day. You
are my love. Attentively, Jorgito.

Figure 8.5   George's first draft of a letter to his parents for St. Valentine's Day
(February 3, 1993).

In the piece shown in Figure 8.5, George wrote "Jorgito 2–3-92" at the
top of the page (he had first written "George" and then erased it, taking
into account his audience, who call him Jorgito, not George). He used
accent marks correctly on "mamá" and "papá," "Valentín," and the
pronoun "Tú." All spelling was conventional except "atenmente," and it
was corrected once again by the teacher. Some punctuation is omitted,
but this was a first draft and George was aware that his teacher will make
corrections for the next draft. For example, he wrote a capital "y"
between "mamá" and "papá," and he omitted a comma after "papá" (a
period or colon would also have been appropriate), exclamation marks
before and after the first sentence (which are optional, depending on the
intonation intended by the writer), the accent mark on the "í" in "dia"
and lowercase "s" on what should be "San," a period after "amor" to
end the sentence, and a comma after "atenmente," a common writing
convention. Also, George added a period after his name and did not
write it on the "proper" line, but his letters do no float above the lines,
as in the previous sample.

In general, George displays considerable proficiency in the letter writing genre in Spanish. Lest this sound trivial or mundane, keep in mind
that this first grader is developing control over the writing system (the
graphophonic, syntactic, and semantic aspects) not in one but in *two*
languages at the same time. Consider the example shown in Figure 8.6,
where he displays similar development with his writing in English.

George's letter writing in English lags behind his development in
Spanish, primarily in terms of conventional spelling. In his first draft of
this letter he starts most of the words with a capital letter, perhaps to

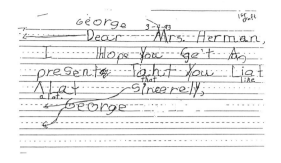

Dear Mrs. Hermen I Hope You Get A present Taht You Liat A Lat
sincerely George A.

Figure 8.6 George's draft of a letter to a teacher assistant for her birthday (March 4, 1993).

convey a certain emphasis, and spells "taht" (for "that"), "Liat" (for "like"), and "Lat" (for "lot"), using a similar phonetic strategy to invent the spelling of the words. George's writing in English, albeit brief, reveals little influence from Spanish grammar, even when writing within the same genre.

In assessing George's progress, as reflected in the writing samples just presented, we must keep in mind that his social conditions for developing biliteracy seem particularly advantageous (cf. Edelsky, 1991a, 1991b). For one thing, he comes from what seems to be a literate family, where his mother is involved in teaching (as part of her duties in the church) and his father has a college degree, and where there is a clear emphasis on literacy learning, including library visits and the reading of scriptures and other church-related activities in Spanish. Furthermore, although his parents recognize and promote the learning of English, they are clearly interested in his development of literacy in Spanish, as emphasized by his mother's comments to the teacher. These background factors are no doubt advantageous. Two other students who developed biliteracy also have a parent with at least some college experience, but the parents of the other five students who excelled do not have this level of formal education. Nevertheless, they also come from a community characterized by binguality, where they come into contact with both Spanish and English on a daily basis, either through oral interactions with monolingual and bilingual members of the community or through contact with print in both languages in varied forms: signs, newspapers, magazines, books, television, institutional forms, and so forth. Thus, regardless of the parents' level of schooling, children enter these classrooms with verbal and written experiences in both languages.

We must also highlight the efforts of the teacher to create an "additive" bilingual situation in her classroom, where the children have an opportunity to speak, read, and write in both languages, and especially where Spanish, the "marked" language in society, is "unmarked" in this particular classroom (see also Edelsky, 1991b). That is, in this classroom, the use of both Spanish and English is legitimate, sanctioned by the teacher, and of equal value for classroom purposes; she does not privilege one language over the other.

The teacher, however, was in control of lessons and the learning process, with little deviation from her assigned tasks. Thus, she determined what counted as reading and writing for the students, although she maintained an emphasis on the children's making meaning through writing. For example, the progress of George in writing in two languages (we only have indirect indicators of his seemingly rapid progress in reading) is most evident in the genre of letter writing, the type of writing that the teacher emphasized and that the children practiced most often. We have no evidence of similar development in the writing of stories, journals, or any writing as part of the children's research or inquiry (but see the next section). Furthermore, the teacher's editing was primarily aimed at correcting spacing, spelling, and punctuation, not at helping the students elaborate or develop what they had already produced. Therefore, the biliteracy of George is at once assisted by the general social conditions created by the teacher and constrained by the scope and emphasis of the specific assignments. That is true of any classroom, we should point out.

But it is the remarkable accomplishment of George that we want to emphasize here. This first grader is achieving control over the complex writing system of *two* languages in order to communicate. That is, in Vygotskian (1978) terms, he is internalizing the essential semiotic system of his culture that will make him literate while transforming it to communicate in two languages. These are the beginnings of writing (conventions) becoming a cultural and bilingual tool for communication and self-regulation, a major transformative moment in Georges' development.

Biliterate thinking: the case of Lupita

Our second case study concerns a third-grade girl who is already able to self-regulate in very important ways: to engage with texts to obtain information and transform it for her own intellectual purposes. Furthermore, she is able to do this in two languages, using her biliteracy consciously as an academic resource. But as in George's case, it is not solely an individual accomplishment; it is mediated and distributed in important ways through the opportunities and assistance she receives in doing her work.

Lupita's classroom consists of 27 children, 12 boys and 15 girls, who either come from the neighborhood or working-class *barrio* surrounding the school (16 children) or who travel from other neighborhoods in the city (11 children) as part of a magnet desegregation program. As is common in bilingual classrooms, there is considerable diversity in the children's language and literate abilities. Fifteen of the children are monolingual English speakers and readers, and of these, two children, Sarah and Brooke, are learning rapidly to speak, read, and write Spanish. Nine children are bilingual: Elizabeth, an English-dominant bilingual speaker, reads in both languages; Veronica, Susana, Francisco, Raymundo, Roberto, and Lupita, Spanish-dominant bilinguals, are reading and writing (with varying proficiency) in both languages; Rosario, David, and Ana are Spanish-only readers. Jaime is a Spanish-dominant speaker who came into the classroom in the fall speaking only Spanish, and by the end of the year he spoke and read some English as well. Acuzena is a monolingual Spanish speaker; she arrived in the United States from Mexico in the spring and reads only Spanish.

The classroom is organized into center activities and theme research projects, where the children work in various ways to accomplish their individual and group academic goals. Adult-directed lessons are relatively rare in this classroom. The children may work alone, but rarely in isolation from other students and adults. There is definitely adult guidance of the children's work; however, that guidance is not controlling but mediating, as we shall show.

Within the theme studies or literature groups, the teacher encourages children to stretch their abilities by taking risks with new experiences, materials, and academic work (see Moll & Whitmore, 1993; Moll et al., 1993). Simultaneously, the organization of instruction and the participation of the teacher support the children, especially those working in their second language. The children are expected to be active participants in their own learning, and are encouraged to be responsible for their own academic development and classroom behavior. In brief, the classroom is socially and culturally organized to support and advance the children's academic work (for details, see Whitmore, 1992).

For present purposes, we will summarize Lupita's participation within a theme study cycle about Native Americans, highlighting her opportuni-

¿Tenian una comida especial?   ¿Cuales eran los nombres de sus jefes?
¿En que teritorio vivían los Sioux?   ¿Como asian las canastas?

Did they have a special food?   What were the names of the chiefs?
In what territory did the Sioux live? How did they make the baskets?

Figure 8.7   A sample of Lupita's research questions.

ties to read and write in two languages as part of her research (for further details, see Moll & Whitmore, 1993). We will also contrast her writing in Spanish within this unit to her writing in English as part of another classroom writing activity. As the teacher explains it, the students have a lot of control over the theme cycle activities:

> The theme cycles are pretty much controlled, the topics anyway, by the kids. Right away at the beginning of the year we go through a group brainstorm process where the kids will put out anything they are interested in studying and we group things together. We put sharks and whales in the list together with someone that said ocean so that related topics are chunked together. And then the kids are asked to vote for their 10 most favorite, and those are the ones that we do as group theme cycles for the year. I put my things on the list, too. (Moll & Whitmore, 1993, p. 30)

The theme study usually begins with some sort of "web," where the students share what they already know about a topic, and then they generate a list of questions that help guide their study and organize their activities. For example, in the Native American theme study, Lupita's web (Figure 8.7, written in Spanish) identified topics she was interested in studying about the Sioux (e.g., food, art, names of chiefs), and then she wrote a list of specific questions (unedited examples) to explore those topics.

Guided by the students' interests and questions and by her own interests, the teacher helped assemble for the classroom a widely varied group of literacy materials in English and Spanish as resources, including about 100 trade books, pieces of art, posters, and artifacts borrowed from the library, support staff, parents, and other adults. These materials formed part of the study centers, small-group activities, and individual research of the students, all helping create a highly literate classroom environment.

Lupita wrote her questions on index cards and then (with the teacher's help) searched for books or other sources to obtain the information necessary to answer her questions. She identified a number of books that seemed helpful (all in English); recorded the title, author, and library call number on a reference sheet; and indicated which of these books she might use as part of her research. These reference sheets became part of every student's bibliography as they wrote reports on their findings. For example, Lupita, who was researching the Sioux, read a trade book (in English) entitled *Plains Indians*, concentrating on a section of the book called "Games and Pastimes." She was interested in finding out about basket weaving and discovered from her readings that the Sioux did not make baskets, information she then recorded (in Spanish) on her index cards.

After identifying, locating, selecting, and recording information from the texts (in English) and writing (in Spanish) the information on index cards to answer her specific questions, Lupita started preparing a report (in Spanish) to summarize her findings. A similar process was used to gather information from local experts. For example, Veronica, another girl in the same class, prepared a set of questions (in Spanish) about the Yaqui Indians to interview a teacher assistant in the school, who is a Yaqui and trilingual in Yaqui, Spanish, and English. Note that through their participation in this theme study, the children develop their own questions in either language and use them to obtain information from both written and social resources (other people).

Lupita and the other students in the class then prepared draft reports on their research that they would eventually edit, type into a computer, print, and compile into a (bound) book that they donated to the school library. A portion of Lupita's first unedited draft is reproduced in Figure 8.8. Note that she can write with fair proficiency in Spanish, regardless of mistakes (later corrected through editing): "del tribo" instead of "la tribu"; "qasi" instead of "casi." She also omits the accent mark on the word "también" (not an uncommon error for novice writers) but accentuates correctly the work "aprendí." In general, however, by building on this initial draft, she produced a final report that was highly readable, and summarized well the information she collected (see Moll & Whitmore, 1993).

More important than the final product, however, are the literate practices that Lupita and the other students learned and developed through these theme studies: the ability to ask questions, obtain information from numerous resources, translate from one language to the other as necessary, and communicate in writing a version of that information to others. After writing the final report, the students did another web summarizing the information they obtained as a way to monitor their own learning. This entire process was graded by the teacher: the quality

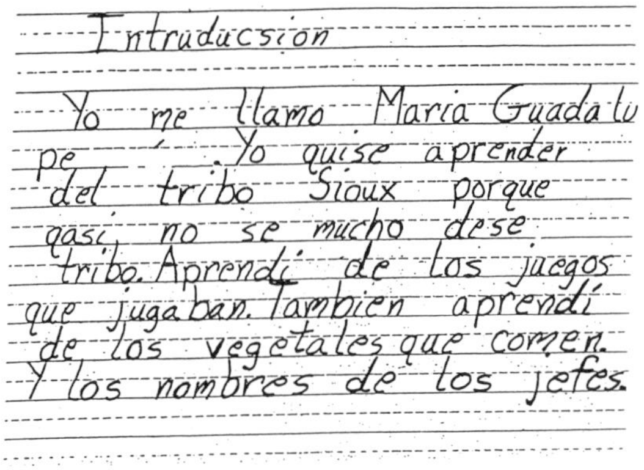
Intruducsion
Yo me llamo Maria Guadalu
pe ´ . Yo quise aprender
del tribo Sioux porque
qasi no se mucho dese
tribo. Aprendí de los juegos
que jugaban. Tambien aprendí
de los vegetales que comen.
Y los nombres de los jefes.

Introduction My name is Maria Guadalupe·...I wanted to learn about the Sioux tribe because I almost don't know much about that tribe. I learned about the games they played. I also learned about the vegetables they eat. And the names of their chiefs.

Figure 8.8 Lupita's first draft of her research report.

of the questions, the first web, the resource list, the note keeping, the final report, and the final web. We must emphasize that the activities were not isolated or occasional lessons but part of the cultural practices of this classroom. It is through these practices that the children learned to use their bilingualism deliberately, consciously, to access and manipulate resources for intellectual and academic purposes.

Consider the next example (Figure 8.9), in which Lupita draws on her (Spanish) cultural experiences to write an essay in English about her mother's home town of Magdalena, Mexico. Note not only her proficiency and eloquence, but how she incorporates into her story cultural details about the "quinceañera" celebration in Mexico. Once again, we take this writing activity as an example of "literate thinking": In this instance, the child uses the occasion for writing in English to reflect on personal experiences that occurred in Spanish and transform them into a literate theme, an object of analysis.

Interestingly, based on the two writing samples presented here, Lupita may be a more proficient writer in English than in Spanish. These are two different genres, and the essay may more easily lead to the inclusion of information that makes for a more interesting and "literate" piece.

Magdalena
by Lupita

Magdalena is where my mother was born! Magdalena is in Sonora, Méxical! I like to go ther because all of my cousins live there! Last month, we went there because my parents were goin to be god parents for 3 fifteen year old girls party! They don't ~~salabrate~~ celebrate a fifteen year old party like any birthday party. They ~~salabrate~~ celebrate it because there out of child-hood and into bieng a woman! They ~~salabrate~~ celebrate it by going to church and they make a big dance and they dress in pretty dresses and a have a big cake In Spanish it's called Quinceañera. They looked very pretty! When we go to Magdalena my brother, Aaron, likes to play in the dirt with his cars. My uncle is building a house for my grandmother. It's turning out very good! I like playing with my cousins. I wish I lived there!!

Figure 8.9 Lupita's essay in English.

Nevertheless, if our assertion is correct, Lupita, whose first language is Spanish, is a more proficient Spanish speaker (and perhaps reader) but a better writer in English. Such is the flexibility of biliteracy, and we can expect her to draw on her writing proficiency in English, her "second" language, to develop her writing in her "first" language, Spanish.

Discussion

We have concentrated on exploring the possibilities and some of the dynamics of biliteracy development in classrooms. As our examples illustrate, there are many paths to biliterate development, and these paths are formed by the history of the student, the social contexts available for learning, and the support the children receive to "engage with topics and texts" (Wells, 1989) in both languages.

A characteristic of the classrooms in our case examples, and one absolutely crucial in mediating external social constraints, is that the teachers create conditions in which both languages are treated, to the extent possible, as unmarked languages (cf. Griego Jones, 1993). The essential element here, we believe, is not necessarily that the children learn to value bilingualism (or Spanish, as the marked language) as an abstract entity, but that they read and write in both languages for academic purposes, where biliteracy is an integral and legitimate part of the intellectual culture of the classrooms and where both languages are involved *substantively* in academic tasks.

In our first-grade example, we highlighted a student's (George) progress in developing his knowledge about language to express himself bilingually, primarily within a letter writing genre that the teacher emphasized. The main point of the writing samples was to illustrate what we take as a landmark in George's intellectual development: his beginning to control the conventions of literacy in two languages. He is appropriating (bilingual) written discourse as an essential cultural tool, in the Vygotskian sense, for communication and self-regulation, both of which he displays through his writing samples. However, to say that he is "appropriating a tool" does not do justice to the complexity of George's accomplishment. This is a child coming to control and transform the complex graphophonic systems of two languages. Writing becomes a cultural-semiotic tool for George through his actions, his bilingual manipulations of this symbol system. But this accomplishment is situated: It takes place within a classroom with specific characteristics, so George's actions are always mediated proximally, by the actions of the teacher, by what counts as writing, and distally by considerations that take place in the culture outside the classroom.

The third-grade example illustrates vividly the dynamic relationship between classroom conditions for learning and biliteracy, especially how children can come to use their two languages consciously to access important resources for their academic learning. The children not only learned information about their theme of study (the Sioux, in Lupita's case) but also came to control literate practices that constituted their research procedures. Recall that the children were not only responsible for conceiving their own questions and guiding their own learning with the selective use of literate materials, but were also expected to articulate their awareness of the learning process and produce a final report summarizing the information collected.

In these learning contexts, biliteracy clearly represents a particularly powerful means for thinking, strategic tools for gaining access to important social and cultural resources (Moll & Greenberg, 1990; Moll & Whitmore, 1993). In Lupita's case, we highlighted her use of cultural experiences that took place in Spanish (the "quinceañera" party in Mexico) to write an expository text in English. In addition, books and other materials in both Spanish and English are available in this classroom, showing the student how bilingualism serves to amplify their resources for thinking. Unlike monolinguals, these children have two literate worlds to draw on. Similarly, when developing, say, questionnaires as part of their inquiry, they can develop a version in English and one in Spanish, facilitating access to the knowledge and opinions of two social and cultural groups. In addition, the recording of data or related writings may be done in either language, as Lupita's examples showed (see also Moll et al., 1992).

Finally, as our examples indicate, in bilingual contexts, especially where literacy in two languages is fostered simultaneously, labels such as *native language* or *second language learners* lose their meaning and may lead to misleading assumptions about children's learning, usually involving a required set or sequences of skills (Flores, 1982; Flores, Amabisca, & Castro, 1988). George is only temporarily a more proficient writer in Spanish than in English; that will probably change in a few months, given what we know about bilingual programs. Lupita, who is already a more proficient writer in English than in Spanish, is usually considered a Spanish-dominant bilingual. It would not be unusual for her to use her ("second" language) English writing proficiency to develop her writing in Spanish (her "first" language). More than likely, if George is to develop his biliteracy, he will use his proficiency in English to develop his Spanish, not the reverse. That is, the propositions of cognitive transfer from the first to the second language may be much more domain specific than we have assumed. These propositions may also change developmentally, both in relation to the students' control over the conventions of literacy and in relation to their sociocultural conditions (see also Valdés, 1991).

The intellectual possibilities of biliteracy, we propose, must be similarly contextualized. These possibilities, at least in terms of the bilingualism, have usually been studied by testing individuals to determine if they possess more of certain psychological characteristics (e.g., metalinguistic awareness or divergent thinking) than monolinguals (Díaz, 1983; Hakuta, 1986). Our studies of biliteracy, however, point to the significance of the social consequences if we are to appreciate fully the intellectual ramifications of bilingualism. As George and Lupita helped us understand, the intellectual power of biliteracy lies in the mediated relationships the learner establishes between symbol system and social world to obtain or create knowledge and transform it for meaningful purposes.

Notes

1 It is also revealing to consider the relationship of bilingualism to the origins of writing. Consider, for instance, Michalowski's (1988) claims about the "fluidity" between language and script in early writing; that early forms of writing were *not* related to the spoken vernacular; and that foreign (and dead) tongues were the main vehicles of written communication: "The writing system began as one that was relatively autonomous from any one language, and then it came into an uneasy truce with a complex linguistic matrix in which multilingualism, dialect differentiation, and social stratification all played a role" (p. 61). In fact, this fluid relationship between script and language is still the case in cultures with "incipient" literacy, as Michalowski also suggests. This fluidity, we propose in this chapter, is also an important characteristic of literacy in bilingual settings, where misconceptions about fixed sequences of literacy learning (e.g., that oral language fluency must precede written proficiency) are distortions introduced from research in monolingual settings (see also Edelsky, 1986).

2 Interestingly, Scribner and Cole (1981) report that it was the presence of Vai-Arabic biliterates that complicated (and enhanced) their research design by making clear the heterogeneity of Vai script literates: "It would have simplified our studies if we could have temporarily set aside Arabic literacy and concentrated on the Vai script/English school/nonliterate comparisons we had in mind at the outset. But the extensiveness of Vai-Arabic biliteracy made that simple solution impractical. . . . We had discovered from an analysis of reading scores that Vai-Arabic biliterates had a higher concentration of top scores on the Vai script reading test than their monoliterate counterparts. We needed that range of skills as part of our studies" (p. 108).

3 The term *Latino*, of course, subsumes tremendous heterogeneity; for example, the

social history of Mexicans in the Southwest is completely different from that of Cubans in Florida or that of Puerto Ricans in New York City, as is the nature of their bilinguality. In fact, there is enormous heterogeneity within each of these groups. All three groups, however, have a history of bilingual education in their communities, where children's becoming biliterate is not only possible but quite common. Our studies have been conducted primarily with working-class U.S. Mexican children and with families in Arizona and California. The children presented in the case examples in this chapter are offsprings of relatively recent immigrants from Mexico.

4 We do not mean to imply that children develop literacy or biliteracy solely in classrooms, but rather that biliteracy is most visible for study within classrooms; not only is life outside the classroom of great importance for the development of literacy, but children may become literate before or without formal schooling. Rosi Andrade and Kathryn Whitmore have contributed greatly to the work summarized in this chapter.

5 Bilingual "maintenance" programs, where both languages are fostered through language arts and other academic components (e.g., mathematics) and where one would expect biliteracy to develop, are rare in the United States. In a recent extensive national study of bilingual education programs (Ramirez, Yuen, Ramey, & Pasta, 1991), only five schools were identified that appeared to offer authentic maintenance programs (also see Dolson & Mayer, 1991).

6 They also report many negative incidents from their personal histories regarding the use of Spanish in schools, such as punishment, ridicule, and other forms of verbal abuse. After all, it was not long ago that Latino children had their mouths washed out with soap for speaking Spanish in school; many of the teachers (and researchers) were victims of these practices.

7 In this context, it is interesting to point out that even in Canadian immersion programs, much lauded for their success, literacy instruction is eclectic, featuring a range of approaches, and the dynamics of biliteracy, especially from the children's perspective, have not been studied in much detail (e.g., Genesee, 1987; Tardif & Weber, 1987).

8 We should point out that writing samples may seriously underestimate the children's proficiency because they result from a request by an outsider to write on demand under artificial and strange conditions; furthermore, there is no indication of what these children could do with some assistance, which may be much more revealing of their proficiency and potential for biliteracy; this contrast (unassisted versus assisted performance) is the essence of Vygotsky's (1978) notion of the zone of proximal development. The following colleagues also participated in this study: Rosi Andrade, Elizabeth Saavedra, and Kathryn Whitmore.

9 We collected the writing samples by following these steps: (a) we asked the children to brainstorm about topics of interest to them; (b) we helped reduce their list to a smaller number of topics for writing; (c) we asked them to write anything they wanted about their favorite topic from that list; (d) we returned a week later and asked them to repeat the process, but in the other language. In allowing the children to select topics, instead of assigning a topic as a prompt, as is usually done, we exchange standardization for motivation to write.

References

Clay, M. M. (1985). *The early detection of reading difficulties* (3rd ed.). Portsmouth, NH: Heinemann.

Cole, M. (1990). *Cultural psychology: A once and future discipline?* CHIP Report No. 131. San Diego: University of California, Center for Human Information Processing.

Cole, M. (1992). *Socio-cultural-historical psychology: Some general remarks and a proposal for a new kind of cultural-genetic methodology*. Paper presented at the First Conference for Socio-Cultural Research, Madrid, Spain, September.

Cole M., & Nicolopoulou, A. (1992). Literacy: intellectual consequences. *The Oxford international encyclopedia of linguistics*. New York: Oxford University Press.

Commins, N. L. (1989). Language and affect: Bilingual students at home and at school. *Language Arts, 66*, 29–43.

Crawford, J. (1989). *Bilingual education: History, politics, theory and practice*. Trenton, NJ: Crane.

Díaz, R. (1983). Thought and two languages: The impact of bilingualism on cognitive development. *Review of Research in Education, 10*, 23–54.

Dolson, D. P., & Mayer, J. (1991). Longitudinal study of three program models for language minority students: A critical examination of reported findings. *Bilingual Research Quarterly, 16*, 105–156.

Edelsky, C. (1986). *Writing in a bilingual program: Había una vez*. Norwood, NJ: Ablex.

Edelsky, C. (1989). Bilingual children's writing: Fact and fiction. In D. M. Johnson & D. H. Roen (Eds.), *Richness in writing: Empowering ESL students*. New York: Longman.

Edelsky, C. (1991a). Writing in a bilingual program: It all depends. In *With literacy and justice for all*. London: Falmer Press.

Edelsky, C. (1991b). Not acquiring Spanish as a second language: The politics of second language acquisition. In *With literacy and justice for all*. London: Falmer Press.

Flores, B. M. (1982). *Language interference or influence: Toward a theory for Hispanic bilingualism*. Unpublished doctoral dissertation, University of Arizona.

Flores, B. M., Amabisca, E., & Castro, E. (1988). *Children's sociopsychogenesis of literacy and biliteracy*. Unpublished manuscript. California State University, San Bernardino.

Genesee, F. (1987). *Learning through two languages: Studies of immersion and bilingual education*. New York: Newbury.

Goodman, K., Goodman, Y., & Flores, B. (1979). *Reading in bilingual classroom: Literacy and biliteracy*. Rosslyn, VA: National Clearinghouse for Bilingual Education.

Goody, J. (1987). *The interface between the written and the oral*. Cambridge: Cambridge University Press.

Griego Jones, T. (1993, April). *Assessing students' perceptions of biliteracy in a two way bilingual classroom*. Paper presented at the annual meeting of the American Educational Research Association, Atlanta.

Hakuta, K. (1986). *Mirror of language: The debate on bilingualism*. New York: Basic Books.

Heath, S. B. (1983). *Ways with words*. Cambridge: Cambridge University Press.

Hornberger, N. (1989). The continua of biliteracy. *Review of Educational Research, 59*, 271–296.

Kjolseth, R. (1973). Bilingual education programs in the United States: For assimilation or pluralism? In P. R. Turner (Ed.), *Bilingualism in the Southwest*. Tucson: University of Arizona Press.

Laboratory of Comparative Human Cognition (LCHC). (1983). Culture and cognitive development. In W. Kessen (Ed.), *Handbook of child psychology* (Vol. 1). New York: Wiley.

Laboratory of Comparative Human Cognition (LCHC). (1986). The contributions of cross-cultural research to educational practice. *American Psychologist, 110*, 1049–1058.

Lamber, W., & Taylor, D. (1987). Language minorities in the United States: Conflicts around assimilation and proposed modes of accommodation. In W. Van Horne (Ed.), *Ethnicity and language*. Milwaukee, WI: Institute on Race and Ethnicity.

Luria, A. (1976). *Cognitive development: Its cultural and social foundations.* Cambridge, MA: Harvard University Press.

Michalowski, P. (1988). Early Mesopotamian communicative systems: Art, literature, and writing. In A. Gunter (Ed.), *Investigating artistic environments in the ancient Near East.* Washington, DC: Smithsonian Institution.

Moll, L. C. (1988). Key issues in teaching Latino students. *Language Arts, 65,* 465–472.

Moll, L. C. (1992a). Bilingual classrooms and community analysis: Some recent trends. *Educational Researcher, 21,* 20–24.

Moll, L. C. (1992b). Literacy research in community and classrooms: A sociocultural approach. In R. Beach, J. Green, M. Kamil, & T. Shannahan (Eds.), *Multidisciplinary perspectives in literacy research.* Urbana, IL: National Conference on Research in English.

Moll, L. C. (1994). Mediating knowledge between homes and classrooms. In D. Keller-Cohen (Ed.), *Literacy: Interdisciplinary conversations.* Cresskill, NJ: Hampton.

Moll, L. C., Amanti, C., Neff, D., & González, N. (1992). Funds of knowledge for teaching: Using a qualitative approach to connect home and classrooms. *Theory into Practice, 31,* 132–141.

Moll, L. C., & Díaz, S. (1987). Change as the goal of educational research. *Anthropology and Education Quarterly, 18,* 300–311.

Moll, L. C., & Greenberg, J. (1990). Creating zones of possibilities: Combining social contexts for instruction. In L. C. Moll (Ed.), *Vygotsky and education.* Cambridge: Cambridge University Press.

Moll, L. C., Tapia, J., & Whitmore, K. (1993). Living knowledge: The social distribution of cultural resources for thinking. In G. Salomon (Ed.), *Distributed cognitions.* Cambridge: Cambridge University Press.

Moll, L. C., & Whitmore, K. (1993). Vygotsky in classroom practice: Moving from individual transmission to social transaction, In E. Forman, N. Minick, & C. A. Stone (Eds.), *Contexts for learning: Sociocultural dynamics in children's development.* New York: Oxford University Press.

Olson, D. R. (1987). An introduction to understanding literacy. *Interchange, 18*(1/2), 1–8.

Olson, D. R., Torrance, N., & Hildard, A. (1985). *Literacy, language, and learning: The nature and consequences of reading and writing.* New York: Cambridge University Press.

Ramirez, D. J., Yuen, S. D., Ramey, D. R., & Pasta, D. J. (1991). *Final report: Longitudinal study of structured-English immersion strategy, early-exit and late-exit transitional bilingual education programs for language-minority children* (Vol. 1). Washington, D.C.: U.S. Department of Education.

Scribner, S. (1986). Thinking in action: Some characteristics of practical thought. In R. Sternberg & R. Wagner (Eds.), *Practical intelligence: Nature and origins of competence in the everyday world.* Cambridge: Cambridge University Press.

Scribner, S., & Cole, M. (1981). *The psychology of literacy.* Cambridge, MA: Harvard University Press.

Street, B. (1984). *Literacy in theory and practice.* New York: Cambridge University Press.

Tardif, C., & Weber, S. (1987, April). *The young child's experience of French immersion schooling.* Paper presented at the American Educational Research Conference, Washington, DC.

Valdés, G. (1991). *Bilingual minorities and language issues in writing: Toward profession-wide responses to a new challenge.* Technical Report No. 54. Berkeley: University of California, Center for the Study of Writing.

Vélez-Ibáñez, C. G. (1988). Networks of exchange among Mexicans in the U.S. and Mexico: Local level mediating responses to national and international transformations. *Urban Anthropology, 17,* 27–51.

Vygotsky, L. S. (1978). *Mind in society*. Cambridge, MA: Harvard University Press.
Wallace, C. (1989). Participatory approaches to literacy with bilingual adult learners. *Language Issues, 3*, 6–11.
Wells, G. (1989). Language in the classroom: Literacy and collaborative talk. *Language and Education, 3*, 251–273.
Whitmore, K. (1992). *Inventing a classroom: An ethnographic study of a third grade, bilingual learning community*. Unpublished doctoral dissertation, University of Arizona.

9 The role of the Black Church in growing up literate: implications for literacy research

Catherine Dorsey-Gaines and Cynthia M. Garnett

Introduction: "A Reading Lesson"

Grandma Dancy was given to praying long and involved prayers. I admired her skill and basked in the esteem her ability brought her and our family at Little Flock Baptist Church. I have to admit though, I often wished she had saved her considerable skills for Sunday services. Grandma Dancy, however, "served the Lord each and every day." If you happened to be with her when one of her good praying spells came upon her, she sweetly but insistently required you to join her on her knees. My uncles, Simuel and Albert, often checked to see that Grandma's eyes were closed and ever so quietly crawled out of the back door and disappeared. I was always afraid God, who was a personal acquaintance of Grandma Dancy, would alert her to my misdeeds and cause her eyes to open at the moment just before my escape. So I stayed and prayed with her often until my knees ached and my legs had gone to sleep.

Collard greens, hot water cornbread, buttermilk and peach cobbler were the treats on which we could rely at our regular afternoons in Grandma Dancy's care. The tasty greens simmered on the back eye of her immaculate white stove. The shiny black iron skillet sat poised on a front eye ready to assist Grandma in the magic she performed with flour, meal, milk, and a touch of sugar. Quart bottles of buttermilk sat chilling in the icebox, and Grandma's peach cobbler called out with warm fragrant breath. As my brother and I could depend on these treats, we could also be sure that not one pot-liquor soaked crumb would cross our palates before we had "joined Grandma on her knees." We hoped, usually in vain, for a short prayer. We were already anticipating crumbling the cornbread in our greens, crunching green and yellow goodness, and washing this whole harmony of tastes down with large glasses of buttermilk. Grandma's mealtime prayers were a hair shorter than at other times during the day. She made up for this brevity with extra helpings of thankfulness and respect for what the Creator had provided. We chimed in a relieved Amen, and greedily smacked our lips around the greens, cornbread, and pieces of ham hock. We then surrendered ourselves to the heaven of Grandma's glorious peach cobbler.

She tidied the kitchen as we ate. We dared not lick our plates as we

247

would have wished, but we spoon-scraped our plates of every last essence of cobbler. It took Grandma only minutes to render her already spotless kitchen debris free. She pulled the cord attached to [the] ancient light fixture above the kitchen table and plunged the kitchen into afternoon darkness. She put her arms on our shoulders, half escorting us and half leaning on us, and said, "you boys come sit with Grandma and read to me a spell." Even if we had minded, our full stomachs forced smiles onto our napkin-wiped faces, and we'd come and sit with Grandma among her starched white doilies and time-worn chairs and sofa.

The spot on the sofa nearest the end of the coffee table that held the Bible was Grandma Dancy's favorite spot. She would settle there, open her gilt-edged Bible to a favorite passage, and hand it to me, since I was the older, and say, "Brother, read this to Grandma." If I stumbled, which at first I often did, she would give me each word without ever looking at the page. As I got less clumsy at my reading, I sometimes noticed Grandma's head tilted back against her sofa scarf. Her eyes were closed and shimmery tears like liquid crystals struggled to stay hidden in their corners. Those that lost their places slipped quickly down Grandma's dark round cheeks, and disappeared in the flowered folds of collar beneath her tiny brown ears.

My brother always read after me and thought he benefitted from observing me and learning from my mistakes. Grandma required that a chapter be read completely before we could stop, so my brother tried to skip verses. These transgressions were met with Grandma's admonishing him with, "Slow down boy, you left out the part that says: 'Deliver me not over unto the will of mine enemies: for false witnesses are risen up against me, and such as breathe out cruelty.' " Sometimes she would wait until he thought he had finished. When his arms were folded in misplaced smugness, then she would say, "Baby boy, you got to go back, you can't just skip over the Lord's words like that. You left out the part where it says, 'Therefore if I know not the meaning of the voice, I shall be unto him that speaketh a barbarian, and he that speaketh shall be a barbarian unto me.' "

In all our afternoons of collard greens, cornbread, peach cobbler, and Bible reading with Grandma Dancy, we never actually saw her read the Bible. We never saw her read a newspaper, or magazine, or any book. As far as we knew she could not "read." But, we could never leave out a single syllable of her precious Bible that she did not stop and make us go back and reread. We never came to a single unfamiliar word in that Bible that she did not supply.

My slick baby brother and I got to be pretty good readers. Grandma eventually had us read aloud in church and she beamed and shed a few of those shimmery tears I'd seen on our afternoons together. When we returned to our seats next to Grandma in her pew, she would lean over to us in her dignified way, hug us warmly and say, "Grandma's boys read just perfectly."

In school I was picked several times to read in assemblies. I was considered one of the best oral readers in my class. My teachers smiled approvingly and told me what a fine job I had done. It was not for their approval I was reading, but Grandma Dancy's. It was she who had invited my reading practice, been critic and audience at my rehearsals, given me greens and peach cobbler for incentive, and allowed me to feel the pleasure of reading well in front of others. Even now when I am called upon to deliver a talk, or when I enter a room of unfamiliar people, I think about Grandma Dancy and feel assured. I see her tear stained cheeks, feel her warm but dignified hug, and hear her whispering, "Grandma's boys read just perfectly." (Garnett, 1994; reprinted by the author's permission)

Much of what is written about the African-American community misses many resources undervalued or ignored by researchers looking for economic and formal educational structures. Although much has been written about the absence of privilege and cultural capital in the African-American community, little has been written about the discourses and literacies and models of transition within the community. The story of Grandma Dancy is familiar to many members of the African-American community. We begin our discussion of the African-American community and the Black Church with this vignette as a way of bringing the reader into one of the intimate spaces where literacy is mentored. This fictionalized account of practices experienced in many families may help the reader to suspend notions of community deprivation and inferiority long enough to examine the ideas developed in this chapter. We hope that Grandma Dancy's ability to mentor will be extended to the readers of this chapter and to the researchers who see communities in terms of what they are not, rather than what they are.

Assumptions about literacy in the African-American community

The church's role in the development of a community's literacies is not always obvious. "A Reading Lesson" illustrates in delicious detail the capacity of church and family to influence literacy development. That scenes like these occur in many communities may be unremarkable. That scenes like these occur in communities that are routinely considered disadvantaged may suggest a need to reevaluate what constitutes literacy advantages. It intimates that perceptions of community inadequacy are inaccurate.

In *Growing up Literate: Learning from Inner-City Families* (Taylor & Dorsey-Gaines, 1988), researchers learned that every part of a child's environment contributes to learning. As the child negotiates and becomes a part of the environment, literacy emerges. Yetta Goodman (cited in Taylor & Dorsey-Gaines, 1988) describes this process in constructivist terms:

> Children in a literate society grow up with literacy as an integral part
> of the personal, familial, and social histories. Interacting with their
> literate environment, children invent their own literacies and their
> inventions often parallel the inventions of literacy by society as a
> whole. (p. 61)

Although this constructivist view of literacy learning is gaining support,
there is still a tendency, even among supporters, to see some communities as having literacy deficiencies.

Before a child enters school, a medical history must be obtained. Beyond finding out whether the child has had asthma, been hospitalized, or
has hearing problems, the health care provider makes observations about
the child's physical well-being and nutritional status. Importantly, the
child's and the child's family's medical history must be indicated. These
steps are deemed necessary to ensure the child's physical health and the
appropriateness of health considerations. Rarely are similar steps taken
to ensure the child's literacy health and the appropriateness of literacy
considerations. We take no literacy histories. We ask for no family literacy
histories or for any information about prevailing literacy conditions in the
child's environment. Lacking literacy histories, educational providers
work in vacuums quickly filled with assumptions about the children, their
families, and their communities. Providers render service based on what
"textbook case" children should do, have, and know at a given time. If
therapies show little effect, stronger therapies are ordered and the children are often labeled "deficient."

Literacy research is rife with theories uninformed by personal and
community literacy histories. "Literacy research theories," suggests Scott
(1991), "explain the language and literacy patterns of nonmainstream
ethnic and social groups more in terms of what they are not than what they
are" (p. 49). The deficit models that dominated earlier research are recy-
cled into contemporary theoretical assumptions. One major research effort of the 1960s, the Department of Education-sponsored Cooperative
Research Program in First Grade Reading Instruction, examined school
instructional practices as they affected different groups of students. The
researchers seemed unaware of the historical context of their work. It
followed by a decade the historic *Brown v. Board of Education* decision
that struck down the "separate but equal" doctrine of education. This
research also celebrated the centennial of the repeal of antiliteracy laws.
During that century, the African-American community achieved a literacy rate of 90% (Bond 1934; Levine, 1977). However, ignoring this historical context and failing to consider the personal and community literacy
histories of learners, researchers labeled groups of students as "culturally

deprived" (Bloom, Davis, & Hess, 1965; Malpass, Williams, & Gilmore, 1967); "psychosocially deprived" (Hodges, McCandless, & Specker, 1967): and, more often, "disadvantaged" (Bereiter & Engelman, 1966; Cohen, 1967; Fite & Schwartz, 1965; Harris, Serwer, & Gold, 1966). Brazziel (1962) described children from "disadvantaged groups," and Chall and Feldmann (1966) identified children from "socially disadvantaged neighborhoods." In contrast, other children in the studies were identified as from "middle class suburban neighborhoods" (Fry, 1966).

Although the labeling or mislabeling of students seems to carefully avoid racial categorizations, the labels tend to be euphemisms for racial designations. Children who are middle class and from suburban neighborhoods are not black. Children who are from urban neighborhoods that are disadvantaged are not white. Indeed, the idea that African-American male children can be both suburban dwellers and middle class is almost inconceivable. When a bus trip took children past one African-American male child's suburban house, the teacher chided the youngster for lying when he exclaimed, "that's my house." The youngster was an avid reader who had always enjoyed school success. He was recommended for special education after a school transfer. When the parents requested to review the assessment instruments, the school's report, and the written plan for remediation, the child was "retested" and recommended for the Gifted and Talented program. In this instance, the child was not being asked to overcome his "disadvantage"; he was being required to overcome the perception of his inferiority. Inaccurate perceptions and mislabeling are bolstered by the theories and assumptions that undergird literacy research and practice.

These assumptions seem clear. Middleclass "surburbanness" provides literacy advantages. Absence of "middleclassness" or "suburbanness" leaves the learner with deficits. When this paradigm fails to explain either success or failure, we are offered notions of "under" and "over" achievement, "learning disability," and medical sounding terms like "dyslexia" and "dyscalclia." Despite what the deficit models fail to explain, they persist in literacy research assumptions and practices. Neither the successes nor school failures of children are adequately accounted for by labels that are often euphemisms for certain groups of learners.

Reconceptualizing literacy in the black community

It is the purpose of this chapter to suggest directions that will modify and expand models of literacy research and practice to appreciate the cultural strengths and resources of diverse cultural groups. It is also our purpose to use these proposed models to begin explorations of the literacy mentoring practices of one of the "major group forces in the Black community" (Asante, 1988, p. 73), the Black Church. The direction and parameters established for the project described in this chapter are oriented by three research questions:

1. What part has the Black Church played historically in the development of literacies (discourses) in the African-American community?
2. What traditions, practices, and teachings seemed to influence most significantly the development of literacies in the African-American community?
3. How do church literacy events and mentoring patterns compare with school literacy events and mentoring patterns?

In this chapter, we report on the initial phases of this research in which we looked at the historical development of the Black Church, and in which we interviewed members, made observations of discourse practices, and collected samples of written materials in Black churches. This chapter also includes insights gained from our own experiences in Black churches.

Important to our research efforts was the growing body of descriptive literacy research studies that explore modes of discourse. James Paul Gee (1989) has defined *discourses* as "ways of being in the world . . . forms of life which integrate words, acts, values, beliefs, attitudes, and social identities, as well as gestures, glances, body positions and clothes" (pp. 6–7). Gee suggests that language socialization occurs early in the lives of children at home, where children acquire a *primary discourse*. Gee's work suggests that primary discourses are not transmitted by direct instruction but are passed on through a process of apprenticeship. Heath (1983) and Cazden (1988) also speak to the role of socialization in the development of discourses. Collectively, this work suggests that discourse is acquired through enculturation into "social practices through scaffolded and supported interactions with people who have already mastered the discourse" (Gee, 1989, p. 7). Researchers like these have also considered classrooms one place of a child's learning that should be dynamic enough to respond to the variety of discourses with which the children arrive. For instance, Moll, Tapia, and Whitmore (1993) describe how a Latino family mobilizes "funds of knowledge" to network for the benefit of the family. They then describe how children establish such networks in whole language classrooms. Overall, these studies suggest ways to look at the Black

Church in terms of its rich funds of knowledge embodied in discourses and mentoring practices.

These ideas helped shape the ways in which we looked at discourse and literacy within the Black Church. African-American families and churches are major socializing forces in the African-American child's acquisition of primary discourses. And where the Black Church's role in helping its members learn to read and write is often cited in the literature, the discussion rarely goes to the manner in which discourses are acquired and the ways in which social forces accomplish literacies. Ideas about the nature of discourse advanced by theorists like Gee (1989, 1990) provide a powerful lens through which to reconceptualize literacy in the Black Church.

The Black Church as a prism of African-American literacies

The Black Church is the first and most enduring social institution created by African-Americans (DuBois, 1962). It began as the invisible church of slavery. As enslaved persons, African-Americans' worship was clandestine or their churches were developed under the close scrutiny of their enslavers (Hughes, Meltzer, & Lincoln, 1983). They managed "through the use of highly allegorical preaching and praying and through the clever use of 'spirituals' . . . to present God's Word and to hear God's Word in a way the slavemaster had never intended" (p. 370). From its beginning, the Black Church had to mold language to inform some, fail to inform others, and communicate a spiritual and political message. The Black Church had "immediate consequences because of the centrality of the spiritual in the African world view and because religion was the only politics possible in the slave regime" (Bennett, 1975, p. 117).

Ironies exist in the evolution of the Black Church. The proselytizing done by missionaries, like Elias Neau in New York and Cotton Mather in Boston, at times included the teaching of reading so that Africans could understand the Bible (Bennett, 1975). Although reading and writing were encouraged, the Christianizing mission was designed essentially to pacify and accommodate Africans to their enslaved status. Plantation owners raised barriers to prohibit the enslaved Africans both religion and education, believing enlightenment would breed discontent (Thompson, 1987). "Often the blame for slave revolts was placed squarely at the door of the missionaries, who were said to imbue the slaves with ideas of insubordination" (Thompson, 1987 p. 219).

Black oral discourses

From its beginnings, bathed in allegory and multimeaning spirituals, the Black Church became a platform for the whole panorama of Black life. The Black Church was a nexus for the formation of African-American discourses. Africans brought a rich legacy of both oral and written traditions to the Americas. Written traditions were more easily frustrated, but oral traditions were pressed into service for survival. James Baldwin (1979) elaborates on the development of Black discourses:

> Blacks came to the United States chained to each other but from different tribes. Neither could speak the other's language. If two black people, at the bitter hour of the world's history, had been able to speak to each other, the institution of chattel slavery could never have lasted as long as it did. Subsequently the slave was given under the eye and the gun, of his master, Congo Square, and the Bible – or, in other words, under these conditions, the slave began the formation of the black church, and it is within this unprecedented tabernacle that black English began to be formed. This was not merely, as in the European example, the adoption of a foreign tongue, but an alchemy that transformed ancient elements into a new language: *A language comes into existence by brutal necessity, and the rules of the language are dictated by what the language must convey.*
>
> There was a moment, in time, and in this place, when my brother, or my mother, or my father, or my sister, had to convey to me for example, the danger in which I was standing from the white man standing just behind me, and to convey this with a speed, and in a language that the white man could not possibly understand, and that indeed, he cannot understand until today. (Section E, p. 19)

African-Americans, through alchemy, passion, skill, sheer intelligence, incredible music, and the Black Church, created oral discourses that conveyed what the denier could not completely comprehend (Baldwin, 1979). Levine (1977) underscores Baldwin's remarks pointing out that in the linguistic dilemma in which they found themselves, Africans forged their oral traditions out of West African work songs, stories, verbal games, allegorical call-and-response sermons, and spirituals. The speeches and sermons of Dr. Martin Luther King, Jr., for example, are part of the long, rich tradition of allegorical preaching and ingenious use of spirituals fashioned to make more bearable, and ultimately to defeat, a system of physical and social enslavement (Hughes et al., 1983). African-Americans forged a new language that retained many of the subtleties and indirection of the African languages but used English to speak new realities.

Black performed discourses: Black music

DuBois (1962) called Black music "America's one real gift to beauty" (p. 125). Black singing, assert Lincoln and Mamiya (1990), is a study of the Africanization of Christianity. Black oral and performed discourses have their origins in Africa. Both are inextricably tied to the Black Church. Lincoln and Mamiya explain that song, worship, and living were one venture. They point out that spirituals were bearers of oral history that developed out of a call-and-response experience in which the preacher chanted some important statement and the congregation responded. Further, they explain that, since music in Africa was always accompanied by movement, shout became a part of the Black Church ritual. The traditions of hymn lining and meter music developed because of "illiteracy" among the congregants and scarcity of hymnals. When the great migrations brought thousands of African-Americans to U.S. urban industrial centers, the Black Church also migrated. The work songs and spirituals of the South became gospel music in urban America (Lincoln & Marniya, 1990).

Black written discourses

Written language was forbidden to enslaved Africans, but far from disappearing, it surfaced in emancipatory narratives. Calvin Hernton (1987) charts the course of African-American literature, a course thwarted but never successfully subdued. In *The Sexual Mountain and Black Women Writers*, Hernton writes:

> The literature of black people began in the cruel ships that transported the Africans to the so-called New World. It began really long ago in Africa. It simply underwent changes in the Americas. Black poetry originated in the fields with the slave songs. It went into the churches with the spirituals and migrated with the blacks wherever they were scattered. When blacks gained enough liberty to be able to write without being killed for doing so they took up the forms and concerts that had been developed and fashioned long before writing. (p. 153)

Forced servitude and proscriptions against reading and writing forced written language underground. These conditions also forced African-Americans to create a new literary form, which was produced and published in unprecedented numbers. Ishmael Reed (1976) suggests in *Flight to Canada* that the enslaved persons who learned to read and write were the first to run away. Those who did run away, who achieved self-emancipation, created literature to tell of their ordeal in bondage – the *emancipator* or *slave narrative*. This genre of literature stood, and stands, as testimony to the enslaved African's thirst for freedom and literacy (Gates, 1987). The *emancipator narrative* was often an "extension of their speeches" (Gates, 1987, p. xi). Those formerly enslaved admitted that often these narratives were edited renditions of spoken stories (Gates, 1987). This spoken work written down enjoyed great popularity between 1830 and 1865, but after the collapse of Reconstruction and the rise of terrorism against African-Americans, this form of discourse went underground and recomposed itself as blues, ragtime, and jazz (Hernton, 1987).

The rise of the Black Church is an important chapter in the literacy history of America. It was created by enslaved Africans. The isolation and hostility encountered by the African-American community created a climate for the emergence of oral, performed, and written discourses. The Black Church is central to the emergence of these discourses in the African-American community, though its role often goes unnoticed. African-American discourses and mentoring traditions are so deeply embedded in the Black Church that they can scarcely be considered separately from it. Although such discourses developed through un-self-conscious social interactions, the Black Church also self-consciously engaged in the education of the Black community. The changing status of African-Americans also made new demands on the Church's funds of knowledge, and new efforts unfolded to educate and support the economic and political aspirations of their members.

The Black Church and community education

The historical efforts of Black churches to provide means for educating their members were monumental. By 1900, Baptist churches alone were supporting some 80 schools, academies, and colleges. The African Methodist Episcopal (AME) Church raised millions of dollars for educational purposes between 1884 and 1900 and supported some 22 institutions providing education above the elementary level. The AME Church established its first education institution, Union Seminary, in 1844. This institution was later merged into Wilberforce University, which the Church purchased from the Methodist Conference in 1856. In 1900, the AME Zion Church as a denomination was supporting eight colleges and institutions of higher learning, and the Colored Methodist Episcopal Church had established five schools in a 30-year period.

Monroe Fordham (1975), in his writings on northern Black religious thought, contends that religious spokesmen were convinced that morality and educational advancement were closely connected. A statement suggesting this was adopted by the Philadelphia Conferences of the Bethel Methodists:

> Education is the only sure means of creating in the mind of those noble feelings which prompt us to the practice of piety, virtue, and temperance and elevate us . . . by assimilating us to the image of maker. (*Colored American*, July 1, 1837)

A similar conviction was voiced later by Booker T. Washington:

> The struggle to attain a higher level of living, to get land, to build a home, to give their children an education, just because it demands more earnestness and steadfastness of purpose, gives a steadiness and a moral significance to the religious life which is the thing the Negro people need at present. (Nilsen, Yokley, & Nilsen, 1971, p. 42)

However, Booker T. Washington saw religion only as a means to imbue African-American people with a moral sense. He ignored a larger part of the history of the Black Church, such as the establishment of First Day School in 1796 and 6 months later, the inauguration of a night school for adults. For instance, at the AME Church during the Nineteenth Session of the Philadelphia Annual Conference in 1831, the following resolution was passed:

> Resolved: That as the subject of education is one that highly interests all people, and especially the colored people of this country, it shall be the duty of every minister who has the charge of circuits of stations to use every exertion to establish schools wherever convenient, and to insist upon parents sending their children to schools, and to preach occasionally a sermon on the subject of education and it shall be the duty of all such ministers to make returns yearly of the number of schools, the amount of scholars, the branches taught, and the places in which they are located, and that every minister neglecting to do so, be subject to the censure of the Conference. (Payne, 1841, p. 100)

Today, churches serving the Black community number more than 65,000. Surveys of a sample of that number reveal that the Black Church "now as in the past, is very much engaged in programs of educational service" (George, Richarson, Lakes-Matyas, & Blake, 1989). Churches are engaged in programs ranging from preschool and day-care programs and after-school and Saturday tutorial programs to college entrance workshops and mentoring programs and GED preparation (George, 1989). The American Association for the Advancement of Science Black Churches-Blacks in College Partnership Program is a recent example of the Black Church's involvement in the education of the Black community.

This partnership assists Black colleges and universities, as well as colleges and universities with significant Black student enrollments, to establish educational programs as sites for preservice field work (George, Malcolm, & Worthington, 1993). Earlier partnerships, report George (1989), have helped more than 1,500 Black churches incorporate science and technology education into their educational programs.

Contemporary literacies

The contemporary Black Church provides numerous literacy experiences for its members. Next to the weekly bulletins that outline the structure of the service, announce the coming events, list the members who are sick and shut in, and remind members of meetings, the hymnal is the most prevalent form of written text. Hymnals are used for the hymns, doxology, and anthems throughout the service. A bimonthly newsletter is mailed to Church members containing articles describing past or current activities, human interest stories, reports concerning issues affecting the African-American community, Bible scriptures, photographs, and announcements. Additional letters may be sent by the Church clerical staff about meetings and events. The Black Church also retains discourse practices that grew out of oral traditions or combine oral and literate traditions. Most hymns are known to the congregation, yet the ministers often *line* the songs throughout the singing. Numerous fliers are posted throughout the church, announcing events. Announcements are also read orally during the course of Church services.

The services and sermon that follow illustrate the literacy traditions that have evolved in the African-American Baptist Church. Dr. Samuel Proctor, Pastor Emeritus of Abyssinian Baptist Church, offered the sermon entitled "Finding Our Margin of Freedom," based on Galatians 3:1–29:

> The Epistle to the Galatians has been called the Magna Carta of the Christian faith. It has been looked upon as the document that spells out the final breach that Paul the Apostle made with the religion of his people, Judaism, and the clear origin of Christianity as a separate movement. (Proctor, 1984, p. 15)

The sermon is outlined and based on biblical scripture, which is read in its entirety aloud. During the presentation of the sermon, personal stories are interwoven throughout – providing the listening congregants with an application of scriptures to their lives, as well as the historical context in which the books were written. This particular minister moves from the historical and actual contexts to other contexts, including an international one, to convey to the congregation the meaningfulness of the scriptures to their lives. He explains that these scriptures highlight the theme of freedom; yet, he continues, with freedom come obligations and responsibilities. Through the spoken word, the minister provides the congregation with relevant examples of this theme – freedom inextricably linked with responsibilities. He also provides several vignettes to support the theme carefully, skillfully interwoven and crafted throughout his sermon, which is interspersed with humor and the necessary signals of an orally delivered speech. The minister speaks using standard American English; however, he highlights aspects of his sermons with language born of and shaped by the community.

Clearly, the contemporary Black Church retains its traditions shaped by the African roots and survival needs of its communicants. It has and continues to shape discourses. It has and continues to act as a literacy mentor. It has and continues to provide leadership training and opportunity for leadership development. By exploring the Black Church in terms of its literacies, this research effort begins to describe the structures available for individual and community development. By looking at the ways individuals and families interact with the Black Church, this research through personal literacy histories also begins to describe the kinds of events that seemed to most influence literacy behavior.

Personal literacy histories

Two separate activities provided the basis for the histories collected: relating family stories and relating the earliest recollections of reading and writing. The two members of the research team had routinely included these activities in their graduate and undergraduate courses. During research discussions, the narratives from these assignments became connected to our questions about the Black Church and literacy. The researchers decided to cull their assignments for narratives that implicated the Church in literacy development. We decided to collect family stories from colleagues and friends, to interview colleagues and Church members about their earliest recollections of reading and writing, and to collect personal narratives from Church members at the churches observed. One researcher attending a family reunion asked the 96 people attending to write their favorite family stories. These preliminary efforts suggest the possibility of a larger, more systematic effort to collect and record literacy reflections. They also suggest the need to record literacy events in the lives of young people as they occur (for instance, instruments like the Primary Language Record can include community activities).

When asked, "Do you remember learning to read or write?", most respondents spoke of those events in which reading and books were specifically designated for reading to be learned or shared. Occasionally a respondent talked about going to silent movies, reading the captions, and surprising older siblings. As participants in the interviews conducted for this research told family stories, and talked and wrote about their experiences with reading and writing, the Church came up repeatedly. In many of these personal narratives, the literacy practices of the Church seemed submerged, embedded in the events, so that learners were scarcely conscious of their educational import. Such embedded literacy learning is illustrated by a passage from Harper Lee's book *To Kill a Mockingbird* (1962), where the character Scout reflects on her literacy learning. On the first day of school, Scout is discovered to be literate. Her novice teacher scolds her for this improper foray into school territory, leaving Scout upset and "meditating upon her crime":

> I mumbled that I was sorry and retired meditating upon my crime. I never deliberately learned to read, but somehow I had been wallowing illicitly in the daily papers. In the long hours of church – was it then I learned? I could not remember not being able to read hymns. Now that I was compelled to think about it, reading was something that just came to me, as learning to fasten the seat of my union suit without looking around, or achieving two bows from a snarl of shoe laces. I could not remember when the lines above Atticus's moving finger separated into words, but I had stared at them all the evening in my memory, listening to the news of the day, bills to be enacted into laws, the diaries of Lorenzo Dow – anything Atticus happened to be reading when I crawled into his lap every night. Until I feared I would lose it, I never loved to read. One does not love breathing. (p. 22)

Long hours of Church or prayer meeting seemed to be the way many respondents remembered their time in Church. In rural southern churches, both Black and White, congregations met often and for long periods of time. One of the personal narratives shared about a man born in the 1880s speaks to the lengthiness of these church services and the learning required for participation in them.

> Papa was the superintendent of the Colored schools in our county. He worked late but was usually home in time to insist that all chores and all homework was completed. Weekends were more relaxed but we still had chores. In the evenings on weekends Papa liked to tell stories about when he was a boy. His favorite was the time he tried to escape from prayer meeting at St. John's. Prayer meetings went on forever, and he and his brother and sisters were required to attend. Prayer meeting was singing, chanting, and different members offering prayers. The children had to behave and try not to fall asleep. At one meeting

Papa was sitting with his friend when the boys heard the preacher drone out that they would hear a prayer from Papa's friend. Papa's friend was caught off guard and asked Papa what to say. Papa told him to say the blessing. Papa's friend said the blessing and the meeting continued. Then Papa heard the preacher drone, "and now we'll hear a prayer from brother Tom." Papa panicked; he had given his one prayer away to his friend and now had nothing to say. Papa and his friend determined to crawl out of the church and escape. They might have gotten away except that the dogs that had accompanied their owners to church were resting under the building, and when the boys reached the dogs they began to bark furiously. They boys ran back into the church. The church broke into hysterics and the prayer meeting ended. Papa was punished with the worst whipping in his memory. He started learning two Bible verses each week from then on, one for himself and one for his friend. The first two he learned were "Delight thyself also in the Lord; and He shall give thee the desires of thine heart" and "Commit thy way unto the Lord; trust also in Him and He shall bring it to pass." (From an interview with P.C., Houston, Texas)

Two additional personal narratives drawn from our interviews reveal how African-American elders, themselves emergent readers, conducted Church services. They used their considerable oral language traditions and assisted the youngsters toward mastery of the written language conventions. Repetition and modeling were key elements of Sunday school and weekday Church activities.

I remember most the repetition, the encouraging of listening strategies. At each Sunday morning Sunday school, each Wednesday evening prayer meeting, each Monday evening Bible study, always the same format. My paternal grandfather, who was unable to decipher the alphabetic configuration, would always pick up the hymnal and "line" a hymn in log or common meter. The members of the Church would follow in beautiful four part harmony. He would recite the scriptures of the Bible, verbatim because this beautiful technique was passed down throughout his generation and much of mine. Deacon Gravely, who was about fifteen years my Grandfather's junior, was Sunday School superintendent. Deacon Gravely could read. He would read to children in Sunday school and have us read the primary class cards to him. We read after him, repeating each word and emphasizing the religious words very loudly. This same method was used when we sang a hymn. The one song I still remember is "Rescue the Perishing, Care for the Dying, Jesus Is Merciful, Jesus Will Save." No matter what other song we sang, "Rescue the Perishing" was always first. The "Card Class" with all the other classes sang with gusto, especially the last part, "Jesus Is Merciful, Jesus Will Save." (From an interview with J.G., New Jersey)

My dad swears that the old people in the church used to make them read the Bible to them aloud. If you messed up they'd tell you to go back over the part, and they could tell you exactly what it was suppose

> to say. You couldn't fool them because they couldn't read. They knew
> that Bible. (From an interview with J.H., New Jersey)

These two narratives reveal something of how reading was encouraged by Church elders. Much of the Bible seems to have become a part of their oral literacy, so that young learners could read while their mentors checked them for accuracy.

Finally, mentoring practices in church, school, and homes were mutually supportive. The opening narrative vignette of this chapter ("A Reading Lesson") suggested the literacy mentoring practices that occurred in home settings, practices that were closely tied to the Church. The following narrative suggests relationships between the Black Church and school literacy practices.

> A five-year-old at Abraham Lincoln Elementary School was explaining to the principal that he knew a particular work on the mosaic mural about the life of Lincoln. He offered, "that word says tom/b/. See, that part *t-o-m*, that's my name, Tom. And teacher said just put a "buh" on the end of it. "So that," the boy beamed, "says Lincoln's tom/buh/." The principal affirmed this youngster's application of a recent school lesson and offered to walk the young man to class. Several years passed before the word *tomb* ever came up again in conversation. As it happened, the boy was preparing to read aloud in Sunday school a Bible passage on the death and resurrection of Christ. While practicing the verse, he came across the word *sepulchre*. When he asked what this *sepulchre* was, his mother suggested that he look the word up in the dictionary. While he was looking at the definition, one of his older siblings injected that *sepulchre* was another word for *tomb*. It was at the moment that the boy connected *tomb* (which he had assumed was spelled *toom*) with the letters t–o–m–b. (From an interview with E.E., Chicago)

These personal literacy histories clearly point to the Church as an influence on individual lives and the collective life of the Black community. Until they were asked to think about time spent in Church and the reading, speaking, and singing they did there, our respondents had not thought seriously about the Church as it had influenced the literacy of their grandparents, their parents, themselves, or their children. The literacy mentoring practices of the Black Church had been scarcely detected by the respondents. Indeed, internalized perceptions of the community's deficiencies may have caused many to suspect that there were limited funds of knowledge. Rediscovering the Church as a rich resource was an exciting part of the storytelling interviewing process. Our interviews usually ended with respondents reclaiming their mentors from Church and cherishing them anew.

The Black Church was and continues to be a nexus for the development of literacies in the Black community. Our historical analyses and personal interviews suggest the rich, multifarious literacies that draw their roots from the Black Church. These early results urge a more accurate appraisal of communities, their literacies, and their funds of knowledge. When literacy researchers ignore such resources, their assumptions, theories, and practices suffer. The perceptions fostered by inaccuracy tend to deprive children rather than encourage their development. Literacy research may be strengthened as it accommodates to the increasing awareness of the discourses and literacies of diverse communities. Explorations in the Black Church persuade us that literacy research agendas should include similar explorations and should develop strategies that describe individuals and communities in terms of what they possess rather than what they appear to lack.

Toward an educational research agenda

All communities create and are created by discourses. Literacy practitioners can scarcely afford simply to declare deficiency in a community and its discourses, and allow that declaration to suffice for research theory or to be a guide for practice. Creating school environments that empower, mentor, and support learners' community-based discourses requires more than paying lip service to the idea that all discourses are to be respected. Often they are not, and each child recognizes when his discourse, and thus his community, are perceived as deficient. An alternative literacy research agenda might begin by recognizing that literacy encompasses more than the ability to negotiate the conventions of written text. To this end, literacy research could be expanded. Descriptive studies could explore communities' discourses and mentoring practices, as well as the harmonies or disharmonies that exist between community and school discourses and mentoring practices. Individual and collective literacy histories could be used as resources for expanding the current repertoire of school discourses. Successful community mentoring practices could be adapted for use in the classroom. Research initiatives like these can provide a clearer picture of the cultural landscapes in which schools operate. More accurate descriptions of learners and the communities from which they come will lessen some of the more nonproductive labeling that obfuscates rather than explicates the issues. These research directions may cause a revision of schools as extensions of the communities they serve, rather than as sites of conflicting discourses.

The function of educational research is to inform practice. Literacy research, it would seem, should labor to provide the most accurate information possible so that practices rest on soundness and not on sluggish, outdated assumptions. The perceived inferiority of the African-American community and its children is an issue that researchers in literacy, as in other fields, must face. It continues to mold the research agendas and underlying assumptions of much of research and practice in literacy education. Children are no longer *"disadvantaged"*, they are *"at risk."* The research effort in which we have engaged grows out of many experiences that remind us that, regardless of fluency in or number of discourses attained, the perception of inferiority is a factor with which many children must contend as they struggle to make sense of the world. Test scores and other research machinations that make comparisons across cultural lines do little to get at the root of the perception. Perhaps this research effort too will not achieve the paradigmatic shift that would be necessary to see all learners as capable meaning makers. However, it will begin to describe how the African-American community supports the development of its members and it will begin to describe how the Black Church, in particular, has had a historic as well as a contemporary role in helping its members create their own discourses and master those of schools and workplaces.

References

Asante, M. K. (1988). (*Afrocentricity*). Trenton, NJ: Africa World Press.

Baldwin, J. (1979). If Black English isn't a language, then tell me what is? *The New York Times*, July 29, Section E, p. 19.

Bennett, L. (1975). *The shaping of Black America*. Chicago: Johnson Publishing.

Bereiter, C., & Engelman, S. (1966). *Teaching disadvantaged children in the preschool*. Englewood Cliffs, NJ: Prentice-Hall.

Bond, H. M. (1934). In *The education of the Negro in the American social order*, Chap. 9. NJ: Prentice Hall. In the *U.S. Department of Commerce, Negro population, 1790–1915*, Chap. 16. (1918). From the *U.S. Department of Commerce, historical statistics of the United States, colonial times to 1957, Chap. H*, (1960). Washington, DC: U.S. Department of Commerce.

Bloom, B., Davis, A., & Hess, R. (1965). *Compensatory education for cultural deprivation*. New York: Holt.

Brazziel, W. F. (1962). An experiment in the development of readiness in culturally disadvantaged groups of first grade children. *The Journal of Negro Education, 31*, 4–7.

Cazden, C. (1988). *Classroom discourse: The language of teaching and learning*. Portsmouth, NH: Heinemann.

Chall, J., & Feldman, S. (1966). First grade reading: An analysis of the interactions of professional methods, teacher implementation and child background. *The Reading Teacher, 19*, 569–575.

Cohen, S. (1967). Some conclusions about teaching reading to disadvantaged children. *The Reading Teacher, 20*, 433–438.

DuBois, W. E. B. (1962). *Black reconstruction in America, 1860–1880*. New York: Atheneum. (Original work published 1902)

Dunn. L. M., et al. (1967). The effectiveness of three reading approaches and an oral language simulation program with disadvantaged children in the primary grades: An interim report after one year of the Cooperative Reading Project. *IMRID Behavioral Science Monograph 7*.

Fite, J. H., & Schwartz, L. A. (1965). Screening culturally disadvantaged, first grade children for potential reading difficulties due to constitutional factors. *American Journal of Orthopsychiatry, 35*, 359–360.

Fordham, M. (1975). *Major themes in northern Black religious thought 1800–1860, (1st ed.)*. Hicksville, NY: Exposition Press.

Fry, E. B. (1966). First grade reading instruction using diacritical marking systems, Initial Teaching Alphabet, and basal reading system. *The Reading Teacher, 19*, 666–669.

Garnett, C. M. (1994). Unpublished short story.

Gates, H. L., Jr. (1987). *Three classic slave narratives*. New York: New American Library.

Gee, J. P. (1989). What is literacy? *Journal of Education, 171*(1), 18–25.

Gee, J. P. (1990). *Social linguistics and literacies: Ideology in discourses*. New York: Falmer Press.

George, Y. S., Malcolm, S. M., & Worthington, V. (Eds.). (1993). *Building blocks for the future student teaching internships in Black Churches*. Washington, DC: American Association for the Advancement of Science.

George, Y. S., Richarson, V., Lakes-Matyas, M., & Blake, F. (1989). *Saving Black minds: Black churches and education*. Washington, DC: American Association for the Advancement of Science.

Halliday, M. (1975). *Explorations in the function of language*. New York: Elsevier.

Halliday, M. (1977). *Learning how to mean: Explorations in the development of language*. New York: Elsevier.

Harris, A., Serwer, B. L., & Gold, L. (1966). Comparing reading approaches in first grade teaching with disadvantaged children. *The Reading Teacher, 19*, 631–635.

Heath, S. B. (1983). *Ways with words: Language, life and work in communities and classrooms*. New York: Cambridge University Press.

Hernton, C. (1987). *The sexual mountain and Black women writers*. New York: Anchor Press.

Hodges, W. L., McCandless, B. R., & Specker, H. H. (1967). *The development and evaluation of diagnostically based curriculum for preschool psychosocially deprived children*. Final Report of Contracts No. 5–0350 and OEC 32–24–0210–1011. Washington, DC: U.S. Office of Education.

Holdaway, D. (1979). *Foundations of literacy*. Sydney, Australia: Ashton Scholastic.

Hughes, L., Meltzer, M., & Lincoln, C. E. (1983). *A pictorial history of Black Americans*. New York: Crown.

Lee, H. (1962). *To kill a mockingbird*. New York: Popular Library.

Levine, L. W. (1977). *Black culture and Black consciousness: African American folk thought from slavery to freedom*. New York: Oxford University Press.

Lincoln, C. E., & Marniya, L. H. (1990). *The Black Church in the African American experience*. Durham, NC: Duke University Press.

Madigan, D. (1991). Family uses of literacy: A critical view. In C. K. Kinzer & D. J. Leu (Eds.), *Literacy research, theory, and practice: Views from many perspectives*. Chicago: National Reading Conference.

Malpass, L. F., Williams, C. F., & Gilmore, A. S. (1967). *Programmed reading instruction for culturally deprived slow learners.* Final Report of Project No. 6–8438 and Contract No. OEC 2–7 – 0684–0069. Washington, DC: U.S. Office of Education.

Moll, L., Tapia, J., & Whitmore, K. (1993). In G. Salomon (Ed.), *Distributed cognitions.* New York: Cambridge University Press.

Nelson, H., Hokley M., & Nelson, H. (1971). *The Black Church in America.* New York: Basic Books.

Payne, D. A. (1969). *History of the African Methodist Episcopal Church: American Negro: His history and literature series #2.* Reproduction 1891 ed. Salem, NH: Ayer Company Publishers.

Proctor, S. (1984). Related by a congregant of a sermon given by Dr. Proctor at the Abyssinian Baptist Church, New York City.

Reed, I. (1976). *Flight to Canada.* New York: Random House.

Scott, J. (1991). Deficit theories, ethnic dialects, and literacy research: when and why recycling is not cost efficient. In C.K. Kinzer & D.J. Leu (Eds.) *Literacy research, theory, and practice: Views from many perspectives.* Chicago: National Reading Conference.

Stuckey, S. (1973). Through the prism of folklore: The Black ethos in slavery. In A. Weinstein & F. Gatell (Eds.), *American Negro slavery.* New York: Oxford University Press.

Taylor, D., & Dorsey-Gaines, C. (1988). *Growing up literate: Learning from inner-city families.* Portsmouth, NH: Heinemann.

Thompson, V. B. (1987). *The making of the African diaspora in the Americas, 1441–1900.* New York: Longman.

Afterword

10   Vygotsky and current debates in education: some dilemmas as afterthoughts to *Discourse, Learning, and Schooling*

James Paul Gee

Vygotsky, or at least the ideas he has bequeathed to sociocultural theories of language, literacy, and cognition, is at the center of much of this volume. The intersection of Vygotsky's ideas and current educational debates are central as well – for example, the distinctions and relations between what we acquire through immersion in communities and what we learn through more typically school-like sorts of instruction. There is, too, in many of the chapters (as in much recent work in the area), a sense that we are looking for ways to move on from where Vygotsky has left us without losing the ground he has helped secure. It is to these themes that I want to turn in some afterthoughts on this volume.

Although Vygotsky's ideas are at the foundation of contemporary sociocultural theories of language and literacy, I believe we are just beginning to realize the extent to which these ideas raise profound dilemmas deeply relevant to current controversies over educational reform. Thus, before I turn directly to Vygotsky, I want to sketch one such controversy now playing itself out in much of the English-speaking world. This is the debate between *progressive* and *postprogressive* pedagogies: a distinction that sometimes turns on arguments about the role and efficacy of explicit instruction in contrast to implicit learning through immersion in rich education environments.

Those on both the right and the left of the political spectrum have called for a renewed emphasis on explicit instruction. The right (as ever) demands a return to "basics," to explicit teaching and testing of traditional grammar, phonics, decoding, and numeracy. Given that contemporary capitalism appears to desire "knowledge workers" who possess not rote knowledge and skills but rather the ability to adapt, learn, and problem solve (Drucker, 1993), I do not believe "back-to-basics" demands are of much importance in the long run, however dangerous they may be in the short run.

More interesting are calls for explicit instruction from the left. Though there are many variations of this position (e.g., Bernstein, 1975, 1990; Delpit, 1986, 1988, 1993), the *genre movement* originating in Australia is

269

one important variant (Christie, 1990; Cope & Kalantzis, 1993; Martin, 1985). People in this movement argue that when the "rules of the game" and the forms of language that society rewards are left implicit, to be discovered (inferred) by students as they are immersed in meaningful activities, we simply privilege children from families where these "rules" and forms are already part of their social practices. Children from families that play by different "rules" and use different forms of language are left to draw the "wrong" inferences or to live out the conflict between what is tacitly expected of them in school and what they experience at home and in their communities. Furthermore, such conflicts cannot become the focus of direct reflection and contestation when "rules" and language forms are left implicit, to be picked up by immersion in practices and activities.

Thus, it is argued, we must (to the extent that we can, of course) explicitly demonstrate and explicate for students (and teachers) forms of language and how they function to express meanings, social relationships, and (ideologically laden) values. These language forms involve not just grammar but also *genres* (patterns of language and behavior used to carry out common communicational tasks, such as reports, explanations, recounts, classifications, and the various specialized versions of these used in academic disciplines) and larger-scale communicational activities (whole lessons, textbooks, research projects, etc.). It is, of course, the focus on how language functions in social contexts and the ways in which language is far more than sentence grammar that, among many other things, distinguishes the genre movement's views on language from calls to return to traditional grammar in the schools.

This argument for explicit instruction is ultimately an argument about access. The genre movement and analogous movements argue for explicitly demonstrating and explicating the "discourses of power," that is, the forms of language and communication that lead to access to the centers of influence in capitalist society. Students, in turn, can choose either to seek "success" within the parameters of their society or to undermine the workings of the social hierarchy with its own tools, so to speak.

This view of explicit instruction runs afoul of those who believe (however sympathetic they may be to some of the genre movement's arguments and political viewpoints) that it is based on a misguided theory of learning (or, perhaps, no theory of learning at all). Its critics argue that presenting people with explicit information, with paradigms of a given genre – a report, for example – is not efficacious for learning. Humans simply do not acquire a repertoire of language forms and functions by being explicitly presented with paradigmatic instances of them. Such explicit information, given the ways in which the human mind/brain just happens to work, cannot translate directly to usable mental representations or embodied practices. (See Gee, 1992, for discussion; see also Edelsky, 1991.) Since the characterization presented here is my own compendium of what I take the central issues to be, and since I do not wish to place people in ideological "camps," I have not singled out by citation here opponents of the genre movement; see Reid, 1987, for papers relevant to the debate.)

Rather, it is argued, people learn the other way around: They (subconsciously) induce patterns and paradigms from actual practice and experience with a broad range of cases. Furthermore, actual instances (say, of reports) are always closely dovetailed to context and, in fact, simultaneously form and are formed by the contexts in which they are used. Anything that we can hold up as a prototypical instance is merely an abstraction from an array of contexts, an abstraction that requires one already to know a broad range of instances that the prototype sums up. Otherwise, the so-called prototype could only function as a particular instance, one that actually fits no particular context very well (Clark, 1993; Harre & Gillett, 1994; Margolis, 1993).

Of course, this dichotomous way of stating the issue is not very helpful, though it is, in fact, how the matter is often put. No one (I presume) would say we should never explicitly tell anyone anything – it is, for instance, useful to tell new drivers in snow and ice that they should steer in the direction of a skid rather than let them discover it through multiple smashes. And no one (I presume) would claim that we could possibly relate everything explicitly or that immersion in communities of practice is not important. The real issue – though too little debated directly in these terms – is when and how explicit information can be efficacious. Put in these terms, we might say that people in the genre movement claim that progressive pedagogies give too little explicit information and proponents of these pedagogies claim that genre-based pedagogies give too much.

However, although this is true, it oversimplifies the issue: We still have to know what sorts of explicit information need to be given in what form and when in the learning process. And this requires theories of learning, of classroom practices, and of the nature and structure of the sorts of knowledge we want people to acquire. Vygotsky, to his credit, had theories of all three (e.g., all three are dealt with, though in a general way, in *Thinking and Speech*, 1987). Whatever we may now think of those theories, it behooves those of us interested in the sorts of educational issues I have just touched on (especially if we wish to make recommendations about practice) to emulate Vygotsky in this regard and offer integrated theories of learning, classroom practices, and the nature of knowledge.

There is another way to situate the educational controversy we have been discussing: This is to consider the nature and relevance of (first) language acquisition. Children acquire their first languages (native languages) "effortlessly" through social interaction within their communities, without direct instruction. In fact, for most of us, this is the most impressive instance of learning in which we engage throughout our lives. The relevant educational question here is: What are the implications of this fact for later forms of learning, such as literacy, second languages, music, and academic disciplines? Should later learning environments, including classrooms, be designed to emulate, as far as possible, the nature of first language development (see Gee, 1994; Halliday, 1993 for discussion)?

Of course, if one believes, as do many American theoretical linguists (e.g., Chomsky, 1986), that the course of first language acquisition is largely directed by human biology, that is, that the development of the "language organ" in the mind/brain is largely the result of an innate endowment, then one may be able to draw few or no implications from first language acquisition for other forms of learning. Things like literacy, literature, and physics have come on the human scene too recently to be largely the products of biological design.

On the other hand, there are those who believe that the course of first language acquisition is determined, by and large, not by biology but by the nature of the child's early activities, social practices, and sociocultural interactions. In fact, even if biology does determine large parts of the grammar of human languages, this fact is germane only to rather formal (and sentence-level) parts of language. It still leaves language as an interactive and communicative phenomenon to be explained in terms of sociocultural aspects of human activities. In this case, we might well ask whether later instances of learning, including education in classrooms, should be patterned on the ways of first language acquisition, given that first language acquisition is an instance of (social) learning where there is widespread success that does not correlate with gender, social class, or any of the other social variables that are hallmarks of education in our hierarchically structured societies.

One can see many forms of progressive pedagogies – such as "Whole Language", process approaches to writing, various sorts of cooperative and collaborative education, and projects-based education – as attempts to re-create, in part at least, the social and cognitive settings of first language acquisition for other instances of learning (rich immersion in meaningful and supported practices, without a focus on overt instruction or form apart from meaning). Just as children are "apprenticed" to the linguistic practices of their home communities and "effortlessly" pick up their first language, so, too, it might be argued, learners should be apprenticed to "communities of practice" or "discourse communities" in such a way that they "pick up" by immersion the mores, conventions, rules, forms, and functions of these communities (whether a community of second-grade writers or a physics classroom). In terms of the distinction I made in Gee (1990) between "acquisition" and "learning" (see Krashen, 1985a, 1985b), we can put the matter as follows: First language development is a key instance where acquisition (immersion in meaningful experience) and not learning (overt instruction) leads to mastery in performance – in fact, it helps us define what constitutes acquisition in a core case. More broadly, then, we might argue that it is a general truth that humans are built in such a way that acquisition, not learning, leads to mastery.

On the other hand, postprogressives of various stripes can simply deny (apart from any arguments about biology) that this analogy ought to be drawn between how children acquire their first languages and how learners learn later skills and knowledge. School-based forms of literacy and academic disciplines like physics or the social sciences, it could be claimed, are much more functionally specific (and historically recent) sociocultural practices than is oral language. They require different forms of learning, including more overt forms of instruction that are germane to schooling precisely because they arose as part of the social practices of (emerging) technologically sophisticated, school-based societies. It is interesting that although Vygotsky is often used as a source for progressive pedagogies, thanks to his emphasis on the originally social nature of learning, he strongly emphasized how the overt forms of instruction typical of modern formal schooling lead to (what he called) "higher" forms of mental functioning.

But, again, the issue does not need to be put as a strict dichotomy: We might instead see the real issue as a question of where *acquisition* (the sorts of things typical of first language development) and *learning* (more overtly focused forms of instruction) are important and how they interact. And, again, here too, there will be those calling for more *learning* and others calling for much less (in the name of *acquisition*), based on their view about the nature of acquisition/learning, classrooms, and the structures and functions of knowledge.

Now to Vygotsky and the dilemmas I referred to at the outset. I consider just two of the leading ideas that Vygotsky has bequeathed to contemporary sociocultural theories of language, literacy, and cognition: the internalization of the social and the zone of proximal development in schooling. It is now taken for granted in many versions of sociocultural theory that the way human minds are "peopled" is by "internalizing" (the interactional semiotics of) the social world:

> Any higher mental function was external [and] social before it was internal. It was once a social relationship between two people. . . . We can formulate the general genetic law of cultural development in the following way: Any function in the child's cultural development appears twice or on two planes. . . . It appears first between people as an intermental category, and then within the child as an intramental category. (Vygotsky, 1960, pp. 197–198, cited and translated in Minick, 1987, p. 21)

Humans use language and other sign systems as social *tools* to accomplish various interactional tasks, and eventually they internalize patterns of tools-within-contexts-of-use as pieces of (intra-)mental furniture, which still bear the hallmarks of their interactive uses. For example, children, by scaffolded participation in the conversational routines of their social groups, get themselves (in mind and body) "in synch" with ways of introducing, sustaining, controlling, and changing topics. Eventually, they internalize "rules" (patterns) about topics and topic formation in conversation, although they can never explicitly state these rules. Or, to take another example, children participate in routines of naming things like shoes – these things are outdoor shoes, those are fancy ones, these are for home, those for work, and so forth: eventually, these patterns of use are organized in the child's mind in such a way that the child shares her community's patterns of use and, indeed, its tacit theories about shoes. What the child *doesn't* do is to gain her conceptual apparatus by asocial experience of the physical world (the world is already fully socialized by the time the child enters it) or by "definitions."

The double-edged nature of this idea is as follows: On the one hand, it demonstrates how crucial cooperative sociocultural interaction is – how riven the mind already is with the social, the cultural, the interactive, the ideological. And, indeed, this is a cornerstone of nearly all sociocultural theories of language, literacy, and cognition. On the other hand, such a process of the translation of the social into the mental does not allow children to gain much, if any, reflective or critical insight into the "representations" they have "swallowed." For example, the intricate "rules" and patterns that "govern" conversational interaction – so well laid bare by ethnomethodologists (e.g., Schenkein, 1978) – are not rules and patterns that we consciously know as we use or internalize them; nor do children have much reflective meta-awareness of their communities' tacit theories of shoes (or anything else). There is nothing in the translation of the social into the (intra-)mental that would give rise to reflective or critical awareness. This is the core problem with immersion learning: Indeed, a child effortlessly acquires her first language, but she ends up with little reflective awareness of the structure or function of language. Vygotsky readily concedes that children have no conscious reflective awareness of or control over their *spontaneous concepts* – his term for what the child comes to know through immersion in experience and interaction, apart from direct instruction.

Vygotsky deals with this problem by a combined use of his concept of the *zone of proximal development* and a notion of (overt) instruction in school. Vygotsky calls concepts over which the child *does* have reflective awareness and conscious control *nonspontaneous concepts* (also, using the term loosely, *scientific concepts*, the sorts of concepts found in academic disciplines). And these, Vygotsky argues, one gets only through working collaboratively with others who "know" more than one does *and* (simultaneously) via overt instruction that focuses on putting things into words, conscious and intentional use of the new concepts, and the relationships among forms and meanings.

As is well known, for Vygotsky the zone of proximal development for a given child is the difference between what the child can do alone and what she can accomplish with help. We have already seen that the child who has been immersed in social experience has acquired spontaneous concepts, but not the ability to deal consciously and reflectively with what she knows. By working with others to carry out joint tasks that require the use of concepts – scientific concepts – in such a way that the child is focused consciously on conceptual connections, verbal links, and connections between form and meaning (not typical of everyday learning outside the classroom), the child accomplishes something that she cannot yet do alone: namely, she uses concepts in a reflective, controlled, and conscious way. Vygotsky argues that this process eventually leads not just to the acquisition of some scientific concepts but also to the transfer of this ability (conscious control and mastery) to the realm of everyday spontaneous concepts.

The child's everyday concepts become reorganized such that the child comes to realize the links and connections among her concepts; she comes to see them as, and to operate with them as, a *system*. The everyday spontaneous concept no longer links directly and singly to the world of experience, but links to experience now only via a whole network of relationships with other concepts. To take one of Vygotsky's examples, the concept of "because" no longer links directly to concrete instances, but reaches reality now only through an intricate network of relationships to other concepts (e.g., physical causation, responsibility, contingency, various sorts of noncausal associations, and so forth). The child becomes aware that the concept has something of a life of its own and that it is related in various ways to other concepts. In turn, the child can now control her attributions of causal relationships with more reflection and mastery.

Vygotsky, to make clear his argument, uses the analogy between learning a foreign language (which is like learning nonspontaneous concepts) and learning a native language (which is like acquiring spontaneous concepts), though it is clear that for Vygotsky this is more than a mere analogy:

> Before we discuss the influence of scientific concepts on the child's general mental development, we will reconsider the analogy between this process and that of learning a foreign language. As this analogy indicates, the developmental path we have outlined for scientific concepts is only a single instantiation of a much broader group of developmental processes that have their source in systematic instruction.
>
> The child learns a foreign language in school differently than he learns his native language. He does not begin learning his native language with the study of the alphabet, with reading and writing, with the conscious and intentional construction of phrases, with the definition of words, or with the study of grammar. Generally, however, this is all characteristic of the child's first steps in learning a foreign language. The child learns his native language without conscious awareness or intention; he learns a foreign language with conscious awareness and intention. . . .
>
> As is true of the development of scientific and spontaneous concepts, however, there is *a mutual dependence* between these two paths of development. The conscious and intentional learning of a foreign language is obviously dependent on a certain level of development in the native language. The child already possesses a system of meanings in the native language when he begins to learn a foreign language. This system of meanings is transferred to the foreign language. Once again, however, the process of learning a foreign language clears the path for the acquisition of higher forms of the native language. Learning a foreign language allows the child to understand his native language as a single instantiation of a linguistic system. As a consequence, *the child acquires a potential for generalizing the phenomena of his native language* and for gaining conscious awareness of his speech operations and mastering them. (1987, pp. 221–222)

Vygotsky believes that it is because scientific, school-based concepts were primarily invented and are learned at a conscious level, and as part of an intricate system of links to other concepts, that they can develop the child's reflective abilities and reorganize the child's early conceptual development. It is clear, then, that Vygotsky has articulated an intricate position on the relationship between instruction (learning) and development (acquisition), as well as on relationships among mind, society, and different forms of knowing and knowledge.

However, it is also clear that Vygotsky leaves us with the need to delineate just what sorts of overt forms of instruction are fruitful – and this is the issue that also emerges from the progressive–postprogressive debate. He clearly does not believe that rote drill or working on "irrelevant" materials is efficacious – he explicitly disowns such approaches (see Vygotsky, 1987, pp. 198–200). He does believe that the sorts of overt instruction that do work involve the learner actively in working on problems with others so as to accomplish things she is not capable of achieving alone. But beyond that, Vygotsky clearly also believes that there are certain sorts of overt focusing on words, relationships, forms and function, on conscious control and reflection, that must supplement mere collaborative problem solving – and we have not yet done well in cataloging these.

Vygotsky's analogy between learning a foreign language versus learning a native one, on the one hand, and learning nonspontaneous concepts versus acquiring spontaneous ones, on the other, is also problematic. Foreign language instruction of the sort he points to has been spectacularly unsuccessful in teaching people to actually use a foreign language; further, the sorts of reflective awareness it gives of one's native language, and of language in general, is, in many cases, better for passing school tests than it is for gaining real insight into language and communication. It remains for us to specify a better account of overt instruction that does lead to the sorts of reflective awareness that is lacking in the acquisition of concepts by immersion in experience.

More interesting, however, is the fact that Vygotsky's account of instruction, and the growth of conscious control and mastery itself, raises a deep dilemma, a dilemma rather like (but at a different level) the one we discussed when we considered the problem that children internalizing the social did not leave much space for conscious control and reflective awareness. This can be seen clearly if we consider further Vygotsky's analogy between acquiring a native language versus learning a foreign one and the process of acquiring spontaneous concepts versus learning scientific ones. Vygotsky makes the following claim in working out this analogy:

When the child learns the foreign word, it is not related to the object in
a direct or immediate way. This relationship is mediated by the words
of the native language. Our analogy remains in force here because this
occurs in the development of scientific concepts as well. The scientific
concept is not related to its object directly. Once again, this relationship is *mediated* by existing concepts.

We can extend this analogy further. The mediating role played by the
words of the native language in establishing the relationship between the
foreign word and the object results in *significant developments in the
semantic aspect* of the native language. Because it can now be expressed
in two different words from different languages, the meaning of the word
or concept is torn from its immediate connection with the phonological
form of the word in the native language. Word meaning is thus differenti-
ated from the sound aspect of speech and acquires a degree of indepen-
dence. As a consequence, the child gains conscious awareness of the
meaning as such. The mediation of the relationship between the scientific concept and the object by the everyday concept has similar results.
As we will see in more detail later, *the everyday concept acquires a whole
series of new relationships with other concepts as it comes to stand between the scientific concept and its object*. Its relationship with the object
is also transformed in this process. (1987, p. 223)

It is clear from the whole of Vygotsky's discussion in the chapter from
which this quote was taken (chapter 6 of *Thinking and Speech*) that he
believes that the conscious mastery of the foreign language or of a
system of scientific concepts *reorganizes* and *transforms* the learner's
understanding of, representation of, and relationship to her native language or system of everyday concepts. The foreign language or system
of scientific concepts *regiments* or imposes a structure or interpretation
on the learner's native language or system of everyday concepts. The
native language or system of everyday concepts is, in a sense, subordi-
nated to, realigned by and with, the foreign language or the system of
scientific concepts.

But this regimentation, structure, or interpretation (whatever we call
it) that is imposed on the native language or on our everyday concepts is
not itself open to a great deal of conscious awareness or critical reflection, however much we become aware of *internal* relations within grammar as a system or within conceptual systems. We gain an analysis of our
native language or everyday conceptual systems (what Habermas, 1984,
called the *lifeworld*), but we gain no real purchase on a critical analysis
of that analysis.

For example, for years the (pedagogical) grammars of languages like
Latin and Greek served as people's meta-analysis, so to speak, of the
structure of English. People who learned Latin and Greek by instruction
came to think of the grammar of English in similar terms, and this

constituted their voluntary control over and reflective abilities about their conscious grammar of English. But such learners did not by any means acquire any reflective or critical abilities about why this analysis of English might be inadequate, the result of historical contingencies, and reflective of an ideologically laden concept of ancient languages and language in general. They could not, for instance, critique the notion of *dative case* applied to English, however much they could consciously use it in analyzing English sentences.

Similarly, the reorganization that science (and academic disciplines in general) has undoubtedly performed on our everyday concepts (our lifeworld), although it has made us more aware of conceptual complexities and associations, has not concomitantly led to any great meta-awareness of the historical contingencies, ideological loadings, or inadequacies of those transformations. We might put the matter as follows: Vygotsky is concerned with how instruction in foreign languages or scientific concepts reorganizes our knowledge of our native language or everyday concepts. He is not concerned with how we might use our knowledge of our native language or everyday understandings (once rendered more conscious and reflective) to regiment and critique traditions of grammar or scientific concepts.

It seems to me an important goal of any adequate (and socially just) education that, for example, an urban African-American student should be able to use her growing reflective knowledge of her Black English dialect to critique traditions of standard English. But how could this happen if her (learned) reflective awareness of her own dialect is the product of a superimposition of norms and representations embedded in overt instruction in standard English or foreign languages taught out of a similar tradition (if we use another tradition, then how does the student critique that one)? How can she simultaneously use her reorganized knowledge of her dialect to critique the very thing that has given her awareness of it in the first place? We need an account of how this can happen as part of development (acquisition) and instruction (learning) if we are to have a full and just theory of education.

Or, to take another example, we all learn, for example, how vague and inadequate the everyday concepts of *force, energy,* and *work* are in comparison to the physicist's neat distinctions among these terms. But we rarely acknowledge how odd the physicist's distinctions are when applied to wider realms of human experience, or even how odd it was in the first place to use these words in this way (e.g., if I push with all my energy – in the everyday sense – on a car and it doesn't move, to a physicist I've done no work). But how do we make such a critique if instruction in these physical concepts is what reorganizes our everyday concepts and gives them their systematic coherence (or judges them in this regard) in the first place?

The problem is that Vygotsky argues that I gain a systematic and conscious analysis of my native language and everyday concepts by instruction, but then it is hard to account for how I can use that analysis to critique itself and the instruction it was part of. It is hard, too, then, to see how we can give an account of instruction that gets us the good things Vygotsky's account does (conscious awareness and reflective abilities) and still gets us the resources (not just the desire) for critique – gets us meta-knowledge of systems, not just awareness of intrasystem relations. Thus, we reach the problem of *critical literacy* (in the political sense of *critical*).

It is precisely here that many people have turned to Bakhtin (e.g., 1986). His stress on the multiple ways in which any concept, piece of language, discourse, or practice that I internalize – make part of my mental and physical apparatus – is always a heterogeneous mixture of different and often conflicting "voices" connected to different social groups and different histories, different interests and desires, is a light leading in the proper direction. It remains to follow the path with anything like the dedication to a full theory that Vygotsky displayed in his work. We still face the problem of how instruction renders this *multi-vocality* consciously and reflectively available and useful while at the same time ensuring that the student learns (yes, even internalizes, in some sense) some coherent and usable system, not just a bag of disconnected, brightly colored, disparate threads. Students must gain a tapestry or they perhaps do no more than pay for our political sins.

The dilemma I am trying to point to here emerges in an interesting way in the Vygotsky-inspired curricula that Ann Brown and her colleagues have developed at the University of California at Berkeley. Using the notion of learners appropriating knowledge out of a rich, collaborative classroom environment containing technological tools and the support of scientific experts and teachers, as well as other learners within an overall community of practice, Brown says (e.g., in Brown, Ash, Rutherford, Nakagawa, Gordon, & Campione, 1993):

> In many forms of cooperative learning, students are left to construct learning goals for themselves; the goals change over time as interests change and groups sometimes concoct goals far different from those envisaged by the authorities. . . . In our classroom, the research direction of the group is not so democratic:. . . .

Teachers are encouraged to hold goals for each research group, hoping that the students will reach those goals through their own efforts. But if they do not, the teacher will invite the students to arrive at a mature understanding by whatever means she can, including, as a last resort, explicit instruction. . . .

Although there is considerable evidence that didactic teaching leads to passive learning, by the same token, unguided discovery can be dangerous too. Children "discovering" in our biology classrooms are quite adept at inventing scientific misconceptions. . . . Teachers are encouraged to see these common problems as fruitful errors, way stages on the route to mature understanding that they can manipulate and direct in useful ways. (pp. 205–206)

Although no one could doubt the excellence of Brown's curricula and pedagogy, we see here also the dilemma between progressive and postprogressive pedagogies. If the child "appropriates" in the zone of proximal development the goals, norms, values, and representations "envisioned by the authorities," if these come for the community of practice to define what *counts* as a mature understanding, then where is a meta-awareness and critique of these goals, values, and norms going to come from? How could it ever be represented, worded, and carried forth without exiting the community? The dilemma again: How can we get *this* and not give up the *instructional* benefits of Brown's curricula, not give up the internalization of some coherent set of norms, values, and representations?

I do not have answers to the dilemmas I have raised, dilemmas that seem to me to play below the surface of many of the chapters in this volume. Here I am only suggesting where the hard questions and very real dilemmas lie in this place to which Vygotsky has led us.

References

Bakhtin, M. M. (1986). *Speech genres and other late essays* (C. Emerson & M. Holquist, Eds.; V. W. McGee, Trans.). Austin: University of Texas Press.

Bernstein, B. (1975). *Class, codes and action: Vol. 3. Towards a theory of educational transmissions*. London: Routledge & Kegan Paul.

Bernstein, B. (1990). *Class, codes and control: Vol. 4. The structuring of pedagogic discourse*. London: Routledge.

Brown, A. L., Ash, D., Rutherford, M., Nakagawa, K., Gordon, A., & Campione, J. (1993). Distributed expertise in the classroom. In G. Salomon (Ed.), *Distributed cognitions*. New York: Cambridge University Press.

Chomsky, N. (1986). *Knowledge of language: Its nature, origin, and use*. New York: Praeger.

Christie, F. (Ed.). (1990). *Literacy for a changing world*. Melbourne: Australian Council for Educational Research.

Clark, A. (1993). *Associative engines: Connectionism, concepts, and representational change*. Cambridge, MA: MIT Press.

Cope, B., & Kalantzis, M. (Eds.) (1993). *The power of literacy: A genre approach to teaching writing*. Pittsburgh: University of Pittsburgh Press.

Delpit, L. D. (1986). Skills and other dilemmas of a progressive educator. *Harvard Educational Review, 56*, 379–385.

Delpit, L. D. (1988). The silenced dialogue: Power and pedagogy in educating other people's children. *Harvard Educational Review, 58*, 280–298.

Delpit, L. (1993). The politics of teaching literature discourse. In T. Perry & J. W. Fraser (Eds.), *Freedom's plow: Teaching in the multicultural classroom*. New York: Routledge.

Drucker, P. F. (1993). *Post-capitalist society*. New York: Harper Business.

Edelsky, C. (1991). *With literacy and justice for all: Rethinking the social in language and education*. London: Falmer Press.

Gee, J. P. (1990). *Social linguistics and literacies: Ideology in discourses*. London: Falmer Press.

Gee, J. P. (1992). *The social mind: Language, ideology, and social practice*. New York: Bergin & Garvey.

Gee, J. P. (1994). Discourses: Reflections on M. A. K. Halliday's "Towards a language-based theory of learning." *Linguistics and Education, 6*, 33–40.

Gee, J. P. (1994). First language acquisition as a guide for theories of learning and pedagogy. *Linguistics and Education, 6*, 331–354

George, Y. S. (1989). Introduction, *In building blocks for the future* by Y. S. George, S. M. Malcolm, and V. L. Worthington. Washington, DC: The American Association for the Advancement of Science.

Habermas, J. (1984). *Theory of communicative action* (Vol. 1) (T. McCarthy, Trans.). London: Heinemann.

Halliday, M. A. K. (1993). Towards a language-based theory of learning. *Linguistics and Education, 5*, 93 – 116.

Harre, R., & Gillett, G. (1994). *The discursive mind*. Thousand Oaks, CA: Sage.

Krashen, S. (1985a). *Inquiries and insights*. Hayward, CA: Alemany Press.

Krashen, S. (1985b). *The input hypothesis: Issues and implications*. London: Longman.

Margolis, H. (1993). *Paradigms and barriers: How habits of mind govern scientific beliefs*. Chicago: University of Chicago Press.

Martin, J. R. (1985). *Factual writing: Exploring and challenging social reality*. Geelong, Australia: Deakin University Press (republished by Oxford University Press, 1989).

Minick, N. (1987). The development of Vygotsky's thought: An introduction. Introduction to L. S. Vygotsky (1987). *The collected works of L. S. Vygotsky: Vol. 1*. (1987).

Reid, I. (Ed.). (1987). *The place of genre in learning: current debates*. Geelong, Australia: Centre for Studies in Literary Education, Deakin University Press.

Schenkein, J. (Ed.). (1978). *Studies in the organization of conversational interaction*. New York: Academic Press.

Vygotsky, L. S. (1960). *The development of the higher mental functions* [in Russian]. Moscow: APN.

Vygotsky, L. S. (1987). *The collected works of L. S. Vygotsky: Vol. 1. Poblems of general psychology*, including *Thinking and speech* (R. W. Rieber & A. S. Carton, Eds.; N. Minick, Trans.). New York: Plenum.

Index

283